T0367170

"Brian Irwin and Tim Perry have given us a comprehensive and compelling book that shows how the apocalyptic imagination has been created over time, and why so many have gotten their interpretations wrong. Drawing on a wealth of historical and hermeneutical expertise, Irwin and Perry provide context for how a certain reading of apocalyptic biblical narratives have acquired the power to mislead generations of Christians. This book should be in pastors' libraries, seminary and university classrooms, and church study forums. If you've ever wondered why folks keep talking about 'the rapture' or the 'blood moon', this book cuts through the confusion with clarity and insight to give the historical and biblical foundations for a more nuanced understanding of contemporary apocalypticism."

—**JEFFREY C. PUGH,** author of *The Homebrewed Guide to the End Times: Theology After You've Been Left Behind*

"For those of us who assumed that the horror show of dispensationalism was a thankfully discarded theological relic, Brian Irwin and Tim Perry provide a lucid primer of dispensationalist history and thought, and persuasively show how its narrative still hums powerfully in the imagination of much popular Christianity. Rather than dismissing this out of hand, Irwin and Perry turn to the same biblical sources that fuel dispensationalism, such as Daniel and Revelation, and find there a hopeful word for Christian living in the here and now. A refreshing book!"

—**THOMAS G. LONG,** Bandy professor emeritus of preaching, Candler School of Theology

"Perhaps no theological mistake has wrought more havoc in the evangelical world than popularized dispensationalism. Bestsellers like *The Late Great Planet Earth* and *Left Behind* have bequeathed an eschatology upon millions of believers that was unknown in the long history of the church. This Johnny-come-lately aberrant eschatology has dire consequences in real life. And this is precisely why *After Dispensationalism: Reading the Bible for the End of the World* is such a welcome addition to Christian eschatology. In this scholarly but accessible book, Brian Irwin and Tim Perry patiently show us how to read the prophetic passages of Scripture in a way that is sound, sane, and hopeful. As such, it is a gentle antidote to the sensationalist, fear-mongering eschatology of recent decades. I do hope that *After Dispensationalism* finds a wide readership."

—**BRIAN ZAHND,** author of *When Everything's on Fire*

"The interpretation of some parts of the Bible is undoubtedly challenging. Some have exploited this difficulty to construct elaborate schemes by combining one bit with another in a way the Bible itself never advocates. The focus is often to give particular and specific focus to the nature of the end times in ways which can bring the church into disrepute because time and again things do not work out as anticipated. In a clear and irenic spirit, Irwin and Perry patiently explain how this relatively new way of Bible interpretation arose and why it can detract from the more important questions of how the Bible was understood at the time it was written and hence how it should be applied to our Christian lives today. 'Rightly dividing the word of truth' must eschew 'wrongly dividing'; this book will help readers escape that danger."

—**H. G. M. WILLIAMSON,** emeritus regius professor of Hebrew, University of Oxford

"In *After Dispensationalism*, Brian Irwin and Tim Perry offer a fair-minded critique of dispensational interpretations of apocalyptic biblical texts—one that is extremely readable and consistently engaging while both practical and scholarly. Speaking with some knowledge of and experience with dispensationalism, Irwin and Perry's superb treatments of apocalyptic texts like Ezekiel, Daniel, and Revelation—texts that are arguably both the most ignored and most abused by many Christian readers—provide an important corrective to dispensational interpretations, while also offering ways that these apocalyptic texts can still speak to contemporary Christian readers in meaningful ways. Thus, this book is commended to any who want to more faithfully read apocalyptic texts found in the Christian scriptures, while at the same time want to learn how dispensationalism has profoundly influenced evangelicalism and American popular culture."

—**ROBERT DERRENBACKER,** Trinity College Theological School, Melbourne, Australia

"My enthusiastic endorsement of this book arises from my context as the principal of the oldest institution for tertiary education in the delightfully diverse nation of Trinidad and Tobago. Discussions often occur here, as they do in many times and places, about God's design for the ages and stages of the world. Irwin and Perry carefully and caringly explain the origins, spread and effects of various theories about the end times. Whether you have thought often about the end times, or whether you never pronounced the word 'dispensationalism' before, this book is for you!"

—**ADRIAN D. E. SIEUNARINE,** principal, St. Andrew's Theological College, Trinidad and Tobago

"I wish I had read this book ten years ago! The terrain of this topic is exciting, confusing, and sometimes dangerous. Brian Irwin and Tim Perry prove themselves to be wise and winsome guides—illuminating an otherwise shadowy and mysterious path. They chronicle the fascinating story that has shaped the modern landscape of end-times speculation, carefully take us through key and much-discussed scriptures, and provide helpful interpretive principles that are both biblical and logical. As a writer and podcaster, and especially as a congregational pastor who is encountering more and more people enamored with (and mystified by) end-times speculation, I appreciate how they caution against cherry-picking scriptures and hunching over calculators, and instead return our gaze to the ever-relevant, big-picture hope and redemption which God is working in human history."

—**MATTHEW RUTTAN,** author of *The Up Daily Devotional*;
host of *The Pulse Podcast* with Matthew Ruttan

"This unique book helps ordinary people as well as professionally trained pastors and academics to understand the history and ongoing influence of the approach to end-times speculation known as dispensational eschatology. *After Dispensationalism* is much more than a history and critique of dispensational eschatology. It offers another way of reading apocalyptic texts such as Ezekiel, Daniel, and Revelation—one that takes the social and historical context of apocalyptic texts seriously, reads individual verses and chapters in their canonical contexts, and wrestles with their significance as words meant to 'to motivate us to greater love and labor for the Lamb, once slain but now alive and exalted.' I wish I had had this book when I first encountered the world of evangelical dispensationalism. I will recommend it to my students, colleagues, and friends.

—**MARION ANN TAYLOR,** professor of Old Testament
and graduate director, Wycliffe College at the University of Toronto

"If you have ever wondered about preachers who see today's headline news 'predicted' in the Bible, this is the book for you. I know of no better book on the topic than this. It starts with the key questions and issues and continues with a fascinating and learned journey into what those 'end-times' texts really mean for us today—and without being unkind or unfair to traditional dispensationalists. This is a must-read for anyone interested in this topic."

—**J. GLEN TAYLOR,** emeritus associate professor of Scripture
and global Christianity, Wycliffe College, University of Toronto

"This is an important book, especially for our times when bizarre end time predictions and interpretations of pertinent scriptures dodge all spheres, including national political life. In easily accessible language yet based in detailed exegetical analysis, the authors manage to write to both a lay and scholarly audience about issues that vex perhaps all readers of apocalyptic scriptures, namely the exact time and location of the events described. We may pick up this book to seek answers to the when and where, but we will be surprised at every turn with the rich history of interpretation that grounds the various approaches from dispensationalism to interpretation of prophecies. Ultimately, we come away with insights on reading this literature that moves us away from what seem unimportant searches to the real purpose of these visions: Jesus revealed then, now, and the future as the glorified Lamb of God. No one can come to the end of this book without their own doxological moments. Insightful and inspiring."

—**ESTHER ACOLATSE,** professor of pastoral theology and world Christianity, Garrett Evangelical Theological Seminary

# AFTER
# DISPENSATIONALISM

# AFTER
# DISPENSATIONALISM

## READING THE BIBLE FOR
## THE END OF THE WORLD

**BRIAN P. IRWIN**
**WITH TIM PERRY**

**LEXHAM PRESS**

*After Dispensationalism: Reading the Bible for the End of the World*

Copyright 2023 Brian P. Irwin and Tim Perry

Lexham Press, 1313 Commercial St., Bellingham, WA 98225
LexhamPress.com

Print ISBN 9781683596813
Digital ISBN 9781683596820
Library of Congress Control Number 2022947471

Lexham Editorial: Todd Hains, Claire Brubaker, Danielle Burlaga, Mandi Newell
Cover Design: Joshua Hunt, Brittany Schrock
Typesetting: Abigail Stocker

To my parents, Paul and Eunice Irwin

To my wife, Elaine

# Contents

## PART 1: The World of End-Times Teaching

## PART 2: The World of Prophecy and Apocalyptic

## PART 3: The Meaning of Biblical Apocalyptic

# LIST OF FIGURES

# List of Tables

# Abbreviations

| | |
|---|---|
| AM | *anno mundi* |
| ASV | American Standard Version |
| BSac | *Bibliotheca Sacra* |
| CTA | *Corpus des tablettes en cunéiformes alphabétiques* *découvertes à Ras Shamra-Ugarit de 1929 à 1939.* Edited by Andrée Herdner. Paris: Geuthner, 1963 |
| ERV | English Revised Version |
| ICC | International Critical Commentary |
| KTU | *Die keilalphabetischen Texte aus Ugarit.* Edited by Manfried Dietrich, Oswald Loretz, and Joaquín Sanmartín. Münster: Ugarit-Verlag, 2013. 3rd enl. ed. of *KTU: The Cuneiform Alphabetic Texts from Ugarit, Ras Ibn Hani, and Other Places.* Edited by Manfried Dietrich, Oswald Loretz, and Joaquín Sanmartín. Münster: Ugarit-Verlag, 1995 (= CTU) |
| NASB | New American Standard Bible |
| NSRB | *New Scofield Reference Bible* |
| PIAU | Proceedings of the International Astronomical Union |
| WBC | Word Biblical Commentary |

# ACKNOWLEDGMENTS

Whatever skills I have brought to this project have been planted and nurtured by the teaching and prayers of others. Gordon Rumford has been a supporter and guide in learning and faith since my youth and remains so today. The Rev. Ian McWhinnie and the congregation of Glenbrook Presbyterian Church have been encouragers and a trial audience for much of what is contained within these covers. Drs. Glen Taylor, Marion Taylor, and Glen Shellrude have over the years modelled what it means to be selfless mentors, supportive colleagues, and effective teachers of Scripture. My former teacher and predecessor at Knox College, the Rev. Dr. Stanley Walters, was key in introducing me to a new way of reading apocalyptic literature and reminding me of the need to connect Scripture with the life of the church.

Like my late mother (with whom she shares an obscure New Testament name) my former principal, the Rev. Dr. Dorcas Gordon, was a gentle prodder and provider of resources, encouragement, conversation, and accountability throughout most of the time this book was in development. Her successor at Knox, the Rev. Dr. John Vissers has continued in that tradition.

Knox College's chief librarian, Joan Pries, is an entrepreneurial and imaginative supporter of students, faculty, and administration and was quick to assist with every request for help with this work.

Thanks goes to Todd Hains, Scott Corbin, Mandi Newell, and Abigail Stocker of Lexham Press for their guidance as this project moved to publication and to Amanda Rodgers and Dr. Laura Alary whose unique skills produced the indexes.

My collaborator, the Rev. Dr. Tim Perry, is a careful theologian, insightful cultural commentator, and man of good humor. His contribution is present on every page and was critical in bringing this project to completion.

Finally, my late parents, Paul and Eunice Irwin, instilled in me a love of God's word and led me to faith in Christ. Their commitment to teaching Scripture and their gracious temperament inspired this book. I hope that the values and character they lived are detected on its pages. I owe a great debt of thanks to my wife, Elaine, who—like her God—is "compassionate and gracious, slow to anger, and abounding in love." Her love and support have been constant throughout this project and our life together. This book is dedicated to all three.

# Prayer for Hearing the Holy Scripture

Blessed Lord,

who caused all holy Scriptures to be written for our learning: Grant us so to hear them, read, mark, learn, and inwardly digest them, that we may embrace and ever hold fast the blessed hope of everlasting life, which you have given us in our Savior Jesus Christ; who lives and reigns with you and the Holy Spirit, one God, for ever and ever.

Amen.

# Introduction

D avid Ben Gurion, Israel's first prime minister, retired from public life to Kibbutz Sde Boker, an agricultural settlement deep in southern Israel, on a stretch of desert highway between Beersheba and the Red Sea port of Eilat. Today, his small house is a museum visited by schoolchildren and tourists willing to make the journey to this isolated and arid corner of the country. Peering into his study, sharp-eyed visitors might spy a small red paperback on a chair beside the former prime minister's desk: a dog-eared copy of *The Late Great Planet Earth*.[1] Why would a prime minister of Israel read a combination of end-times biblical interpretation and political speculation written by an American seminary graduate and Christian Bible teacher?

On January 10, 2003, the *Los Angeles Times* noted the passing of John Walvoord, aged ninety-two.[2] The obituary noted Walvoord's three-decade-long career as a theologian and president of Dallas Theological Seminary. Of the thirty or so books that Walvoord had written during his lifetime, none drew more attention than his bestselling volume relating Bible prophecy to oil and the Middle East, a book requested by the White House for President George H. W. Bush and his staff at the outbreak of the first Gulf War in 1990.[3] Why would the president of the United States and his advisers take this book into account at a time of war?

The two books in question, Hal Lindsey's *The Late Great Planet Earth* and Walvoord's *Oil, Armageddon, and the Middle East*, are examples of dispensationalist eschatology, an approach

1

to interpreting Scripture and the end times common among conservative evangelical Christians in North America and globally. Rooted in the writings of early nineteenth-century Anglo-Irish Bible teacher John Nelson Darby, this way of reading the Bible now influences a significant swath of Christianity and has moved into pop culture. Even so, the view of the future it offers remains impenetrable to many inside and outside the church today.

This book sketches the origins of this approach, identifies its current proponents, and describes the future it predicts. It also examines the genres of biblical writing that this approach uses most, their original contexts, and how their original audience likely understood their contents. Finally, this book considers dispensationalism's main texts to show how a reading of the final form of these biblical books yields important messages for the church today. In short, this book commends dispensationalism's scriptural zeal even as it finds that its way of reading often misses what the biblical authors wished to communicate. This shared commitment to Scripture is why we opened this book with the old Anglican "Prayer for Hearing the Holy Scripture." As a young Church of Ireland curate, the founder of dispensationalism, J. N. Darby, would have spoken these very words over those in his pastoral care. Like Darby, we are grateful for the word of God that points us to Jesus Christ and the everlasting life he brings.

# PART 1

## THE WORLD OF
## END-TIMES TEACHING

# 1

# End-Times Prediction through the Ages

End-times enthusiasm seems to erupt every few decades, and not only among evangelical Protestants. In the latest round, in 2010 pop culture turned to the ancient "Mayan calendar" that predicted the end of the world on December 21, 2012. The world, however, still exists. It seems the foreseen end had more to do with our misunderstanding of how one ancient civilization tracked time.

Mayans employed several overlapping means of reckoning dates. The Calendar Round was a cyclical calendar that endlessly repeated in units of fifty-two years. While this calendar is suitable for tracking basic events (indeed, a form remains in use today), it didn't and doesn't provide unique dates beyond its cycle. It cannot point to events more than a half-century into the past or future. To move outside the cycle, whether for dates on monuments or historical reckoning, the Maya developed the Long Count Calendar, which took its starting point from their date for creation (August 11, 3114 BC). This calendar was at the center of the speculation around 2012 and the end of the world. The Long Calendar's basic unit, the *tun*, roughly corresponds to a solar year. It also measures entire eras, called *bak'tun*, which lasted 144,000 days or 394.3 years. When one *bak'tun* ended, another was simply added. The Maya believed that three worlds had preceded their own and that the third of those worlds had ended after thirteen *bak'tuns*.[1] December 21, 2012, marked the end of the thirteenth *bak'tun* since creation of their world in 3114 BC.

As the fateful date approached, bizarre internet- and New Age–fueled speculation emerged. What would happen on December 21? A new dawn in which the world would be renewed? A catastrophic reversal of earth's magnetic field? A visitation by beings from the planet "Nibiru," or Earth joining an extraterrestrial federation?[2] The Maya left no mythic texts revealing what they thought would accompany the close of the thirteenth *bak'tun*.

Eager to leverage the free publicity around all things Mayan, Hollywood responded with the John Cusack vehicle *2012*, a story of global catastrophe foretold by an ancient civilization. Museums in North America and elsewhere took stock of their Mesoamerican collections and launched exhibits on Mayan civilization and chronology.[3] Even Christian TV preachers took advantage of the Mayan phenomenon. Noted end-times preacher Jack Van Impe produced two DVDs, *World War III: 2012?* and *December 21st 2012: History's Final Day?*, in which he cautiously suggests that 2012 might mark the beginning of a period of turmoil known as the great tribulation.

But what about the Mayans themselves? Some Mayan inscriptions recently discovered in Guatemala refer to dates beyond the thirteenth *bak'tun*. Were they alive today, the

Mayans would have done what so many of us do on January 1: hung up a new calendar. The Mayan sensation was harmless in the end. At worst, it parted many North Americans from their money in theaters and museum gift shops.

The fallout from the end-times predictions made a year earlier by Christian broadcaster Harold Camping of the US-based Family Radio ministry was graver. A civil engineer and Bible teacher, Camping cofounded Family Stations, Inc., or Family Radio, in 1959. From a single FM station in San Francisco, Family Radio eventually grew to sixty-five US radio stations and a shortwave facility. Camping's eschatological interests intensified in the 1980s. When he began to teach that the church age had ended and that all existing churches were apostate, many evangelicals and other Christians distanced themselves from his ministry.[4]

His first prediction of the end is found in a 1992 book that employed numerology and allegorical interpretation to determine that Christ would return to earth sometime in September 1994.[5] Undefeated by his failure, Camping continued to study Scripture. By 2005 he felt confident enough to announce that on May 21, 2011, Christ would rescue the saved from five months of torment, with final global destruction on October 21. As the May date loomed, Family Radio sponsored a nationwide media campaign announcing the coming rapture of believers and the destruction of the earth and its remaining inhabitants. Billboards blaring, "Judgment Day, May 21. The Bible Guarantees It!" sprang up across America while the ministry's friends held signs and distributed tracts warning of "The End." When May 21 came and went, Camping responded through his Family Radio call-in program, *Open Forum*. Christ had indeed returned, he said, but in an unexpected, mystical way. Explaining the absence of torment as an example of God's mercy,[6] Camping insisted that the world would still be destroyed on October 21. After that date too passed uneventfully, Camping resigned as head of Family Radio and pledged to refrain from any further end-times predictions.

The spectacular failure of Camping's predictions came at a cost for Camping specifically and Christian churches in general. Not only had the ministry squandered millions of dollars on advertising, but the failed predictions gave rise to widespread ridicule of Christians generally—touching even those churches that had critiqued Camping and which he had attacked as apostate.

The New Age friends of the Maya and Bible teachers such as Harold Camping are just the latest in a long line of end-times prognosticators that began long before the advent of mass media and the internet. The catalyst for this obsession—for with some, that is what it truly is—can be found in Jesus's last words in the New Testament, "Yes, I am coming soon" (Rev 22:20). This promise of return, coming at the end of a book pregnant with turmoil, persecution, and deliverance, seeded in Christianity both end-time expectation and an ongoing interest in what Scripture has to say about Christ's return. For millions of Christians globally, time has dimmed neither.

While there have been periods in which Christians have settled into a sense of comfort with the world, Christianity's history is peppered with periods of intense apocalyptic speculation. Examining these different episodes can remind us that recent conjecture is nothing new and help us approach the future with a more sober and helpful understanding of the end and how we should live in anticipation of the return of Christ.

## END-TIMES SPECULATION
## THROUGH THE AGES

### RABBINIC ESCHATOLOGY

From the beginning, Christian end-times speculation has been inextricably linked to both studying Scripture and counting time. It sprang from a rich seedbed of messianic expectation that featured prominently in first- and second-century AD Judaism. Several factors coalesced to intensify Jewish messianic interest during this period. A widely held view associated the world's lifespan with the days of creation. Interpreted according to a formula derived from Psalm 90:4—"A thousand years in your sight are like a day that has just gone by"—the result (with some variation) was an understanding that the world would exist for a period of six thousand years, corresponding to the six days in which God created, followed by one thousand years of rest, parallel to the Sabbath, on which God rested (fig. 1.1).[7] Connected to this was the view that as the end approached, there would be increasing warfare, tribulation, heresy, and unfaithfulness that would signal the arrival of the Messiah, the "Son of David," as God intervened to usher in the Sabbath (Babylonian Talmud Sanhedrin 97a).[8]

The date of Messiah's arrival was a matter of some rabbinic debate. Some authorities foresaw Messiah's arrival anytime in the final third of earth's existence: "A Tannaite authority of the house of Elijah [said], 'For six thousand years the world will exist. For two thousand it will be desolate, two thousand years [will be the time of] Torah, and two thousand years will be the days of the Messiah'" (Babylonian Talmud Sanhedrin 97a; also Babylonian Talmud Avodah Zarah 9a; Babylonian Talmud Rosh Hashanah 31a).[9] First-century AD historian Josephus believed the world was already five thousand years old, on the cusp of Messiah's appearing (*Against Apion* 1.1; see fig. 1.2). Combined with the harsh reality of subservience to Rome, this chronology made the period ripe for messianic expectation. Josephus records the rise of several charismatic figures who attempted to break the Roman yoke,[10] any of whom might have inspired messianic expectation.

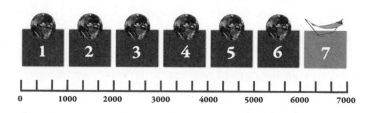

*Fig. 1.1. The days of creation and the lifespan of the earth*

These isolated and sporadic insurrections culminated in the failed first revolt against Rome and the destruction of the Jerusalem temple in AD 70. Far from eliminating messianic expectation, however, this catastrophic loss was entirely consistent with what was to be expected. As one of the "birth pangs" of the Messiah, it only increased hope for imminent divine intervention. When the second revolt against Rome broke out in AD 132, it is no surprise that its charismatic leader Simon ben Kosiba (also known as bar Kokhba) declared himself to be the messiah (Babylonian Talmud Sanhedrin 93b).[11] Indeed, this messianic identity was confirmed by no less an authority than Rabbi Akiva, who is said to have given him the name Bar Kokhba, "Son of a Star" (Jerusalem Talmud Ta'anit 4.5), playing on a messianic understanding of Numbers 24:17. Only after this disastrous second revolt, the subsequent expulsion of Jews from Jerusalem, and its transformation into Aelia Capitolina did messianic fervor wane.

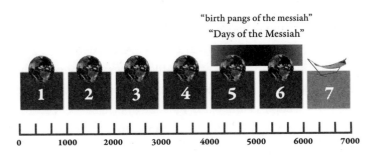

Fig. 1.2. Josephus on the end of the world

It did not, however, die out completely. Periodically Jewish messianic pretenders arose with predictable results. Church historian Socrates of Constantinople records the sad fifth-century story of Moses of Crete. Claiming to be the Moses of the exodus, this Moses spent a year traveling the island, gathering followers, and promising to lead them through the Mediterranean Sea to their ancient homeland. On the appointed day, Moses directed his followers to a promontory overlooking the Mediterranean Sea and commanded that they leap off. Many did, dying on the rocks or drowning in the surf below. Survivors were pulled from the water by nearby Christian fishermen. Realizing they had been deceived, Moses's followers sought their leader to kill him. Their "Moses," however, was never seen again (Socrates of Constantinople, *Ecclesiastical History* 7.38).

## EARLY CHRISTIAN ESCHATOLOGY

Messianic expectation and (failed) revolution was endemic to the world of Jesus's first followers. In Luke's nativity, the heavenly army that announces Jesus's birth would have conformed well to the conviction that the Messiah would remove the Romans and restore Israel (Luke 2:13–14).[12] Later, Jesus corrected and restrained similar misconceptions of his identity and mission among his own followers (Matt 16:13–21; 26:51–52; Mark 8:27–29; 14:46–50; John 18:3–10; Acts 1:6–8).

More important, however, was the church's adoption of the six-thousand-year eschatological timeline popular in Judaism. The early second-century text Epistle of Barnabas reflects the acceptance of this schema and its application to Christ:

> the Lord will make an end of everything in six thousand years, for a day with him means a thousand years. And he himself is my witness when he says, "Lo, the day of the Lord shall be as a thousand years." So then, children, in six days, that is in six thousand years, everything will be completed. "And he rested on the seventh day." This means, when his Son comes he will destroy the time of the wicked one, and will judge the godless, and will change the sun and the moon and the stars, and then he will truly rest on the seventh day. (Epistle of Barnabas 15.4–5; see 2 Pet 3:8–14)[13]

Irenaeus (ca. 130–ca. 202) expresses the same view a generation later (Irenaeus, *Against Heresies* 5.28.3). In subsequent centuries, the combination of the six-thousand-year schema and the expectation that Jesus would return soon drew attention to the signs of Christ's coming and gave rise to multiple premature announcements that his appearing was at hand.

The calendar itself shaped speculation about Christ's return. Evidence suggests that the early church's first calendar was adopted in the third century AD by Hippolytus of Rome (ca. 170–ca. 236) and Julius Africanus (ca. 180–ca. 250). Like its Jewish predecessors, this system began its reckoning with the creation of the world, *anno mundi* (AM).[14] According to Hippolytus, Jesus was born in 5500 AM I, which placed Hippolytus himself in the early 5700s AM I (Hippolytus, *Commentary on Daniel* 4.23; see fig. 1.3).

### *Anno Mundi* I

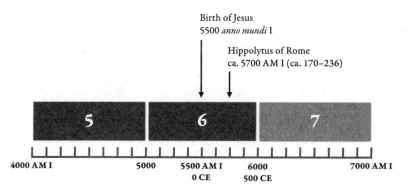

Hippolytus of Rome (ca. 170–236)
Julius Africanus (ca. 180–250)

Birth of Jesus
5500 *anno mundi* I

Hippolytus of Rome
ca. 5700 AM I (ca. 170–236)

5    6    7

4000 AM I    5000    5500 AM I    6000    7000 AM I
0 CE    500 CE

*Fig. 1.3. Anno mundi I*

In his commentary on Daniel, Hippolytus accepts the six-thousand-year-plus Sabbath-era framework earlier espoused by the rabbis, the author of Barnabas, and Irenaeus, placing Jesus's birth in 5500 AM I and noting that the eschatological Sabbath will arrive at the six-thousand-year mark (Hippolytus, *Commentary on Daniel* 4.23).[15] He also recognized the dangers that accompanied such speculation. By pushing Christ's return far into the future, Hippolytus significantly modified the expectation of the early church that Christ's return was imminent.[16]

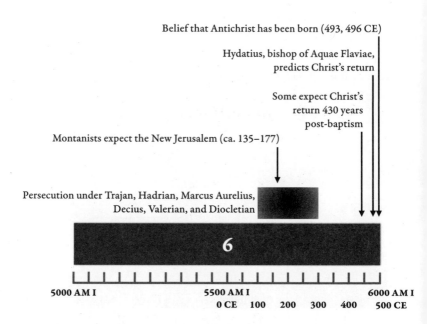

*Fig. 1.4. Anno mundi I and fifth-century concerns about the end*

The use of AM I, however, merely *delayed* concern about the end. As 6000 AM I (AD 500) approached, millennial expectation increased. Periodic persecutions in the second and third centuries recalled the book of Revelation's predictions of suffering and the belief that Christ would return near the arrival of the seventh millennium. Unsurprisingly, then, in Asia Minor in the mid- to late second century AD a group gathered around a charismatic figure named Montanus, who proclaimed that the new Jerusalem would soon be lowered in Phrygia. Later, Jerome (ca. 347–ca. 420), in his commentary on Ezekiel, documents the belief that the end would come 430 years after the baptism of Christ, a date close to the year 500.[17] In the late fifth century in northwest Spain, Hydatius (ca. 395–ca. 470), bishop of Aquae Flaviae, predicted the second coming of Christ on

May 27, 482.[18] In 493 and 496, marginal notes in tables used to calculate the timing of Easter record that certain "ignorant" and "delirious" people claimed that the antichrist had already been born[19] (fig. 1.4).

## THE CALENDAR AND ESCHATOLOGY IN
## THE EARLY TO MEDIEVAL CHURCH

Even as millennial speculation around the year 6000 AM I (AD 500) waxed, however, theological and chronological developments within the Mediterranean world worked against it. Christians who embraced allegorical interpretation of the Bible rarely understood the millennium and antichrist concretely. Origen (ca. 185–254) decried the carnality of those who anticipated the millennium as a time of indulgence and repose; he dismissed all notions of a literal, earthly kingdom (Origen, *First Principles* 2.11.2–3).[20] In the early fourth century, Rome's new toleration of Christianity ended persecution, a key motivator of apocalyptic speculation. Rome's subsequent adoption of Christianity as its official religion left millennial apocalypticism—which presupposed worsening conditions—significantly out of step with both reality and the interests of a church whose political influence was on the rise. St. Augustine of Hippo (ca. 354–ca. 430) further diminished the influence of millennial speculation. Repulsed, like Origen, by the carnal view of the millennium, Augustine retained the familiar six-part schema of world history but understood the millennium to name the present era. The millennium was initiated at Christ's incarnation and corresponded to his rule through the church (Augustine, *City of God* 20.8–9).[21] This amillennial solution to apocalyptic imaginings profoundly influenced the church for centuries to come.

Chronologically, the problem of the year 6000 AM I in a context of peace, stability, and a now-Christian Roman Empire was ameliorated through the work of Eusebius of Caesarea (ca. 260–ca. 339). Eusebius, a church historian and biographer of Emperor Constantine, also authored a major work on world history. His *Chronicle* dates creation some three hundred years after the earlier date given by Hippolytus so that Eusebius's own time became circa 5500 AM II, pushing the doomsday ahead to AD 800 (fig. 1.5). Jerome's adoption of this revised chronology ensured its eventual acceptance in the Latin West and in early medieval Europe. Predictably, however, this postponed speculation; as 800 (6000 AM II) approached, evidence suggests that—at a popular level at least—end-time concerns increased. From the late seventh century onward, for example, some historical works included dates in the format of AM II along with calculations of the years remaining until the millennium[22]—despite the dominance of amillennialism among church elites.

## *Anno Mundi* II

Eusebius of Caesarea (ca. 260–ca. 339)
adopted in the West by Jerome (ca. 347–420)

Fig. 1.5. *Eusebius and the shift to anno mundi II*

In 703, English monk the Venerable Bede (ca. 672–735) produced a chronicle, *De temporibus*, that shaved twelve hundred years from the earth's age and redated the birth of Christ to 3952 AM III. Once again, the close of the sixth millennium was pushed into the distant future (fig. 1.6).

## *Anno Mundi* III

Bede the Venerable (ca. 672–735)

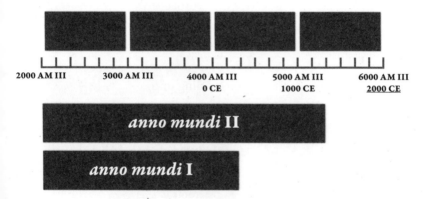

*Fig. 1.6. Bede the Venerable and the shift to anno mundi III*

In a later chronicle, *The Reckoning of Time*, Bede adopts the *anno domini* (AD) dating schema. Taking the birth of Christ as its starting point, this broke the connection between the six-age schema of history and systems of dating (fig. 1.7).

Despite the theological influence of Augustine and the chronological work of Bede, however, comments in various sources show the stubborn persistence of the six-thousand-year system. Bede himself in *The Reckoning of Time* urges his readers to ignore those who announced Christ's return at the close of the sixth millennium (Bede, *The Reckoning of Time* 67). As the year 6000 AM II (AD 800) approached, many ordinary people were anxious. Frankish and Saxon annals from the late eighth century note various celestial phenomena that unsettled the populace.[23] In his commentary on the book of Revelation, late eighth-century Spanish monk Beatus of Liébana predicts the end of the world in 838. Other sources from the era state that on one occasion, his Easter end-time proclamation resulted in panic and fasting.[24]

### *Anno Domini*

Bede the Venerable (ca. 672–735)

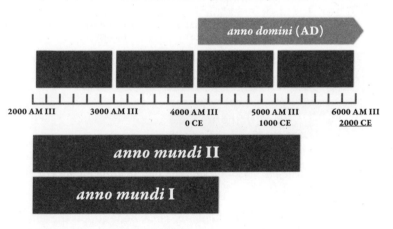

*Fig. 1.7. Bede the Venerable and the shift to anno domini*

Even as the triumph of the *anno domini* system of chronography severed the calendric tie between the six-day view of the world and the *anno mundi* system, concern about the end of the world did not disappear entirely. The millennial anniversary of Christ's birth saw apocalyptic expectation grow again. The run-up to 1000 was marked by political uncertainty in Western

Europe precipitated by the sudden death of the last Carolingian king of West Francia, Louis V (ca. 966–987), and fueled by Hugh Capet's (ca. 941–996) consolidation of his power. Many took the appearance of Halley's comet in European skies in 989 to be a portent of Christ's return one thousand years after his birth.[25] When the second advent did not occur, many looked to the one thousandth anniversary of the crucifixion. In subsequent centuries, apocalyptic flare-ups accompanied unexpected or calamitous events, spiking between 1346 and 1349, when bubonic plague killed off a third of Europe—a scale of destruction frightfully consistent with predictions of global plague found in the book of Revelation (Rev 9:14–19).[26] By 1516, the disruption wrought by end-time preaching prompted the Catholic Church to ban it. Christians were "in no way to presume to preach or declare a fixed time for future evils, the coming of antichrist or the precise day of judgment; for Truth says, it is not for us to know times or seasons which the Father has fixed by his own authority. Let it be known that those who have hitherto dared to declare such things are liars."[27]

## END-TIMES SPECULATION FROM THE REFORMATION TO THE EIGHTEENTH CENTURY

Just one year later, Augustinian monk Martin Luther (1483–1546) nailed his Ninety-Five Theses to the door of All Saints' Church at Wittenberg, dividing the church in a way not seen since the East-West schism of 1054. The Lateran Council's ban couldn't restrain Protestant reformers who responded to church-led persecution by identifying successive popes with the antichrist.[28] Once again, on both sides, interest in end-times prediction accelerated. Even Luther took part. His 1541 chronology of the world, *Supputatio annorum mundi*, calculated his own present to be about halfway through the sixth millennium; Christ would return about five centuries hence. Diseases arriving from the new world, heavenly disturbances during the reign of Holy Roman Emperor Maximilian I, the devilish character of Pope Julius II, and the Peasants' Revolt of 1525, however, all led Luther to expect it even sooner.[29]

The threat to Europe posed by the advancing Ottoman armies of Sultan Suleiman the Magnificent (1520–1566) almost certainly also affected Luther's predictions. In the decades since the fall of Constantinople (1453), the Ottoman Empire continued to advance so that by Luther's day it threatened Vienna itself. Luther had his perfect apocalyptic pair: "But just as the pope is the Antichrist, so the Turk is the very devil incarnate. The prayer of Christendom against both is that they shall go down to hell, even though it may take the Last Day to send them there, and I hope that day will not be far off."[30]

End-times speculation was further fostered in 1650 with the publication of a landmark work on history and chronology by the Reverend James Ussher, Church of Ireland archbishop of Armagh. Following Bede and others, Ussher produced detailed scholarship that drew on the biblical material as well as all the relevant extrabiblical texts available to him. The result was a nine-hundred-page history that began with the world's creation in 4004 BC and laid out its progression in seven ages, the last of which began at the birth of Christ.[31] For those interested in end-time predictions, the wide dissemination and adoption of Ussher's chronology provided a then-authoritative foundation for calculating dates. Ussher inadvertently became a catalyst for the detailed, mathematically oriented end-times speculation that followed in the nineteenth century.

## WILLIAM MILLER AND APOCALYPTIC FERVOR IN NINETEENTH-CENTURY AMERICA

William Miller (1782–1849), a farmer and lay preacher from Low Hampton, New York, built on Ussher's chronological and historical foundation. Shortly after his conversion in 1816,[32] Miller began to study the Bible earnestly. As he pondered Daniel's words, "Unto two thousand and three hundred days; then shall the sanctuary be cleansed" (Dan 8:14 KJV), Miller became convinced that "sanctuary" referred to the church and that "cleansed" described the redemption from sin that would take place following the resurrection. Beginning with 457 BC as the date from which the seventy weeks commenced, Miller reckoned that the twenty-three hundred days referred to twenty-three hundred years (based on the familiar principle drawn from Ps 90:4 and 2 Pet 3:8), arriving at 1843 as the world's last year (fig. 1.8).[33] By 1831 Miller felt compelled to share this news with the world, and by 1833, his church had granted him a license to preach.[34] A lack of formal theological training did not inhibit the growth of Miller's influence in his Low Hampton church. He soon developed a reputation for being harsh in theological disagreements and becoming so consumed with the question of prophecy that one local observer described him as a "monomaniac."[35] Nevertheless, Miller soon began to receive numerous invitations to speak on his findings in local churches and farther afield.

In 1838 he published his calculations in a 280-page book (*Evidence from Scripture and History of the Second Coming of Christ, about the Year 1843*). The next year, he traveled to Boston, where he met a Baptist pastor named Joshua Himes and gave twice-daily public lectures in his church for a week. Taken with Miller's message and presentation, Himes was shocked that Miller had waited so long to publicize his findings. He arranged to have Miller's lectures published and subsequently became Miller's main promoter. Himes designed a large chart, founded two journals, recruited additional speakers, and published books and tracts—all to publicize Miller's message of the approaching end and the need for repentance.[36] Running up to 1843, Miller held forth at churches, tents, and outdoor camp meetings to growing numbers.[37]

By 1843, an estimated fifty thousand people counted themselves as Miller's disciples; close to a million more followed from a distance. As the frequency and urgency of Miller's speaking increased, however, so did the objections and ridicule of those unconvinced by his theory.[38] In one mocking cartoon, a devoted "Millerite" thumbs his nose at the rest of the world before locking himself in a fireproof box with a block of ice, a bottle of brandy, and a few other essentials (fig. 1.9).

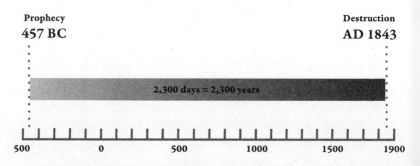

*Fig. 1.8. William Miller's prediction of the end of the world*

*Fig. 1.9. "The salamander safe. A millerite preparing for the 23rd of April."*

Until this point, Miller had claimed only that Christ would return sometime in 1843. With an anxious public pressing him to be more specific, Miller elaborated. When Christ returned he would "destroy the bodies of the living wicked by fire, as those of the old world were destroyed by water, and shut up their souls in the pit of woe, until their resurrection unto damnation." Once the earth was thus cleansed, Christ and his saints would take possession and dwell there forever.[39] All of this would unfold, he announced, sometime in the Hebrew year from March 21, 1843, to March 21, 1844.[40]

Miller's apocalyptic calculations were frighteningly confirmed by what has since become known as the Great March Comet of 1843.[41] From February to April this immensely bright, long-tailed comet appeared nightly and at its March peak was visible in daylight. Throughout the northeastern states where Miller's preaching had been concentrated, tens of thousands were convinced. March 21, 1844, however, came and went. A devastated Miller issued a public apology in late May.[42]

Some of Miller's followers, however, were not so willing as their teacher to relinquish hope in the imminent return of Christ but revised the timeline. Miller's spirit revived, and he soon concurred: a new date of Christ's return was announced—October 22, 1844.[43] The impact of Miller's teaching in America is measured by an October 15 dispatch by the American correspondent to the faraway *Times of London*. Appearing in the October 31 edition, the article captures the turmoil and anxiety that gripped the northeastern United States as the clock ticked down.

New York, Oct. 15. The excitement which at this moment pervades the American community is without example in the history of the country. ... The religious community seems, as it were, convulsed to its centre. Nor is it strange or wonderful, if the credulous, from the signs of the times, should become alarmed, and apprehensive of the approach of some dread event or revolution. All is fanaticism, feigned or real. ... Then come the Millerites. The leader of this sect was, I believe, a Presbyterian minister (sic); so far as I am informed, a respectable, pious man, of medium talents. At length, however, according to his own view of the case, he became inspired with the gift of prophecy; or, as his followers say, he discovered in the holy Scriptures the precise time of the second coming of the Saviour, when the world should be judged. Having made this discovery, he felt it his duty to proclaim it aloud, which he accordingly did, until the day of judgment had passed by. In the meantime, however, many of his followers, being of weak mind, became deranged. After the prophet had proved to be a false prophet, the presumption was that the sect would become extinct. Not so the fact. Miller continues to preach with new and fiery zeal, that the last day is near at hand, and his followers are rapidly increasing in number. One of them has gone so far as to designate the 22d of this month as the end of all things on this earth. ... Many of their converts have become maniacs, wasting their property, and leaving their families to suffer in indigence. Miller is not of this class. He takes care of the one thing needful in this life. But charity forbids considering him either a hypocrite or an impostor. He is a self-deluded fanatic. But he is making an inroad upon long-established churches, and will probably continue to make such inroad where anything like fanaticism prevails.[44]

After this failure, October 22, 1844, became known to Miller's followers as "The Great Disappointment." Miller himself was shattered. In January 1845, he presented his predictions in language from the book of Daniel, "My visionary scheme was demolished at a blow, and became like Nebuchadnezzar's image, as the chaff of the summer threshing floor." Later that same month, Miller and most of his followers in Low Hampton were removed from the Baptist denomination.[45]

Miller's lament and excommunication, however, were nothing compared to the confusion and crisis that ensued for many of his followers. Having been entirely convinced that the Lord would take them away to heaven on the appointed day, many of Miller's followers had given away their possessions or sold their homes and businesses. Confident in the Lord's soon return, others had not planted crops. Poverty, hunger, and property disputes with relatives and neighbors, not to mention thoroughgoing humiliation, were tragically common. In the wake of the Great Disappointment, most of Miller's followers drifted away. Enough remained, however, that by the time Miller died in 1849, the "Adventist" movement he began had grown into a variety of sects. The best known of these today is the Seventh Day Adventist Church.

## CONCLUSIONS

What is the lesson in this historical parade of end-times prediction? While predictions of the world's end often have spawned intense evangelistic outreach, when the appointed date has passed, there has just as often been profound disappointment, embarrassment, and loss of credibility. A single statistic helps put the value of end-times date-setting in perspective. In the over two-thousand-year history of the church, the accuracy of end-times predictions has been exactly 0 percent. Here's the lesson: there is a danger in setting a date for the end of the world.

With 0 percent accuracy in mind, here are four ways to avoid the embarrassment of a failed end-times prediction.

### 1. DON'T MAKE A PREDICTION ABOUT THE END OF THE WORLD

If you don't feel comfortable doing your own taxes, steer well clear of end-times calculations. Even if you are good with numbers, it's impossible to use biblical numbers to do precise projections. Sometimes biblical authors use numbers for literary effect or theological meaning and don't expect readers to tally them. Moreover, these authors were sometimes selective in their presentation of history; the record given is representative, not exhaustive. For example, the twelve judges in the book of Judges likely represent a selection of Israelite leaders whose periods of influence may have overlapped and not been sequential. Biblical numbers do sometimes convey chronological information;

sometimes they are symbolic. Readers must be discerning. Given the stakes involved, caution should be the order of the day.

## 2. REMEMBER THAT THE BOOKS OF THE BIBLE WERE NOT GIVEN TO US FIRST

This basic fact and its ramifications are often lost in excited end-times discussions. The books of the Old and New Testaments were *first* given not to us, but to ancient Israel and the early church. This material made sense first to *those* audiences in *their* sociohistorical contexts. If while reading Ezekiel, Daniel, or Revelation, you become convinced that your knowledge of current world or regional politics equips you with unique insight into those texts, you're wrong. As we'll show in later chapters, in almost all cases, biblical prophecies were *fulfilled during the lifetime of the original audience*. Because the dominant purpose of prophecy is to warn people to turn from their sin and obey God, it makes sense that its consequences are foreseeable. If a prophecy given to a person or group could only be fully understood and fulfilled thousands of years after the original audience had died, who would pay attention? It would be the Holy Spirit's cruel joke to impart a message that could not be understood by, or helpful to, its original audience. Prophetic Scripture is certainly *for us*; that does not mean that it is *all about us*.

## 3. READ A BIBLICAL BOOK AS A WHOLE FOR ITS OVERALL MEANING

End-times expositors typically have spent a great deal of time reading and pondering Scripture. However commendable this is, they often focus on minutiae, comparing the details of individual verses in various biblical books with scant consideration of any book as a whole. Treating Scripture as a collection of matching clues, puzzle pieces, or codes, however, is not how biblical authors expected readers to approach their works. They wrote expecting that their audience(s) would read and consider their book in its entirety. They wrote so that their overall message would be conveyed in the final form of their work. In the final section of this book, we will apply this principle to look at how consideration of the final form of Daniel and Revelation is key to appreciating the message of those books.

## 4. REMEMBER THAT JESUS HIMSELF
### TOLD US NOT TO BOTHER

In Matthew 24:3, the disciples ask Jesus, "What will be the sign of your coming and of the end of the age?" In Matthew 24:36, Jesus finally gets around to an answer: "About that day or hour no one knows, not even the angels in heaven, nor the Son, but only the Father" (see also Mark 13:4, 32). Modern teachers from William Miller to Jack Van Impe have avoided this plain warning, claiming that they have only predicted the year, not the day or hour.[46] And yet, in each case they have been wrong. The Lord's caution and their error invite us to ask, "Why follow them?" Perhaps it is God's wisdom that we don't know when Christ will return. Imagine a teenager certain her parents were returning from vacation on Sunday at 8 p.m. She might spend most of the week avoiding housework only to launch into a tidying frenzy at 7:45 on Sunday night. The New Testament's consistent witness is different: always be ready.

The popular bumper-sticker slogan summarizes our conviction well—"Jesus is coming soon. Everybody look busy!" Jesus expects us to live his kingdom in the world and make disciples of all nations. That doesn't leave much time for math.

# 2

# WHO ARE THE
# END-TIMES TEACHERS?

## EVANGELICALS, FUNDAMENTALISTS,
## AND DISPENSATIONALISTS

The previous chapter identified key theological beliefs and calendric developments that birthed and perpetuated interest in Christ's return and the world's end. But what about more recent history? Which Christians today are most invested in the end of time? What has fueled that interest? According to secular media, they are at best indifferent to the threats the world faces; at worst, they are actively looking for ways to bring it about. Pop culture also casts evangelical Christians as odd, unbalanced, or wicked. Films such as *Saw*, *Money Train*, *See No Evil*, *Contact*, *The Mist*, *Frailty*, *There Will Be Blood*, *White Oleander*, and *Escape from Los Angeles*, and TV series such as *The Dead Zone* and Dick Wolf's *Law and Order* franchise all pile it on. The zeitgeist makes it easy to imagine that the Christians most interested in end times might go to any length to bring them.[1]

Jim Jones and David Koresh seem to validate this judgment. It would be wrong, however, to confuse these apocalyptic cult leaders with well-known end-times teachers such as Tim LaHaye, Hal Lindsey, and Jack Van Impe, or the many ordinary

Christians who follow them. Koresh and Jones were not evangelicals or fundamentalists; both were self-appointed, mentally unbalanced, authoritarian figures with messiah complexes. Their self-styled teaching led to destruction—for them and their followers. Neither practiced the interpretative approach known as dispensationalism that informs, guides, and constrains the teaching of most evangelical end-times teachers.

At the time of his death, David Koresh (1959–1993) led a small sect known as the Branch Davidians. Located at a compound near Waco, Texas, this tiny, apocalyptically minded group traced its pedigree through a tumultuous line of schisms back to the Seventh Day Adventists discussed in the last chapter. Vernon Wayne Howell combined the names of two Old Testament messianic characters—David and Cyrus—for himself: "David Koresh." Midwesterner Jim Jones (1931–1978) briefly associated with Methodist, Baptist, Independent Assemblies of God, and the Disciples of Christ denominations before founding the Peoples Temple. Although often appearing in a clerical collar, Jones was far from orthodox. A Marxist, Jones settled in San Francisco, where his status as an urban cleric led to influence in civic affairs and allowed him to promote his own unique vision of a religious socialism.[2] Jones denounced the Bible-centric religion of most evangelicals from his Peoples Temple pulpit in 1973, declaring,

> Your Bible religion and all churches say, that man is born a sinner. We say no, he's not born a sinner. He is a child of the most high. He's born with light, he's born with truth, that man has the highest potential evolution. We do not accept religion. Religion says man's born a sinner. No, he's not born a sinner. Ah— We've got to get this question settled here, because I hear some of this bullshit

still preached from this pulpit, that man's born in sin. Man, the only sins you're born in, is the society, the kind of community you live in. If you're born in a socialist community, then you're not born in sin. (Pause) If you're born in this church, this socialist revolution, you're not born in sin. If you're born in capitalist America, racist America, fascist America, then you're born in sin. But if you're born in socialism, you're not born in sin.[3]

Religious iconoclasts, Koresh and Jones rejected denominational associations that might have constrained their views or behavior. Their rejection of any outside boundaries to their biblical interpretation meant that they never had to justify their readings to anyone. Both claimed messianic status and with it unique authority to interpret the Bible. This also justified their extraordinary demands—including that husbands offer up their wives, and parents their daughters, for their sexual gratification. Thus, they could lead their followers into armed compounds in Guyana or Waco. Most tragically, adopting messianic status deluded them into taking a direct role in end-times events, leading them to suicide and mass murder.[4] Jones and Koresh had apocalyptic obsessions; neither represents the history, literature, and people connected to the kind of end-times teaching associated with conservative evangelical Christianity in America and around the world.

If not people such as Koresh and Jones, then, just who are the Christian teachers behind most of the end-times speculation that we encounter in today's churches?

To answer this question, we need to draw some distinctions within Protestant Christianity. Who are evangelicals, fundamentalists, and dispensationalists? Contrary to common misconceptions inside and outside the Christian faith, they are not synonymous. "Evangelical" and "fundamentalist" describe over-lapping movements within Protestant Christianity; "dispensa-tionalist" names a specific biblical and theological approach adopted by many within them.

Focusing on the first two terms, we can think of "evangeli-cal" as broadly describing any Protestant Christian who holds a "high" view of Scripture: that the Bible is the sole authority for faith and practice. "Fundamentalism" is a particular flavor of evangelicalism.[5] Defining either more precisely, however, is difficult, especially with "fundamentalism." After the rise in the 1970s of Iran's Ayatollah Khomeini, the phrase "fundamentalist Islam" associated the word "fundamentalist" with something religiously intolerant, reactionary, and violent. Evangelicals who might have been reasonably comfortable with the label "fundamentalist" complained that the term was now an inap-propriate and inaccurate descriptor of Christians. Brian Stiller, then head of the Evangelical Fellowship of Canada, penned a nationally distributed op-ed denouncing "fundamentalist" as being as offensive to Christians as the "N-word" was to African Americans.[6] Clearly an overstatement, Stiller's piece nonetheless demonstrates that many once self-identified "fun-damentalists" are today more comfortable with terms such as "conservative evangelical."

The term "fundamentalist" dates to the early twentieth cen-tury and was then a much broader term. America was under-going rapid demographic change. The preceding decades saw massive immigration from Catholic parts of Europe—nota-bly Ireland and Italy—and the advance of new ideas such as Marxism, evolution, and German higher criticism of the Bible. The influx of new ideologies and influences led a pair of American Christian businessmen to publish a series of ninety pamphlets on *fundamental* Christian beliefs along with essays on a number of the pressing issues of the day. Published from 1910–1915, these tracts were eventually combined into twelve volumes (available today in four) titled *The Fundamentals: A Testimony to the Truth*.[7] Written by sixty-four authors drawn from evangelical clergy, laypeople, and theological faculties from a wide range of Protestant denominations in the English-speaking world, the pamphlets were offered free to American clergy, Sunday school teachers, and missionaries. Those who subscribed to the views contained in these volumes became known as "fundamentalists."

Subsequent events in American society caused the fundamentalist movement to fracture, with some making different choices about how they lived in the world and related to those who believed differently. A key example was the Scopes monkey trial of 1925. Legal titans Clarence Darrow and William Jennings Bryan squared off over the teaching of evolution in Tennessee public schools. Although initially a legal win for fundamentalists, the trial quickly became a public relations catastrophe, as fundamentalists' opposition to evolution was widely lampooned. Bryan, a former democratic presidential candidate and US secretary of state, championed the anti-evolutionist side. His death shortly after the trial robbed fundamentalists of their most articulate spokesperson. Because of these setbacks, some fundamentalists withdrew from American civic and cultural life to create parallel education, literature, and music. Others went even further, limiting association and cooperation in activities such as evangelistic endeavors.[8] Those fundamentalists who remained theologically conservative but resisted the urge to withdraw took the name "neo-evangelical" or later "evangelical."

Theologically, fundamentalists (and many evangelicals) affirm the "verbal, plenary inspiration" of Scripture, that it is "inerrant." Many also promote the King James Version of the Bible over newer translations that they feel undermine key doctrines. They value the "literal" readings of Scripture over those that turn to symbolism and metaphor. To preserve the faith's purity, fundamentalists sometimes openly critique other evangelicals who stray into "doctrinal error." Their avoidance of practices that might lead to sin has often led to a long list of "don'ts" (don't drink, don't smoke, don't go to movies, etc.). Certain types of higher education are to be avoided because of "controversial" subject matter (evolution in biology; critical theory in the humanities). Fundamentalist-owned private businesses might avoid being "unequally yoked" to unbelieving partners to live out Paul's injunction in 2 Corinthians 6:14. Modesty in style and dress especially for women is stressed. Church membership typically rests on conformity in one or more of these areas. Distinct in belief and lifestyle, caricatured in film and television, fundamentalists—rightly or wrongly— have a reputation for intolerance, which only encourages their inward-looking tendencies.[9] Although more pronounced among fundamentalists, many of these characteristics are sometimes true of other evangelicals. Because the two groups share history, and because individuals, churches, and institutions drift sometimes imperceptibly from one to the other, it is difficult to demarcate one from the other: the boundary is porous.

As a proportion of evangelicals, fundamentalists' numbers have shrunk since the mid-twentieth century. After World War II, the National Association of Evangelicals (1942) and the World Evangelical Fellowship (1951) were established as parallel structures to the mainline-dominated National Council of Churches (1950) and the World Council of Churches (1948), respectively. By their nature, these organizations meant cooperation across denominational lines and despite theological differences—something not characteristic of fundamentalists. While evangelism has been a key interest of all evangelicals, fundamentalists have tended toward cultural isolationism, while evangelicals have been more willing to engage others and to adopt contemporary cultural language.

Let's turn now to the reading method. Dispensationalism is a theological approach to understanding Scripture and how God works in the world. It emphasizes the literal interpretation of Scripture and the precision and reliability of prophetic prediction. Because it conforms well to the predispositions described above, many evangelicals and fundamentalists find it attractive. Yet it is not universal. Alongside those who interpret Scripture through a dispensational lens, other evangelicals and fundamentalists read it through a different system—perhaps covenant theology; others have not consciously adopted any system at all. Indeed, many Reformed evangelicals, in the vein of Old Princeton Presbyterians Charles Hodge and B. B. Warfield, and nineteenth-century British Baptist C. H. Spurgeon, reject dispensationalism outright. This skepticism ought not to surprise since dispensationalism really only took shape in the mid-nineteenth century. As a theological latecomer and outsider, therefore, dispensationalism took some time to penetrate the world of Protestant biblical interpretation. Dispensationalism is practiced by many evangelicals and fundamentalists; it has never been universal among them.

Being clear about the origin and nature of fundamentalism, evangelicalism, and dispensationalism is important if we are to assess how these terms are popularly used. Often, the term "fundamentalist Christian" is used only pejoratively and to label figures to whom it does not properly apply. A sad case study is that of Denis Michael Rohan (1941–1995). In 1969, when Rohan arrived in Israel from Australia, he had already been diagnosed and hospitalized as a paranoid schizophrenic. Uncomfortable around other people, he did not attend any church, but listened to the radio broadcasts of Herbert W. Armstrong, the founder of the US-based Worldwide Church of God. The previous year, he had taken out a subscription to the church's magazine, *The Plain Truth*. Originally planning to travel to England to attend Armstrong's Ambassador College, Rohan abandoned the idea en route and continued on to Israel, where he ended up as a volunteer on a kibbutz. In August 1969, hearing voices and believing himself to be the "king of Jerusalem," Rohan stole into the al-Aqsa mosque at the south end of the Temple Mount and there set fire to the building's ornate and prized twelfth-century pulpit.[10] The event and its aftermath sparked outrage and rioting around the Muslim world, and the event is still annually commemorated in Palestine. Quickly arrested and prosecuted in the Jerusalem District Court, Rohan was found not guilty by reason of insanity and deported to Australia, where he died in a mental institution in 1995.

Since the event, it has become common to see Rohan labeled a "Christian," an "evangelical Christian," or a "Christian fundamentalist." Because Israeli media and ordinary citizens commonly designate any white person who is neither Muslim or Jewish as "Christian," this ought not to surprise. Given our discussion, however, the error is obvious. Rohan had no serious religious commitment. The group with which he was associated—tenuously—is considered by most evangelical Christians to be a cult or pseudo-Christian religion.[11] Writing to supporters at the time, church leader Armstrong vigorously and rightly denied the widely circulating idea that Rohan was a dedicated member.[12]

Despite these easily discoverable details, many continue to refer to Rohan as an evangelical or fundamentalist Christian.[13]

The sad truth remains that Rohan was directed by voices inside his head; his profile is miles removed from dispensationalist Christians interested in the return of Christ and strongly connected to a denomination or a Christian congregation. Dispensationalists are keen spectators of events in the Middle East and anxious observers of the signs of the times. Unlike Rohan and others like him,[14] however, their commitment to prophecy, a divine plan, and the sovereignty of God accentuates their awareness of God's unalterable timing. There is no question of taking action, forcing God's hand, or hastening Christ's return. To do so would challenge God's dominion.

While dispensationalism has lost considerable ground within evangelical denominations and seminaries over the past half-century, like the supertanker that moves forward long after its engines have been cut, its vision of the future remains deeply embedded in evangelical consciousness and American popular culture. To understand this vision, we must dig deeper into the system. What is dispensationalism? How does it work? What does it teach about Scripture and the end of the world? These are questions we will turn to next.

## THE IDEAS, INSTITUTIONS, AND INFLUENCERS OF DISPENSATIONALISM

### JOHN NELSON DARBY AND THE BIRTH OF DISPENSATIONALISM

Just off the main path of the Wimborne Road Cemetery in Bournemouth, England, stands a plain white gravestone bearing the epitaph "As unknown and well known." In 2 Corinthians 6:9 the apostle Paul uses these words to describe the extremes he experienced in his work for Christ. Standing over this unassuming nineteenth-century grave, they are an apt description of the legacy left by its occupant, John Nelson Darby (1800–1882), a leading figure in the Plymouth Brethren movement and founder of modern dispensationalism. Although unknown to most Christians today, Darby so shaped Protestant Christianity that one church historian dubbed him the fourth most influential figure in the formation of present-day Protestantism.[15]

John Nelson Darby was born into a wealthy Anglo-Irish landowning and mercantile family. His father, John Darby (1751–1834), was a successful trader who had assembled sufficient wealth to acquire an estate in Sussex and a house in London. Later, a series of premature deaths among his relatives allowed the elder Darby to inherit Leap Castle and its forty-six hundred acres in the Irish midlands. The family also had connections to the Irish legal world and the Royal Navy: Darby's middle name, Nelson, was given in honor of close family friend Admiral Horatio Nelson, the hero of Trafalgar. His mother, Anne Darby (née Vaughn; 1757–1847), came from an equally—if not more—successful Irish family that a generation earlier had moved to America and from there had established a flourishing trade between Boston, Jamaica, and London. In America, Darby's maternal grandfather, Samuel Freer Vaughn (1720–1802), fully immersed himself in the life of the young republic. Well-established among the social elite, he was a member of the American Philosophical Society and counted Benjamin Franklin among his close friends.[16] For a young John Nelson Darby, this pedigree meant easy movement among the Irish upper class and access at a young age to a first-rate education at Trinity College, Dublin, where he graduated in 1819 with the gold medal in classics.

While respectable, neither side of the family was particularly devout. For John Nelson Darby, a spiritual awakening seems to have occurred following his graduation from Trinity

College while preparing for a legal career. At the time, Darby's sister and brother had each settled in nearby County Wicklow, then a center of evangelical Church of Ireland piety. While the details of his spiritual transformation remain obscure, by 1825, Darby emerged as a deacon in the Church of Ireland in the newly formed backwater parish of Calary.[17] Over the next few years in this poor and isolated region of Wicklow, Darby demonstrated a frenetic pattern of travel, teaching, and evangelism that characterized the rest of his life. This commitment to the Church of Ireland ended, however, as a result of Darby's own mercurial personality and an apparent falling out with the archbishop of Dublin, William Magee.

Relocating to predominantly Catholic Dublin, Darby stumbled upon other Protestants who were meeting outside their denominational affiliations to share Communion. Fascinated, he soon began to take part. Eventually, this small ecumenical group developed into what would become known as the Plymouth Brethren movement, with Darby its most indefatigable (and ultimately divisive) teacher, evangelist, and writer.[18] As the Brethren movement grew and even after it began to splinter, Darby's influence remained high. He traveled frequently through Britain, Europe, and North America preaching and evangelizing. Along the way he translated the Bible into English, French, and German and produced theological letters, treatises, and tracts that today fill thirty-five volumes.[19]

Darby's work suffers from a dense writing style that leaves even the most earnest reader befuddled and defeated. Furthermore, he rarely wrote systematic treatments of particular theological topics; rather, most of his *Collected Writings* are letters and transcriptions of loosely organized public addresses responding to specific questions or criticisms. Add to this an almost rabbinic attention to detail and a tendency to range

widely and quickly through Scripture, and contemporary igno-
rance of his work becomes understandable. As an upshot of this,
while many claim Darby's support on this or that point of theology or eschatology, seldom are his own works cited. For our
purposes, three aspects of Darby's work are germane: (1) his
development of the dispensational approach to Scripture and
theology, (2) his understanding of Israel as a separate people
of God, and (3) his belief in the so-called rapture prior to the
final return of Christ.

## DISPENSATIONALISM

Dispensationalism, the theological scaffolding for most end-
times teaching today, takes its name from Darby's division of
world history into dispensations (economies or ages) in which
God in various ways has reached out to humanity, who have
always fallen short. A dispensation is "any arranged dealing of
God in which man has been set before his fall. And having been
tried, has failed, and therefore God has been obliged to act by
other means."[20] In each failed dispensation there nevertheless
remains a remnant faithfully responding to God's work. Prior
to the judgment that invariably ends each dispensation, God
discloses his plans to this remnant. Thus, the fate of Sodom
is revealed to Abraham (OT) even as the fate of Babylon the
Great is revealed to the church (NT).[21] Members of the remnant begin with a perception of God's glory, which by contrast
leads to a consciousness of their own fallen condition and to
their being called out of the world to intercede for it and stand
as a testimony to God's grace. At the close of each dispensation, the faithfulness of the remnant testifies to the failure of
the majority. In each case, God does not judge humanity until
it has rejected every remedy.[22]

Darby divided all human history into six dispensations (see fig. 2.1; this is a schema differing from the sevenfold approach popularized by C. I. Scofield). Five of these present similar combinations of disobedience, faithfulness, and judgment: (1) Noah, (2) Abraham, (3) Israel, (4) the church, and (5) the millennium.[23] Missing is any dispensation prior to Noah. Since an essential feature of a dispensation was a form of divine government by which God related to human beings, and since he could detect no such arrangement prior to Noah, Darby thought that prior to the flood no dispensation existed. The dispensations themselves are summarized in this way.

| 1 | 2 | 3 | 4 | 5 | 6 |
|---|---|---|---|---|---|
| **Noah** | **Abraham** | **Israel under the law** | **Gentiles** | **Spirit/ Church** | **Millennium** |
| (flood to the call of Abraham | (call of Abraham to the giving of the law) | (giving of the law to the exile) | (Nebuchadnezzar to Christ) | (first to second advents of Christ) | (second advent of Christ to the end of 1,000 years) |

*Fig. 2.1. Dispensations according to Darby*

1. NOAH

The period of Noah was a time God governed through judgment and "committed the right of the sword to man."[24] This dispensation ended in the flood. The preservation of the righteous Noah and his family sets a pattern that subsequent dispensations follow and explains both the evangelistic and separatist impulses that characterized Darby's approach to ministry.

## 2. ABRAHAM

In the next dispensation, named after Abraham, God relates to people through calling, election, and promise.[25] A key to understanding this dispensation (and also the church age) is that "separation from the world for the enjoyment of promise by faith becomes the divine principle of blessing."[26] The blessings promised to Abraham are unconditional and therefore endure despite Israel's later disobedience and fall. For Darby (and for dispensationalists today), the enduring nature of these promises explains Israel's abiding claim to the promised land and its role in end-times events.

## 3. ISRAEL UNDER THE LAW, PRIESTHOOD, AND KINGS

The dispensation of Abraham ends with judgment on the Egyptians for their abuse of Abraham's seed, giving rise to the dispensation of Israel.[27] The giving of the law at Sinai unites the first dispensation's principle of government to the second's principle of calling. Like the second, this one also includes promises, but these are now conditional on Israel's obedience to the law, which is given to show Israel what God intends it to be and to which end God gives Israel priests, prophets, and kings.[28]

## 4. GENTILES

The exile marks God's removal of the principle of government from Israel and passes it to the gentiles (though God's second-dispensation calling and promises remain with Israel).[29] Because the gentile nations are also fallen, they administer human government as "beasts" of the kind found

in the book of Daniel.[30] This dispensation ends with Jews'
and gentiles' joint rejection of Jesus. Since Christ himself
was the source of Israel's blessing, Jewish rejection of Jesus
means that, while the promises abide, they are cut off from
earthly blessing until he returns.[31]

## 5. THE AGE OF THE SPIRIT/CHURCH

The sin of Israel and the nations and the judgment incurred
inaugurate the dispensation of the church or the Spirit: that is,
the present, a dispensation defined by an "earthly versus heavenly" dynamic. Although Satan is "the prince and god of this
world," God visits the gentiles through the gospel to call out a
people for his name—the church.[32] While Jews are still God's
chosen people, they remain excluded from his presence through
their rebellion and rejection of Jesus. Similarly, the gentiles
retain the power of human government, but exercise it in a state
of ruin.[33] During the church age, Christ is both in heaven and
mystically united to Christians as his heavenly people, associated with him as a "better Eve." Through this union, the church
"fills the gap" left by the failure of the gentiles and Jews.[34]

Darby understood this fifth dispensation to be at the point
of failure. Against those who hoped for the global growth
of Christianity, Darby asserts that "there is no prophecy in
Scripture, or promise … that the gradual diffusion of the gospel
shall convert the world."[35] Passages of Scripture such as the parable of the tares (Matt 13:24–30) convinced him that the church
too, at least as an outward system rather than the mystical body
of Christ, would be judged.[36] Corruption and nepotism in the
nineteenth-century Church of Ireland and elsewhere in Britain
convinced Darby that the organized church was in "ruins."[37]
Darby was not alone. Many contemporaries shared this conviction. The massive popularity of John Wade's *The Black Book,*

*or, Corruption Unmasked!* (2 vols., 1820–1823) and its later revisions and reprints (1831, 1832, 1835) is evidence. Though Wade chronicled state corruption generally, the church in Britain and Ireland was rebuked for nepotism, forced tithing, clergy sloth (e.g., clergy reliance on curates and purchase of sermon collections), pluralism (i.e., income double-dipping), nonresidence of bishops and clergy, and so on.[38] Charges such as Wade's, combined with the repeal of restrictions for dissenters in public life, made leaving the established church a realistic option. This backdrop of ecclesial corruption, Darby maintained, provided a context for potent testimony on the part of the faithful remnant, whom God would gather prior to the judgment.[39]

Consequently, faithful believers should leave their denominations, meeting instead according to exclusively New Testament principles. Combined with Darby's idea that the basis of unity was correct doctrine, this meant that his tireless evangelism and teaching were also divisive. This separatist impulse came so strongly to characterize Darby's movement that W. H. Griffiths Thomas, dispensationalist and cofounder of Dallas Theological Seminary, observed that "the Brethren are remarkable people for rightly dividing the word of Truth, but wrongly dividing themselves."[40]

### 6. THE MILLENNIUM

Darby's final future dispensation, the millennium, will begin when the power of the gentiles ends and the church is taken to heaven.[41] He understood this period to be a literal one-thousand-year reign of Christ on earth, a time of universal knowledge when "men shall no more say, 'know the Lord.'" God's chosen people Israel, set aside following the third dispensation, now experience blessing under the returned Christ, who rules from Jerusalem. Old Testament prophecy predicting an ideal future state for

Israel not literally realized during the dispensation of Israel will be fulfilled in this era (e.g., Isa 65:13–25).[42]

According to Darby's dispensational understanding of God's work in the world, one's interpretation of a particular portion of Scripture varies according to the dispensation to which it was given. For example, ardent dispensationalists downplay the Beatitudes. Being given prior to the crucifixion, they fall into a period when Israel exists but the church does not. They are thus intended for Jews, not the church. Similarly, David's plea in Psalm 51:11, "Do not cast me from your presence or take your Holy Spirit from me," has no bearing on debates about salvation today. Belonging to the dispensation of law, this passage has been displaced by Acts 2, when the Holy Spirit is given in the dispensation of the church.

Did Darby invent dispensationalism or recover a lost doctrine? Dispensationalism's opponents have tended to argue that it was Darby's own invention; allies have sought to show how it was anticipated from the earliest church fathers until Darby's own time.[43] The answer lies somewhere in between. The division of the history of the world into six preordained one-thousand-year eras was common in early Judaism and early and medieval Christianity, as we have seen. In a sense, Darby was not proposing anything new. His innovation lay in the specific pattern of divine work and human response that he saw in each dispensation and how this influenced specific scriptural interpretations. Darby, we conclude, founded a theological movement, which innovates by building on something previously well-established.

## ISRAEL AND THE CHURCH

Darby's understanding of the relationship between Israel and the church has also had significant consequences for end-times teaching. Where it was once common to emphasize the church as the new Israel or the new people of God,[44] Darby affirms that God has done a new work in the church as the *heavenly* people of God. For him, Israel remained God's *earthly* people. "All the doings of God upon the earth," he writes, "have reference entirely and directly to the Jews, as the center of His earthly counsels and of His government." For support, Darby cites Deuteronomy 32:8 (KJV), which suggests that even the number of the nations was ordained in relation to the number of the "sons of Israel."[45] Indeed, Darby argues, "Israel, as a nation, will be saved. 'There shall come out of Zion a deliverer.' He has not cast away His people. As touching the gospel they are enemies, and they will so remain until the fulness of the gentiles come in, but the Deliverer will come."[46]

For Darby, the catastrophic judgment on Israel's unbelief that was the destruction of Jerusalem and the Babylonian exile ushered in the dispensation of the gentiles. Israel was set aside.[47] The promises given to Abraham and his descendants (the second dispensation), however, were not. The unconditional promises of blessing the nations and living in the land remained valid, allowing Darby to boldly predict—when the Ottoman Empire controlled the Middle East and much of the Mediterranean—that the Jewish people would return to their ancestral homeland.[48] Once nationally reestablished, they would receive the rule of Christ upon his future return to earth.[49] Thus Darby harmonized God's shift to the church as his agents in the world with the abiding promises given to the chosen people. That Israel remained *a* people of God with vital promises yet to be fulfilled meant that they still had a role in God's prophetic plans. This explains why Israel commands such attention from dispensationalist evangelicals today and the strong support for the modern state of Israel and for Jewish groups domestically.

## THE RAPTURE

Darby's theory of the rapture has gained the most currency in the evangelical world and spread to popular culture.[50] The historic view of the church had been expressed in the Apostles' and Nicene Creeds: Christ would someday "come to judge the quick and the dead." Darby, however, questioned this long-standing doctrine, discerning not one resurrection, but two. The first of these—the rapture—denotes the return of Christ to receive resurrected saints and living believers into heaven, ending the dispensation of the church. The second resurrection is of the wicked to judgment and occurs following the millennium.[51] Christ, having long returned to the earth with the saints, judges the wicked as they stand before his great white throne. Anticipating the objection that this two-stage view was novel, departing from the church's traditional teaching, Darby counters that the church's "traditional teaching" could and had misread Scripture throughout history. He concludes that "there is no such thing in Scripture as a common resurrection."[52]

Parallel lines of scriptural reasoning led Darby to this two-stage resurrection.[53] He could not accept the traditional belief that the righteous and unrighteous were raised together. The deceased faithful, he maintained, are raised by virtue of their union with Christ (1 Cor 15:12–23; Col 2:12), who has been judged in their stead. The resurrection of the faithful to judgment is impossible.[54] Darby asks, If redeemed souls are immediately with Christ upon death, dwelling with him in heaven, then why would their bodies be raised to judgment later?[55] Noting Paul's words—"If by any means I might *attain* unto the resurrection of the dead" (Phil 3:11 KJV)—Darby wonders why the apostle would be anxious over something he and the wicked shared.[56] In Luke 20:35, says Darby, Jesus also seems to suggest that the resurrection of the righteous is distinct from that of the wicked.[57] Furthermore, differing descriptions point to two distinct events. First Thessalonians 4:14–16 does not mention the wicked but describes the saints meeting Christ in the air.[58] The resurrection of the wicked, described in Revelation 20, is markedly different. Not a resurrection "to be attained" but a forced removal to judgment, this resurrection occurs at the end of Christ's millennial reign, long after his return.[59] These differences allow Darby to assert that Scripture speaks of the resurrection of the righteous *and* the resurrection of the wicked.[60] The physical and complete return of Christ occurs between them when, accompanied by the saints, Christ returns to judge the living and initiate the millennium (Zech 14:5; Col 3:4).[61]

## CONCLUSIONS

Understanding each dispensation's predictable pattern allowed Darby and his followers to situate themselves and their spiritual work within the flow of salvation history: they were their dispensation's remnant, making them both keen to evangelize and skeptical about whether faithfulness might be found in "fallen" churches. Darby's doctrine of the rapture, with Christ appearing to rescue his people, gave their evangelistic efforts peculiar urgency. Evangelical urgency and ecclesial skepticism explain why dispensationally minded churches and individuals have so focused on evangelism and world missions. Darby's idea that God reveals his future intentions to the remnant of each dispensation helps explain why eschatological study has so defined the Plymouth Brethren and dispensationalists generally.

Also important is Darby's understanding of Israel's ongoing identity as an earthly people of God and the recipient of the prophecies of the Old Testament. This understanding, undergirded by the solemn warning of Genesis 12:3, explains dispensationalists' interest in the Middle East, support for the modern state of Israel, and most notably the almost complete absence of anti-Semitism among their number.

Negatively, Darby's system leads to a pessimistic worldview. Since each dispensation ends with things getting worse, there is little to animate collective action for world peace or improved environmental stewardship. While dispensationalists do share the common human interest in maintaining a peaceful world and a healthy planet, their perception that human behavior worsens as each dispensation ends predisposes them to passivism.

## CYRUS INGERSON SCOFIELD:
## DISPENSATIONALISM FOR THE MASSES

By the time of his death in 1880, Darby had made a remarkable seven transatlantic crossings and many more journeys elsewhere.[62] Advancing the cause of dispensationalism in North America, however, largely fell to Cyrus Ingerson Scofield (1843–1921), remembered today as both saint and scoundrel. Even the sympathetic biographical sketch found in the first chapter of *The Scofield Bible: Its History and Impact on the Evangelical Church* is subtitled "A Controversial Life."[63]

Born in Clinton, Michigan, in 1843, Scofield was the youngest of seven children. Following the death of his mother and stepmother, a teenage Scofield moved to Lebanon, Tennessee, to live with his sister and her husband and to attend Cumberland University. At the outbreak of the Civil War, however, Scofield, apparently swept up in local fervor, enlisted with the Seventh Tennessee Infantry.[64] Scofield—a northerner—proved a fickle Confederate. When conscription threatened to extend his military service, a now ill and hospitalized Scofield petitioned for exemption on the grounds that he was not a citizen of the Confederacy, but a northerner who had enlisted while on a visit south.[65]

Shortly after his discharge, Scofield traveled to the Union-controlled St. Louis, where he lived with another sister. Her husband, a prominent lawyer and city tax assessor, helped the young Scofield acquire work; he began training to be a lawyer. It was also in St. Louis that he met and married Mary Leontine Cerré, a Roman Catholic and member of a prominent local family of French descent.[66] Shortly thereafter, the Scofield family moved to Atchison, Kansas, where his legal career flourished; he served in the state legislature and chaired the judiciary committee. In 1873, President Grant appointed the twenty-nine-year-old to the post of US state attorney for the district of Kansas.[67] Within six months of his federal appointment, he resigned, suspected of accepting bribes. So began a downward spiral: failure to establish a private law practice, debt, and drinking. In 1877, an unemployed Scofield abandoned his family and embarked on a short and desperate series of fraud schemes.[68]

In 1879 the ruined Scofield experienced a profound religious conversion back in St. Louis. In the years that followed, the Rev. Dr. James H. Brookes, a prominent Presbyterian minister and dispensationalist Bible teacher, mentored him. Through Brookes, Scofield met evangelist D. L. Moody, beginning what would become a lifelong association. Under the tutelage of Brookes and another minister, C. L. Goodall, Scofield put his scandalous past behind him, emerging in 1882 as pastor of the First Congregationalist Church of Dallas.[69] The rest of Scofield's life cycled between pastoral ministry, conference speaking, and writing. He died at his home in Douglaston, Long Island, in 1921, aged seventy-eight.

Scofield made two significant contributions to the promotion and development of dispensational thinking among American evangelicals. First, his short book *Rightly Dividing the Word of Truth*, published in 1888, clarified Darby's sometimes dense and disorienting work, presenting the basics of Scofield's method of personal Bible study along with his dispensational assessment of time and Scripture.[70] Like Darby, Scofield organized God's redemptive dealings with humanity into dispensations, with each of these dealings culminating in human failure. Scofield's numbering and characterization, however, differed from Darby's in the following way (see fig. 2.2):[71]

1. *Man innocent.* This first dispensation begins with the creation of Adam, who must obey God by abstaining from the fruit of the tree of the knowledge of good and evil. Disobedience results in judgment and expulsion from the garden (Gen 1:26; 2:16–17; 3:6, 22–24).

2. *Man under conscience.* In the second dispensation, humans have a conscience and are responsible for choosing between good and evil. God judges the universal unchecked growth of evil with the flood (Gen 3:7, 22; 6:5, 11–12; 7:11–12, 23).

3. *Man in authority over the earth.* During this dispensation, Noah's descendants repopulate the earth and are given the opportunity to form human government. Instead, they attempt to become independent from God, leading to the confusion of languages at Babel (Gen 9:1–2; 11:1–4, 5–8).

4. *Man under promise.* In this era, God calls Abram, giving him and his descendants conditional and unconditional promises. Repeated violation of the conditions culminates in slavery in Egypt (Gen 12:1–3; 13:14–17; 15:5; 26:3, 12–13; Exod 1:13–14).

5. *Man under law.* This dispensation was inaugurated by God's gift of the law at Sinai. Israel repeatedly breaks this law and is judged through exile from the land and dispersion (Exod 19:1–8; 2 Kgs 17:1–18; 25:1–11; Acts 2:22–23; 7:51–52; Rom 3:19–20; 10:5; Gal 3:10).

6. *Man under grace.* Commencing at the crucifixion of Christ, this dispensation—Scofield's present day—is characterized by God's undeserved favor, which brings righteousness. This era will end with judgment on an unbelieving world and an apostate church (Luke 18:8; 17:26–30; 2 Thess 2:7–12; Rev 3:15–16), and the removal of Christ's followers at the rapture with judgment for those left in the form of the great tribulation (Jer 30:5–7; Dan 12:1; Zeph 1:15–18; Matt 24:21–22), ending with the final and personal return of Christ in power (Matt 24:29–30; 25:31–46).

7. *Man under the personal reign of Christ.* Christ's return with his saints, which corresponds with his millennial reign on earth over a restored Israel (Isa 2:1–4; 11:1–16; Acts 15:14–17; Rev 19:11–21; 20:1–6), begins the seventh dispensation. It will end with the loosing of Satan, his subsequent judgment along with the wicked dead, and the creation of a new heaven and a new earth (Rev 20:3, 7–15; 21:1–22:21).

Scofield also discusses the distinction between Israel and the church, and the two resurrections, repeating Darby's essential dispensationalist ideas, but simpler and clearer.[72]

| Darby | | | Scofield | | |
|---|---|---|---|---|---|
| Paradise | Garden of Eden to the fall | (no government; not a dispensation) | 1 | Man innocent | (creation to the fall) |
| Conscience | Fall to the flood | (no government; not a dispensation) | 2 | Man under conscience | (fall to the flood) |
| 1 | Noah | (flood to the call of Abraham) | 3 | Man in authority over the earth | (flood to the tower of Babel) |
| 2 | Abraham | (call of Abraham to the giving of the law) | 4 | Man under promise | (call of Abraham to the law at Sinai) |
| 3 | Israel under the law | (giving of the law to the exile) | 5 | Man under law | (law at Sinai to Calvary) |
| 4 | Gentiles | (Nebuchadnezzar to Christ) | | | |
| 5 | Spirit/Church | (first to second advents of Christ) | 6 | Man under grace | (Calvary to the second coming) |
| 6 | Millennium | (second advent of Christ to the end of 1,000 years) | 7 | Man under the personal reign of Christ | (second coming to the end of the millennium) |

Fig. 2.2. Dispensational systems of Darby and Scofield compared

If *Rightly Dividing the Word of Truth* introduced readers to dispensationalism's essential elements, Scofield's famous reference Bible took the second step: systematically applying this approach to Scripture as a whole. Although Scofield himself was first a Congregationalist and later a Presbyterian, his grand Bible project was influenced and aided by others,[73] including members of the Plymouth Brethren. One of Scofield's long-time friends from the Bible conference circuit, Methodist Bible teacher, publisher, and evangelist to Jewish immigrants Arno Gaebelein, connected Scofield with several wealthy Plymouth Brethren businessmen who provided seed money for the project. Gaebelein himself was listed as a consulting editor.[74] More importantly, these connections introduced Scofield to Plymouth Brethren member Henry Frowde, the savvy manager of Oxford University Press's London Office and bearer of the title "publisher to the university."[75] Now, Scofield had a publisher with global distribution and—most importantly—respectability. The publisher in turn received a steady income that sustained it through the lean years of the First World War and beyond.

*The Scofield Reference Bible*'s two editions (1909, 1917) used cross-references to trace key themes through Scripture;[76] footnotes elaborated on these and provided brief commentary about the dispensational relevance of various passages. It brilliantly transposed an entire theological system onto the biblical text: always at hand to guide one's private reading of Scripture or sermon preparation and permitting those listeners or readers of others' works to judge how closely they hewed to accepted dispensational teaching. Scofield's influence on the spread of dispensationalism is difficult to overstate. Although a global promoter of dispensationalism, Darby was throughout his career a combative, divisive figure and intolerant of what he considered to be doctrinal error. Scofield's entrepreneurial disposition and ability to enlist others in his efforts, by contrast, made him a linchpin of dispensationalism. He passed Darby's ideas on to a new generation and a much wider audience.

## DISPENSATIONALISM AND THE SEMINARY

In 1896, D. L. Moody invited Scofield to leave Dallas to assume leadership of Moody's church and Bible training school in East Northfield, Massachusetts.[77] There, Scofield met a bright and resourceful student named Lewis Sperry Chafer. As James Brookes had done for him, Scofield mentored Chafer and in the years that followed relied on him as a gifted administrator and teacher. When Scofield needed someone to lead his New York–based correspondence school, and later to set the curriculum for and teach at the newly established Philadelphia School of the Bible, he turned to Chafer. When Scofield died, his congregation at First Congregational Church in Dallas called on Chafer to fill the empty pulpit.[78]

From Dallas, Chafer continued to spread the dispensational message. He established the first seminary in America with dispensationalism as a founding principle. Originally named the Evangelical Theological College, it is known today as Dallas Theological Seminary. Its dispensationalist ministers soon served churches across North America. Its doctoral program, established in 1927, ensured that dispensationally minded students would soon serve as faculty in evangelical colleges and seminaries. In 1934, Chafer's savvy acquisition of the journal *Bibliotheca Sacra* further broadened the seminary's dispensational influence by providing an outlet for promoting dispensational thinking in the academic world.

Among the thousands of students and faculty produced by Dallas Theological Seminary since 1924, three stand out for their impact on end-times teaching in America.[79] First,

J. Dwight Pentecost (1915–2014) began his ordained ministry in the Presbyterian Church and eventually became professor of biblical exposition at Dallas Theological Seminary. His most influential end-times book, *Things to Come: A Study in Biblical Eschatology*,[80] laid out Pentecost's understanding of prophecy and end times and critiqued competing views methodically and accessibly. Since its publication in 1964, it has been foundational for many popular end-times writers and teachers. Pentecost cast a long shadow over Dallas, teaching there occasionally until well into his nineties.

Like Pentecost, John Walvoord (1910–2002) also first served as a Presbyterian minister before spending his academic career of fifty years entirely at Dallas Theological Seminary. The primary academic interest of Walvoord, who served first as professor of systematic theology and later as seminary president, was eschatology. He produced several books influential among dispensationalists, including works on the rapture and the millennium and commentaries on Daniel and Revelation.[81] His most widely read work, however, was the paperback *Armageddon, Oil and the Middle East Crisis*.[82] In the run-up to the first Gulf War (1990–1991), renewed interest led the book's publisher, Zondervan, to print one million new copies.[83] Among the book's many new readers were members of the White House staff of President George H. W. Bush, who requested copies directly from the publisher.[84]

More easily overlooked but no less important is Walvoord's contribution to *The New Scofield Reference Bible*.[85] Published in 1967, the *New Scofield* featured an editorial panel of nine respected dispensationalists, including Walvoord, by then the president of Dallas Theological Seminary, and Frank E. Gaebelein, son of Arno Gaebelein, who had done much to launch the original. The new edition revised footnotes, added cross-references, and updated maps, dates, and headings, all in a new typeface. The new notes eliminated perspectives from the original that were no longer acceptable. Thus the original note on Genesis 9:1, which foretold for Ham (the "father" of the African peoples) "an inferior and servile posterity," was replaced with the more restrained comment that Ham's descendants "would be servants to their brethren." *New Scofield* also incorporated archaeological and textual discoveries that had been made since 1917, such as those from Qumran, Ugarit, Nuzi, and Mari. *New Scofield*'s editors also adamantly reaffirmed their commitment to inerrancy, the virgin birth and deity of Christ, his imminent coming for the church, and his physical premillennial return to the earth. A significant update to Scofield's original, *New Scofield* brought dispensationalism to a new generation of conservative Protestant readers who could read it with one eye on the text and the other on events that were unfolding at that moment in the Middle East. Like the first two editions, *New Scofield* was published and distributed by the venerable Oxford University Press. Walvoord's stature within the crowded world of end-times publishing is attested by the multiple editions of his books, many of which remain in print more than a decade after his death, to say nothing of his conference speaking and video-based teaching.

Our third Dallas Theological Seminary figure was not a member of faculty but a student. Hal Lindsey (b. 1929) published his best seller, *The Late Great Planet Earth*,[86] shortly after graduating. Just as Scofield popularized Darby, so Lindsey took what he had learned from his professors Pentecost and Walvoord and presented it (with the help of ghostwriter C. C. Carlson) in the form of a fast-paced thriller. This approach clearly paid off. A recent paperback edition proclaims over fifteen million copies sold. Reading Lindsey's dated prose today, one might wonder why it had such immediate and wide popular appeal.

One explanation is, simply, its context. The anti-establishment ethos of the 1960s created a ready market for books that took on established theories with new and radical proposals that captured the popular imagination. Even as readers devoured Lindsey's book, they were also captivated by *The Ra Expeditions*, Thor Heyerdahl's idea that ancient Egyptians traversed the Atlantic to influence Mayan civilization. A year before Lindsey's book was published, Eric von Däniken's *Chariots of the Gods?* argued that aliens had visited earth to give a technological boost to civilizations around the planet. In the same year, Alvin Toffler's *Future Shock* described the disorientation and anxiety that results from a world characterized by radical change and information overload.[87] All of these books quickly became global sensations because of their arrival at a culturally serendipitous moment.

*Late Great* also arrived at a key moment historically and theologically. In the New Testament, Jesus says his return will be preceded by "wars and rumors of wars" (Matt 24:6; Mark 13:7). For many Americans, that described the decade that had just ended. When *Late Great* hit the shelves in 1970, the United States had just emerged from the turbulent 1960s. Race riots had occurred in Los Angeles, Chicago, and elsewhere; prominent national figures Martin Luther King Jr. and Bobby Kennedy had been assassinated in short succession; and the country was embroiled in an unpopular war in Vietnam. The dawn of the 1970s also saw growing tensions in the Middle East and the rise of PLO terrorism. In this context, the book's message that Bible prophecy predicted much of what was unfolding in current events seemed startlingly accurate and relevant.

A further attraction of Lindsey's book was its unabashed application of the more sober eschatological teachings of Pentecost and Walvoord to recent history and current events. Consider Lindsey's treatment of the parable of the fig tree in Matthew 24, specifically Jesus's statement in verse 34 that "this generation will certainly not pass away until all these things have happened." In his *Things to Come*, Pentecost evaluates different understandings of "generation" and concludes that it refers to the nation of Israel as a whole. The parable shows that Israel as a people will endure to the end.[88] By contrast, Lindsey simply asserts "generation" to mean a forty-year period. After identifying the "tender" leaves (v. 32) with Israel's 1948 rebirth, he suggests that Christ's return could well take place within forty years of that event.[89] This dramatic date-setting might have unsettled Lindsey's professors, but combined with the book's catchy section titles and use of sixties slang, it made *Late Great* perfectly suited to its time.

## DISPENSATIONALISM IN THE MEDIA:
## THE END TIMES AS NEWS

As sales of *Late Great* and its many follow-ups dwindled, Lindsey shifted to Christian television, hosting the *International Intelligence Briefing* on the Trinity Broadcasting Network from 1994 to 2005 and later *The Hal Lindsey Report*. In this he followed several other notable end-times teachers, including Canadian brothers Paul and Peter Lalonde, whose *This Week in Bible Prophecy* pioneered the prophecy newsmagazine format. Along with *Jack Van Impe Presents,* these programs connected current events to Bible prophecy while mimicking the style of secular newsmagazines such as *ABC News Nightline.*

The most enduring of these TV-based end-times teachers has been Jack Van Impe (1931–2020), who along with wife,

Rexella (b. 1932), hosted a weekly prophecy–current affairs program broadcast on the Daystar Television Network and streamed over the internet. The program's format had Rexella reviewing media headlines from newspapers and asking husband Jack how they related to the Bible and end-time events. Each presentation concluded with an urgent evangelistic appeal, a feature common to dispensational end-times teaching generally. If Scripture and current events suggest that Christ could return at any moment, then it's vital to accept Christ before it is too late. Over the years Van Impe openly piggybacked on popular apocalyptic fervor to make semiguarded predictions about Christ's return, producing videos based on different dates—for example, 2000 and 2012.[90] When questioned about the propriety of such predictions, Van Impe consistently pointed to Jesus's words in Matthew 25:13, "Keep watch, because you do not know the *day* or the *hour*." Jesus apparently said nothing about the *year*.

While Van Impe's combination of ancient prophecy, analysis of current events, and evangelistic appeal may seem bizarre, it is a natural impulse *if* one assumes (1) that much biblical prophecy refers to the end times and (2) that the world is rapidly approaching those times.

## THE END TIMES AS ENTERTAINMENT

Over his long career, Tim LaHaye (1926–2016) was a Baptist minister, Christian writer, and political activist. Concerned by the secularization of American society, LaHaye founded such organizations as the Institute for Creation Research and San Diego Christian College (formerly, Christian Heritage College), sat on the board of Jerry Falwell's Moral Majority, and endorsed or otherwise promoted political candidates perceived to be friendly to conservative evangelical interests. Today, however, LaHaye is best remembered for teaming with Christian writer

Jerry B. Jenkins to launch the most popular series of Christian novels ever produced. At its completion, the Left Behind series of end times–themed novels ran to thirteen volumes, sold over sixty-five million copies, and spawned children's editions of the series, graphic novels, films, and video games.

To franchise the books into films, LaHaye turned to Canadians Paul and Peter Lalonde. With considerable experience as dispensational end-times teachers and broadcasters, the Lalondes had wound down their weekly prophecy program and branched into religious filmmaking through their production company, Cloud Ten Pictures. Its first release was 1998's *Apocalypse*. Produced on a modest budget, this film enjoyed wide distribution through video and showings in evangelical churches, and led to three follow-up pictures starring actors such as Gary Busey, Mr. T, Corbin Bernsen, and Carol Alt. When the first Left Behind novel was published, the Lalonde brothers purchased the film rights and produced five films based on the series. While box-office success and critical praise have proved elusive, the Lalondes' films have found an audience among North American evangelicals who have valued these movies for their evangelistic potential. The Left Behind movies enjoyed strong DVD sales and have been screened in many conservative evangelical churches across North America.

The Lalondes, of course, were not the first to see the entertainment and evangelistic potential of end times–related drama. In 1972, Christians gathered in churches and at special cinema screenings to watch the film *A Thief in the Night*, a gripping story of life during the tribulation. Three more pictures followed in the Thief in the Night series before it wound down in 1983. *Late Great* itself was adapted for the screen in 1979. Combining documentary and dramatization, and narrated by

Orson Welles, it had wide theatrical release and grossed $19.5 million at the box office.[91]

When compared to the average feature film, end-times movies (like Christian movies in general) have always been made on modest budgets for limited theatrical release. Many are released straight to video and screened through churches. Because they tend to fly under the radar, they may have more of an impact than first imagined. The main interest in producing these pictures is evangelism.

## CONCLUSION

Ministers today, unless they graduated from one of the few theological schools that takes dispensationalism as its guiding principle, are unlikely to have any knowledge of the system. Most laypeople, even those within evangelical contexts, would struggle to define it. And yet, through popular resources such as the Scofield Bible, *The Late Great Planet Earth*, prophetic news analysis, and the Left Behind phenomenon, dispensationalism's view of end times has so permeated popular culture that a 2010 Pew Research poll found that 41 percent of Americans believed that Jesus would definitely or probably return prior to 2050. By contrast, only 27 percent of white mainline Protestants agreed.[92] These statistics reveal a significant pastoral issue and opportunity for clergy. To engage with a significant swath of American culture on what lies in its future, ministers will need to understand dispensationalism and its reading of the biblical books on which most end-times teaching rests. So, what does premillennial dispensationalism think about the last days, and how does it arrive at those conclusions? Importantly for the church, what kind of behavior can be expected by those who hold to these beliefs? These are questions we will look at next.

# 3

## THE DISPENSATIONAL
## END-TIMES STORY

"Reverend, when are you going to preach on prophecy? Russia is on the move in the Middle East, and Israel is under threat. The signs are lining up, and our church could use some teaching on this so we understand what happens next." Because so few seminary curricula are designed from the dispensational perspective, many ministers might well wonder how to respond. While they are keen to meet the needs of their congregation, they may have likely *avoided* studying books such as Ezekiel and Daniel; if, perchance, they ventured into Revelation, they likely got no further than the letters to the seven churches in chapters 1–3. With so much else going on in congregational life, they may think, eschatology is best left on the back burner—and understandably so. On this subject, it is likely the parishioner who has devoured books on the end times and regularly watches television and internet-streamed prophecy teachers who is in the know. We'll bridge this cultural gap by describing in greater detail how dispensationalism's vision of the future unfolds.

Complicating our task is the sheer number of end-times teachers writing, blogging, and broadcasting on the subject. Although the basic end-times narrative is broadly shared, the details vary, sometimes a lot. So does temperament. Where older writers such as Darby and Scofield were cautious about connecting Scripture to contemporary events, restraint is rarely a hallmark of more recent ones. Many are quite ready to tie biblical passages to world events—and to do so on a weekly basis! Sometimes prophetic understanding is a moving target. The person who was the antichrist ten years ago may not be the antichrist today. To avoid getting caught in the weeds, we've distilled the drama of the end times, focusing on the premillennial, pretribulation rapture position that might be heard in most dispensationalist-oriented churches today.[1]

So, what does the future look like? For most dispensationalists, today is the dispensation of grace or the church age. From here forward, there looms the restoration of Israel, the rapture, the great tribulation and the dominance of antichrist, the battle of Armageddon, the return of Christ to earth, the millennium, and the new heaven and the new earth. We'll examine each of these and more in turn, listing the key biblical passages that contribute to the dispensationalist understanding of the future. We'll show how dispensationalism uses various genres and passages of Scripture to formulate its vision. Hopefully we'll describe more than we criticize and so provide a snapshot of how dispensationalism sees the future.

## RESTORATION OF ISRAEL TO THE PROMISED LAND
### (Key Passage: Ezek 36–37)

Since Darby's days, dispensationalists have pointed to the restoration of Israel to the promised land as a sign of the end.[2] They see the regathering of Israel reflected in many prophetic passages, including Isaiah 11:11–12; Ezekiel 36:10–38; 39:25–27; Amos 9:11; Micah 4:1; and Zephaniah 3:9–10. The most dramatic of these is Ezekiel 37, where God tells Ezekiel to prophesy to a vast expanse of dry bones. After the prophet sees them miraculously reassembled and revived, God addresses his prophet: "Son of man, these bones are the people of Israel. They say, 'Our bones are dried up and our hope is gone; we are cut off.' Therefore prophesy and say to them: 'This is what the Sovereign LORD says: My people, I am going to open your graves and bring you up from them; I will bring you back to the land of Israel'" (Ezek 37:11–12). The images of dry bones restored to life and of two sticks being bound together (37:15–22) depict the resurrection of Israel as a nation. It's easy to see why this vision authenticates the dispensational view of the future for so many. As early as 1840, Darby matter-of-factly wrote that Scripture foretold that Israel would one day be restored to its ancestral land.[3] At the time, this was a laughable sentiment because the ancient Jewish homeland was firmly within the sprawling Ottoman Empire, and the Jewish people were scattered around the globe. Half a century later, when European Jewish intellectuals founded a "Zionist" movement to champion the formation of a Jewish state in Palestine or elsewhere, few Christians noticed. In 1917, however, when British foreign secretary Arthur James Balfour penned the words "His Majesty's Government view with favor the establishment in Palestine of a national home for the Jewish people," the idea of a Jewish state suddenly had the support of a great world power, and a Jewish homeland did not seem so far-fetched. Jewish immigration to Palestine dramatically increased,[4] and new communities were established. Jewish inhabitants of Palestine began once more to speak to each other in the resurrected sounds of Hebrew.

Jewish migration to Palestine continued through the 1930s and 1940s as persecution in Germany culminated in the Holocaust. Trying desperately to maintain control of its mandate in Palestine, Britain attempted to limit demographic change by detaining Jewish migrants in internment camps in Cyprus. Hoping to relieve itself of this burden, the British government relinquished control of the region's future to the United Nations, which proposed to partition western Palestine into a Jewish and an Arab state. When, in 1948, the UN General Assembly voted in favor of the partition of Palestine, the Jewish community declared its independence, and the state of Israel was born. Can you imagine how remarkable—supernatural even—the creation of the state of Israel seemed to many at the time? In 1946, many around the world were still numb at the realization that six million Jews had been exterminated in the death camps of Nazi Germany. Those who had escaped and survived were often bereft of all family and possessions. Thousands of those who had attempted to travel to Palestine had been intercepted by the Royal Navy and were now in indefinite internment in British-run camps on the island of Cyprus. Within *two years*, there was an independent Jewish state in Palestine.

For many dispensationalist Christians around the globe, the birth of the modern state of Israel was nothing less than a miracle and confirmation that God was faithful in fulfilling prophecy.[5] Two decades later, when Israel captured the West Bank and the city of Jerusalem from Jordan, and Israelis gathered once again to pray at the western wall of the Temple Mount, dispensationalist Christians were ecstatic once more. As promised in Ezekiel's vision of desiccated corpses being brought to life, a people hunted to near extinction was now an independent nation in its ancient homeland. The dispensational understanding of prophecy had seemingly been astonishingly and powerfully validated. No wonder *The Late Great Planet Earth*, published in 1970, just three years after the Israeli capture of Jerusalem, quickly became a best seller.

## REBUILDING THE TEMPLE IN JERUSALEM
*(Key Passages: Dan 9:27; Matt 24:15–16)*

For dispensationalist end-times teachers, Israel's reestablishment and Jerusalem's reoccupation clear the way for the rebuilding of the temple—another major sign. Although Scripture does not clearly establish the date, they insist that the temple must exist during the tribulation period. Jesus seemingly predicts its defilement in Matthew 24:15–16 (cf. Dan 9:27)—"When you see standing in the holy place 'the abomination that causes desolation,' spoken of through the prophet Daniel ... then let those who are in Judea flee to the mountains."[6] End-times teachers see the future rebuilt temple and the restoration of the ark of the covenant throughout the Bible: Isaiah 18:7; Jeremiah 3:16–17; Ezekiel 39:21–22; 40–43; 2 Thessalonians 2:3–4; and Revelation 11:1–2. While the temple may not be rebuilt until after the rapture, excitement among dispensationalists abounds around the details of its reconstruction. Consider the Temple Institute in Jerusalem, a conservative Jewish organization dedicated to disseminating knowledge about the temple and researching the practices and equipment associated with its operational life.[7] It has even commissioned the preparation of garments and vessels for use in a future "third temple."[8] That it has generated considerable excitement among many dispensationalists is understandable.

Some dispensationalist Christians are particularly fascinated by the institute's efforts to breed the "red heifer." Animal husbandry, end-times teaching, and restored temple worship? Let us explain. In ancient Israel, priests maintained their ritual purity in part by washing with water mixed with the ashes of a sacrificed red heifer (Num 19). The Old Testament and the Mishnah describe the animal as entirely red and never having been used for work (Num 19:2; Mishnah Parah 2:2, 5). If the third temple is to be built, then it will require priestly staff. The ashes of the red heifer are a necessary component of the water of purification needed to consecrate them. The Temple Institute today not only seeks to raise a red heifer in Israel but has developed rigorous protocols to be used by any Jewish farmer wishing to do so also.[9]

Others have invested imagination and effort in a related quest: locating the ashes of the red heifer used at the time of the destruction of the second temple in AD 70. In the 1980s some Christians were captivated by eccentric independent researcher Vendyl Jones (1930–2010). Working from an idiosyncratic interpretation of a passage from the Qumran Copper Scroll, he spent much of the 1980s and 1990s—and a great deal of donor money—looking for the resting place of not only the ashes of the red heifer, but also the Second Temple incense and the ark of the covenant.[10] In the end, Jones succeeded only to dislocate a great deal of Jordan Valley soil.

Breeding a new red heifer, recovering ancient ashes, preparing to rebuild the Jewish temple on the Temple Mount—together they have sometimes been used to mischaracterize this group as eager to destroy the Dome of the Rock and Al-Aqsa mosque that today sit on temple grounds. Although reinforced by the plotlines of novels, television dramas, and films,[11] dispensationalist Christians are not keen to manipulate events in order to hasten the return of Christ or bring on the apocalypse. As we noted in our last chapter, documented activities such as these have been the purview of a few troubled individuals with no connection with the dispensationalist movement. Such caricatures malign the character and identity of many interested in how Scripture relates to the end of time and the return of Christ. While many dispensationalist Christians share an interest in developments that might precede the return of Christ, the dispensationalist understanding of the sovereignty of God and his working through prophecy means that no human endeavor can force his hand or change his timing. Sinister dispensationalist plots to remove the Dome of the Rock or the Al-Aqsa mosque to make way for a Jewish temple are conspiracies suited to Dan Brown novels and no more.

## THE RAPTURE
*(Key Passages: John 14:1–3;*
*1 Cor 15:51–52; 1 Thess 4:16–18)*

According to most end-times teachers, the advent of the last days will see deteriorating world conditions: a time of international conflict and persecution of those who truly follow Christ. Jesus put it this way:

> You will hear of wars and rumors of wars, but see to it that you are not alarmed. Such things must happen, but the end is still to come. Nation will rise against nation, and kingdom against kingdom. There will be famines and earthquakes in various places. All these are the beginning of birth pains. Then you will be handed over to be persecuted and put to death, and you will be hated by all the nations because of me. (Matt 24:6–9)

When things look most dire, however, Jesus appears in the sky to rescue his followers in an event known as the rapture.[12] The rapture is not the traditional second coming of Christ. As the Apostles' Creed testifies, Christians have long believed in the eventual return of Christ to the earth "to judge the quick and the dead." J. N. Darby demurred, positing instead a two-stage event: first a "secret return," and later the physical return of Jesus to the Mount of Olives as announced to the disciples following the ascension (Acts 1:11). The "secret return" would not be the loud, triumphant, physical return of Christ, but a midair meeting to remove his followers from the world prior to the tribulation. Darby based his belief in this secret removal of Christians in part on his interpretation of 1 Thessalonians 4:16–18.

> For the Lord himself will come down from heaven, with a loud command, with the voice of the archangel and with the trumpet call of God, and the dead in Christ will rise first. After that, *we who are still alive and are left will be caught up together with them in the clouds to meet the Lord in the air*. And so we will be with the Lord forever. Therefore encourage each other with these words.

Paul's words are often cited alongside Jesus's: "If I go and prepare a place for you, I will come back and take you to be with me that you also may be where I am" (John 14:3).

Premillennial dispensationalists have adopted Darby's "two return" vision (fig. 3.1). First, Jesus will appear to snatch away his followers—deceased and living—who rise to meet him in the air and return with him to heaven (John 14:3; 1 Thess 4:17). Later, he will return to reign on the earth for one thousand years—the millennium (Matt 24:29–31; Mark 13:24–27; Luke 21:29–33; 2 Thess 1:7–10).

Dispensationalists disagree among themselves over the rapture's timing. Will it take place before, during, or after the tribulation?[13] Today, most dispensationalists would hold that the rapture will take place prior to the tribulation, sparing Christians from its suffering, citing verses such as 1 Thessalonians 1:10 ("wait for his Son from heaven ... Jesus, who rescues us from the coming wrath") and Revelation 3:10 ("I [Jesus] will also keep you from the hour of trial that is going to come on the

## Pre-Tribulation Rapture

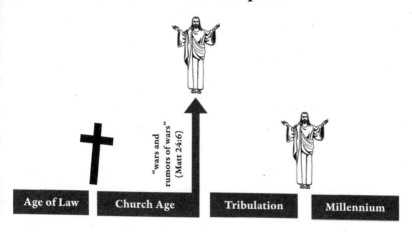

*Fig. 3.1. The pretribulation rapture*

whole world to test the inhabitants of the earth"). For them, the rapture is an imminent, signless occurrence; believers simply wait for Christ to be revealed. The second coming of Christ, on the other hand, will be preceded by the turmoil of the tribulation (e.g., 1 Cor 1:7; 15:52; 16:22; Phil 3:20–21; Titus 2:13; 1 Pet 1:13).[14] Based on Titus 2:13, "we wait for the blessed hope—the appearing of the glory of our great God and Savior, Jesus Christ," the rapture is also sometimes known as "the blessed hope" or "his glorious appearing."

Dispensationalists may well debate whether the rapture occurs before, during, or after the tribulation.[15] Outside dispensationalism, the rapture itself is controversial.[16] That it is a novel doctrine departing from the traditional view of the church is a common observation from Darby's time. He countered that the Protestant Reformation showed that long-accepted teaching could be wrong. Another objection concerns the kind of behavior to which rapture-belief might lead.[17] On the one hand, as we've seen, belief in the rapture has made dispensationalists among the most energetic evangelists, and the reason is obvious. If Jesus could return at any moment with only tribulation and judgment to follow for those not ready, then there is a sense of urgency about spreading the good news of salvation to others. On the other hand, however, the doctrine's pessimism may well leave one disinclined to strive in the present for world peace or environmental preservation. Other rapture critics focus on scriptural exegesis; 1 Thessalonians 4:13–18, they say, refers to the return of Christ to earth as traditionally understood. Nowhere does the passage indicate a lordly descent and ascent. Rather, it describes how citizens in ancient times left a city to greet an approaching dignitary to accompany him back through the city gates.[18]

## JUDGMENT SEAT OF CHRIST
### (Key Passages: Rom 14:10; 1 Cor 3:9–15; 9:24–27; 2 Cor 5:10; 2 Tim 4:8; Rev 22:12)

Following the rapture, believers now in heaven experience the "judgment seat [Greek *bēma*] of Christ" (2 Cor 5:10). That is, Christ will assess believers' works, stewardship of spiritual gifts, and opportunities for service during their earthly lives (Rev 22:12). Writing to the Corinthians, the apostle Paul summarizes what believers can expect: "We must all appear before the judgment seat of Christ, so that each of us may receive what is due us for the things done while in the body, whether good or bad" (2 Cor 5:10). Writing earlier to the same audience, Paul assures his readers "if what has been built survives, the builder will receive a reward" (1 Cor 3:14), and encourages them to run in order to attain the prize (1 Cor 9:24–27). Among those rewards are crowns (1 Cor 9:25; 2 Tim 4:8; Jas 1:12; 1 Pet 5:4; Rev 2:10) and robes of white linen (Rev 19:8). Since this judgment determines the nature of eternal reward, Paul's statement about the possibility of being "disqualified for the prize" (1 Cor 9:27) does not mean the loss of eternal salvation, but merely of heavenly station (1 Cor 3:14).[19] This has nothing to do with earthly wealth, a prominent element of the so-called prosperity gospel promoted by many television evangelists. The crowns will be cast at the feet of the Lamb who has died for them (Rev 4:10–11) in worship and gratitude.[20]

## THE MARRIAGE SUPPER
## OF THE LAMB
### (Key Passage: Rev 19:7–9)

Throughout the New Testament, Christ is likened to a groom (Matt 9:15; 22:2–14; 25:1–13; Mark 2:19–20; Luke 5:34–35; 14:15–24; John 3:29), while the church is described as Christ's betrothed (2 Cor 11:2). Following the rapture, when the church is finally fully united to Christ in heaven, a wedding feast is celebrated (Rev 19:7–9).[21] John records how a multitude announces the arrival of the bride dressed in white:

> Let us rejoice and be glad
>     and give him glory!
> For the wedding of the Lamb has come,
>     and his bride has made herself ready.
> Fine linen, bright and clean,
>     was given her to wear."
> (Fine linen stands for the righteous acts of God's holy
>     people.)
> Then the angel said to me, "Write this: Blessed are those
>     who are invited to the wedding supper of the Lamb!"
>     And he added, "These are the true words of God."
>     (Rev 19:7–9)

According to dispensationalist author and teacher Ron Rhodes, the sequence of the church on earth, rapture, and the marriage supper of the Lamb conforms to the three stages of a Hebrew wedding, in which "the bride was betrothed to the bridegroom, the bridegroom came to claim his bride, and the marriage feast was celebrated."[22] The marriage supper of the Lamb thus concludes the long physical separation of bride and groom that was the church age.

## THE GREAT TRIBULATION AND
## THE REVIVED ROMAN EMPIRE
*(Key Passages: Ezek 38–39; Dan 7:8, 24–26;*
*9:26–27; 12:1; Matt 24:4–28; Rev 6–19)*

The great tribulation shifts us back in time and back to earth. The rapture removes all Jews and gentiles who have accepted Jesus from the world but leaves unbelieving Israel and gentiles behind. Thus the aptly titled LaHaye and Jenkins novel *Left Behind* is set in the great tribulation, a seven-year period of earthly suffering that overlaps with the heavenly judgment seat and marriage supper we've just outlined above.[23] The great tribulation is described in Daniel's seventieth week, referred to by Jesus (Matt 24:4–28), and outlined by Revelation's tumultuous time of seals, trumpets, and bowls (Rev 6–19; see fig. 3.2). With believers removed—along with the restraining power of the Holy Spirit (2 Thess 2:7)[24]—the world goes to pieces, and the nation of Israel once again takes center stage as God's earthly people.

Although preceded by the rapture, the tribulation properly begins with the inauguration of a covenant or treaty between the nation of Israel and the antichrist, leader of a revived Roman Empire. There *may* be some lapse of time between these two events. From the moment this treaty is signed, however, the clock begins ticking toward Armageddon and the return

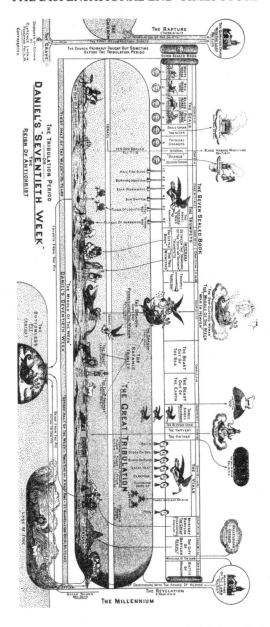

Fig. 3.2. The seventieth week of Daniel and the tribulation
(Larkin)

of Christ—a period of seven years. Prominent in this under-standing of events is Daniel 9:27: "He [antichrist] will confirm a covenant with many [Israel] for one 'seven.' In the middle of the 'seven' he will put an end to sacrifice and offering. And at the temple he will set up an abomination that causes desolation, until the end that is decreed is poured out on him."

"Seven" here refers to a "week of years," part of Daniel's time-line of seventy weeks. According to Daniel 9:24–26, the seventy weeks of Daniel's vision commence with the order to rebuild the ruined temple in Jerusalem,[25] with the end of the sixty-ninth week coinciding with the death of the "Anointed One"—the crucifixion of Jesus. Since dispensationalism maintains that the church age was not revealed to the Old Testament prophets, the entire period from the death of Christ to the rapture is one that it believes to be unrepresented in Daniel's schema.[26] As a result, a gap of unknown length is thought to exist between Daniel's sixty-ninth and seventieth weeks (fig. 3.3). This pro-phetic ellipsis corresponds to the legs of iron depicted in the vision of the statue experienced by King Nebuchadnezzar and interpreted by Daniel in Daniel 2:31–45. These two legs of iron are understood by most end times teachers to represent the ancient Roman Empire, which eventually split into eastern and western halves. The feet of iron mixed with clay and their ten toes are thought to correspond to a *revived* Roman Empire that figures prominently in the seventieth and final week, the great tribulation that precedes Christ's triumphal return to earth.[27] Thus, in the dispensational understanding of the future, there is an overlap between Daniel's seventieth week, the feet of iron and clay, the revived Roman Empire of the antichrist, and the seven-year period of the tribulation.

All of this makes a single verse—Daniel 9:27—a linchpin passage in dispensationalist eschatology. While not wrong—the

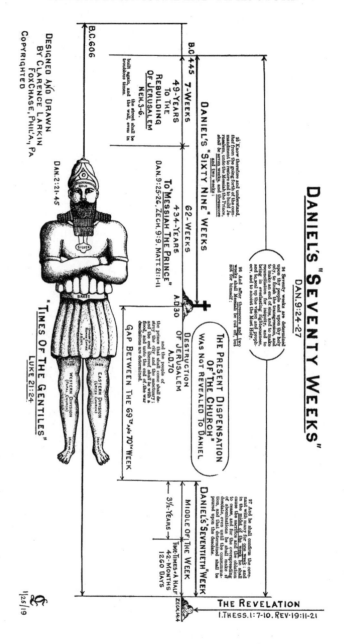

*Fig. 3.3. The gap in Daniel's seventy weeks (Larkin)*

church has often placed a great deal of doctrinal weight on single passages (see Col 2:11–12 and the connection between circumcision and infant baptism)—if such a verse has been misunderstood, then all that is built on it can be at risk. The greater the theological superstructure, the greater the potential wreckage.

So, what occurs following the rapture and during the tribulation?[28] Daniel 9:27 provides a summary: At the outset of the tribulation, the antichrist establishes a seven-year treaty with the nation of Israel, bringing stability and security to the region.[29] Given the disruption caused by the sudden removal of millions of Christians globally and the resultant weakening of nations such as the United States, the world tilts toward confusion and turmoil.[30] Power shifts to Europe, and the antichrist is globally lauded for his gifts as a world leader and peacemaker. With the restraints to evil removed, however, things soon begin to sour. The beastly nature of the antichrist's empire, outlined in Daniel 7:8, 23–24, "will be different from all the other kingdoms and will devour the whole earth, trampling it down and crushing it" (Dan 7:23). End-times teachers connect Daniel's vision with the seven-headed, ten-horned beast that emerges from the sea in Revelation 13:1. According to many, the ten horns of this beast represent the ten constituent nations of the revived Roman Empire, often equated with the European Union—which was brought into existence by the Treaty of Rome (1957).[31] The antichrist, who leads this new political union, received his power from Satan himself (Rev 12:3–4; 13:2). He is described in 2 Thessalonians 2:3–4, 8–9 as the "man of lawlessness."

At the midpoint of the seven-year pact with Israel, the antichrist precipitates a crisis. He defiles the temple in Jerusalem by setting up a statue—"an abomination that causes desolation"—and demanding that he be worshiped (Dan 9:27b; 11:40–43;

THE DISPENSATIONAL END-TIMES STORY

Rev 13:4–6). This midtribulation act is taken by most end-times teachers as evidence that the Jerusalem temple will be rebuilt and sacrifices will be reinstituted either early in or prior to the tribulation. The antichrist's global status and his role in bringing about world peace explain why most TV prophecy teachers regard the European Union, the United Nations, and international peace initiatives with such profound suspicion. This results in the paradox that for many dispensationalists today, the world figure most successful in promoting peace and ending bloodshed becomes the person who might raise the greatest concern.

In Revelation 13:18 the faithful are warned to be watching for the rise of this figure and are given a clue to help identify him. His number is 666. Who is this enemy of Christ and his followers? Since the first century, speculation has abounded, with Nero, Mussolini, Hitler, Henry Kissinger, Mikhail Gorbachev, and pretty much every pope and US president being advanced as possible candidates. Many creative proposals have claimed to connect some aspect of these and other figures with some detail connected with the antichrist. During the early 1970s, the role played by American National Security Adviser and later Secretary of State Henry Kissinger in ending the Vietnam War convinced many that he was a possible candidate. The later claim that in Hebrew his name added up to the number 111, one-sixth of 666, was further proof. A decade later, suspicion fell on Ronald Wilson Reagan, because, in addition to leading the world's greatest superpower and promoting a fantastic "Star Wars" space-based antimissile system, each of his names had six letters, corresponding to the number 666. After he was shot and nearly died, many recalled that the antichrist would recover from a fatal wound (Rev 13:13). At the same time, others suggested that Reagan's Soviet counterpart, Mikhail Gorbachev, was the antichrist, this based on the fact that he was widely celebrated as a man of peace who had a mysterious birthmark on his forehead (Rev 13:15–17).

Before we dismiss such wide-ranging and far-fetched speculation as a frivolous waste of time, let us not forget that such speculation simply follows the direction of Revelation 13:18 to be wise and to "calculate the number of the beast" in order to recognize him when he arises. For many, therefore, efforts such as these flow from a serious warning given in Scripture. Earnest motivation aside, however, these efforts are problematic. Since dispensationalists read Revelation as predictive, changes in news and politics means unending speculation regarding the antichrist. Surprisingly little weight is given to the document's original context and audience. If it was first given to first-century Christians, presumably searching for the antichrist should start there.

The great diplomatic success of the antichrist leads to increasing public adulation. His rise to global authority and his persecution of the faithful are aided by "the harlot Babylon," a woman robed in scarlet and purple, riding a fearsome seven-headed beast, and drunk on the blood of the saints (Rev 17:1–6). From the Reformation to the twentieth century, Protestant writers often reckoned her to be the Roman Catholic Church. After all, the seven heads of the beast on which the woman sits are seven hills—a clear if coded allusion to Rome (Rev 17:9).[32] Recently, however, the common cause that many evangelicals and Catholics have found over moral and cultural issues has weakened the stark equation between Babylon and the Roman Catholic Church.[33] Instead, the ecumenical movement or a global apostate Christendom, perhaps with Rome, are now sometimes mentioned.[34] Since 9/11, the efforts of some Christians to dialogue with Muslims have led end-times teachers such as Jack Van Impe to equate the harlot Babylon with "Chrislam," a future one-world religion combining Christianity and Islam.[35]

## THE FALSE PROPHET AND THE DRAGON

Alongside harlot Babylon, the antichrist is also aided by the false prophet. He promotes the worship of the antichrist (Rev 19:20; 20:10). As the promoter of and spokesperson for a false god, his title is apt. Also thrown into the mix is the dragon—Satan—cast down to earth, where he attacks the Jewish faithful (Rev 12:7–12, 17). As the persecution increases, the followers of God are economically marginalized so that none are able to do business unless they accept the mark of the antichrist on their forehead or hand (Rev 13:16–18). Over the years, end-times writers have wondered whether this meant a tattoo, a barcode, or lately microchip implants.[36] Profound suspicion of data collection and analysis, and of moves to a cashless economy, is frequently voiced by Jack Van Impe, Hal Lindsey, and other end-times teachers. As this period progresses, God begins to intervene from heaven, with ever more severe judgments, described in Revelation 6–19.

## THE 144,000 AND THE TWO WITNESSES

Those left on earth after the rapture are not doomed; they may still be saved. News of salvation is brought to the world through the work of 144,000 Jewish evangelists—12,000 from each tribe of Israel—divinely commissioned and sealed for God's service (Rev 7:1–8). In the escalation of persecution, many of these are martyred (Rev 14:1–5).[37] Also active on God's behalf in this period are "two witnesses," dispatched to Jerusalem (Rev 11:1–14). For 1,260 days, they traverse the city in sackcloth under divine protection, performing miracles and preaching God's message. They are assassinated once their work is done, and their corpses are left unburied in the street for three and a half days while the entire world watches and celebrates. Writers such as Rhodes attribute this global audience to television and the internet.[38] Many end-times writers equate the 1,260-day or three-and-a-half-year ministry of these prophets with the first half of the tribulation. Their martyrdom marks its midpoint, when the antichrist exalts himself. After three and a half days, however, the watching world is stunned to see the two prophets rise from the dead and ascend into heaven. This unexpected event shifts the global mood from celebration to fear—the message of the prophets has been divinely validated. Simultaneously, an earthquake strikes Jerusalem, bringing death and destruction to thousands and causing the survivors to give glory to God (Rev 11:11–14).

## THE BATTLE OF ARMAGEDDON AND
## THE RETURN OF CHRIST
(Key Passages: Isa 33:1–34:17; 63:1–6; 66:15–16;
Ezek 38–39; Dan 11:40–12:1; Zech 12:1–9; 14:1–8;
Rev 16:12–16; 19:1–19)

At the end of seven years, the tribulation culminates in history's final showdown: the battle of Armageddon (Rev 16:16). A Greek transcription of the Hebrew har məgiddô ("Mount of Megiddo"), Armageddon refers to a city on the western edge of the Jezreel Valley in northern Israel. In ancient times, the fortified city of Megiddo guarded the northern entrance to a strategic pass through the Mount Carmel range, a potential choke point for any army traveling through the region (fig. 3.4). Whoever controlled Megiddo controlled all north-south traffic along the highway through Israel. Its strategic significance is summarized by Pharaoh Thutmose III (1504–1450

BC)—"The capture of Megiddo is the capture of a thousand cities"[39]—and this significance later made it one of the cities fortified by Solomon (1 Kgs 9:15). Given this history and the innumerable battles that took place there,[40] it is not surprising that this is the site the book of Revelation identifies as the place where history's final battle unfolds.

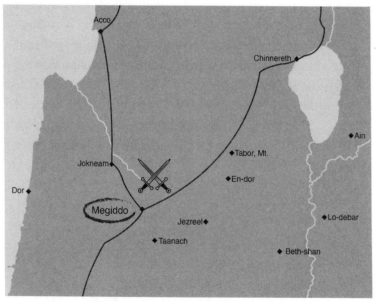

*Fig. 3.4. Megiddo ("Armageddon") in the Jezreel Valley*

Precisely how the battle of Armageddon unfolds is a subject of debate.[41] Most identify this final battle at least in part with that described in Ezekiel 38–39: the attack by Gog of Magog on an unsuspecting Israel. Commending this understanding to dispensationalists is the way the order of material in Ezekiel matches the prophetic timeline. The restoration of Israel (Ezek 36–37) is followed by the attack on Israel and the destruction of her foes during the tribulation (Ezek 38–39), and finally the advent of the millennial kingdom (Ezek 40–48). Alas, the matter is not so easily settled. Because Ezekiel's postbattle cleanup requires seven years (Ezek 39:9; the length of the tribulation), others hold that Ezekiel 38–39 narrates a separate event that precedes the tribulation entirely or occurs immediately at its outset.[42] Still others see the invasion as the first phase of a battle of Armageddon that unfolds over a longer period of time. This last view is Pentecost's, who sees Gog's invasion occurring midway through the tribulation and initiating a response by the antichrist, which culminates with the final battle at Armageddon.[43]

For the sake of simplicity, the description of the battle of Armageddon offered here follows the eight-stage sequence laid out by Pentecost, supplemented with details from other sources.[44]

1.  In the first half of the tribulation, Israel is at peace under the covenant made with the antichrist and his revived Roman Empire (Ezek 38:8, 11; Dan 9:27).

2.  Perhaps around the midpoint of the tribulation, seeing Israel as easy prey, the king of the north (i.e., a northern confederacy headed by Russia) invades (Ezek 38:11; Joel 2:1–21; Isa 10:12; 30:31–33; 31:8–9),[45] motivated by Israel's wealth (Ezek 38:12–13). Hal Lindsey believes that one attractive source of wealth will be the mineral resources of the Dead Sea.[46]

3.  The antichrist then invokes his covenant with Israel and moves into the land with the armies of the revived Roman Empire (Dan 11:41–45). It is

perhaps at this point, or following the battle (see stage 5), that he enters the temple and sets up an image of himself there (Dan 9:27).

4. The battle described in Ezekiel 38–39 and in Daniel 11:40–43 follows.[47] The reference in Daniel 11:40 to "the time of the end" places these events in the tribulation. In determining the participants involved in this conflict and who attacks whom, much depends on antecedents of "him" and "he" in Daniel 11:40–45. Pentecost believes that these pronouns name the antichrist, the king who "will do as he pleases" and who "will exalt and magnify himself above every god" (Dan 11:36).[48] If so, then the king of the south (perhaps a confederacy of African and Middle Eastern nations) advances against the forces of the antichrist, located in Israel (Dan 11:40a). At the same time, a northern confederacy led by Russia (the "king of the north") also advances by land and sea (Dan 11:40b) to lay siege to Jerusalem (Zech 12:2).[49] Lindsey understands the destruction of Gog's forces by "fire and brimstone" (Ezek 38:22) to refer to the use of tactical nuclear weapons.[50] Pentecost is more sedate: while the king of the south is destroyed by the beast, Gog's destruction is an act of God.[51] At the war's end, the antichrist and the forces and allies of the revived Roman Empire remain; the invaders, both north and south, are destroyed (Ezek 39; Zech 12:4). Rather than secure the peace, however, Daniel 11:40–43 details how the antichrist will then press the attack.

> He [antichrist] will invade many countries and sweep through them like a flood. He will also invade the Beautiful Land [Israel]. Many countries will fall, but Edom, Moab and the leaders of Ammon will be delivered from his hand. He will extend his power over many countries; Egypt [the king of the south] will not escape. He [antichrist] will gain control of the treasures of gold and silver and all the riches of Egypt, with the Libyans and Cushites in submission.

The scale of destruction is enormous. The local inhabitants take seven months to bury the dead, while the abandoned military hardware is scavenged and provides fuel for seven years (Ezek 39:9, 12). Interpreting literally and attempting to draw points of connection with current events, some have made the spurious claim that many Russian weapons are made with a compressed wood product known as lignostone, which explains why the weapons can be burned.[52]

5.  The victorious antichrist and his army then occupy Israel (Dan 11:45). If he hasn't already (see stage 3), the antichrist now erects an image of himself in the temple at Jerusalem and demands that he be worshiped as a god (Dan 9:27).

6.  The victory's magnitude enables the antichrist to assemble a vast coalition (Ps 2:1–3; Rev 13:7), though it may take some time following the destruction of the king of the north (Ezek 39:9, 12).

7. At some point thereafter, the antichrist learns of a new threat: "But reports from the east and the north will alarm him, and he will set out in a great rage to destroy and annihilate many" (Dan 11:44). The defeat of the northern confederacy under Gog of Magog (i.e., Russia and her allies) creates a power vacuum filled by the kings of the east—likely Communist China and her regional allies. They assemble an army two hundred million strong and advance toward the Middle East (Dan 11:44; Rev 9:13–21; 16:12).[53] The sixth trumpet is sounded, and the sixth bowl of judgment is poured out on the Euphrates River, drying it up and allowing this eastern army to cross over and proceed south toward Israel and confrontation with the forces of the antichrist (Rev 9:13–21; 16:12).

8. Eventually, the two coalitions engage in battle in the hill country around Jerusalem (Zech 14:1–3) and the Valley of Jehoshaphat (Joel 3:12), which Pentecost places nearby.[54] For Pentecost, this is the climax of a perhaps three-and-a-half-year-long sequence. He labels this final phase the "battle of Armageddon." The name, therefore, is somewhat misleading, for it is not the location of the conflict, but the muster point for participating troops (Rev 16:16). The battle itself stretches throughout the Judean hill country; the center of conflict is Jerusalem.[55] At just this moment Christ returns to earth, fulfilling the promise made to his disciples at his ascension (Acts 1:11). When his feet touch the Mount of Olives, it splits in two, providing

an escape route for those trapped in Jerusalem. Accompanying Christ are his heavenly forces, which rout the antichrist's armies:

> On that day his feet will stand on the Mount of Olives, east of Jerusalem, and the Mount of Olives will be split in two from east to west, forming a great valley, with half of the mountain moving north and half moving south. You will flee by my mountain valley, for it will extend to Azel. You will flee as you fled from the earthquake in the days of Uzziah king of Judah. Then the LORD my God will come, and all the holy ones with him. (Zech 14:4–5)

The descent of Christ and his forces is also related in Revelation 19:11–15:

> I saw heaven standing open and there before me was a white horse, whose rider is called Faithful and True. With justice he judges and makes war. His eyes are like blazing fire, and on his head are many crowns. He has a name written on him that no one knows but he himself. He is dressed in a robe dipped in blood, and his name is the Word of God. The armies of heaven were following him, riding on white horses and dressed in fine linen, white and clean. Out of his mouth comes a sharp sword with which to strike down the nations. "He will rule them with an iron scepter." He treads the winepress of the fury of the wrath of God Almighty.

The armies of the nations are vanquished, the faithful rescued (Isa 33:1–34:17; 63:1–6; 66:15–16; Jer 25:27–33; Zech 12:1–9; 14:1–4), and the antichrist and the false prophet are captured and consigned to the lake of fire (Rev 19:17–21). His enemies destroyed and Satan bound, Christ establishes his millennial rule on earth (Rev 20:1–10).

Having covered the events leading up to and including the battle of Armageddon, let's return briefly to the invasion of Israel by Gog of Magog for an additional comment. Does it refer to Russia? Most popular end-times teachers think "Gog of the land of Magog, the prince of Rosh, Meshech, and Tubal" (Ezek 38:2) names Russia, Moscow, and the lesser-known Tubolsk respectively.[56] But there are problems. The Russian identifications depend on the 1833 edition of the Hebrew and Aramaic lexicon of Wilhelm Gesenius (1786–1842).[57] Scholarly knowledge of Hebrew and the ancient Near East, however, has advanced significantly since the early nineteenth century. The most recent edition of Gesenius no longer contains these identifications.[58] Indeed, when scholars began to read Akkadian texts only after 1857, they encountered references to the Mushki and Tabal, a pair of tribes in eastern Asia Minor that pestered the Assyrians from the twelfth to ninth centuries BC. Meshech and Tubal in Ezekiel 38:2 do not name faraway Russian cities, but two ancient regional actors.

Furthermore, "Rosh" does not appear in the vast majority of English translations including the Geneva Bible (1560) and the King James Version (1611), for good reason.[59] Translators from the Reformation to today correctly understand "Rosh" to mean "chief" or "head"; thus, Gog is "*chief* prince of Meshech and Tubal." "Rosh" as a place name is found in the Septuagint, an early Greek translation of the Old Testament that often transcribed as names words its translators didn't completely understand. What might have been a possibility given the state of knowledge in the early nineteenth century is now ruled out. There is no biblical reason to see Russia as a prophetic actor on the end-times stage. Although this has been accepted for decades, even by some dispensational scholars, it is either unknown to or ignored by almost all popular end-times teachers today.[60]

### THE MILLENNIUM AND THE GREAT
### WHITE THRONE JUDGMENT
*(Key Passages: Ezek 40–48; Zech 2:4–13;*
*8:1–8, 20–23; 14:8–21; Rev 19:20–20:15)*

Following Christ's victory, Satan is imprisoned in the abyss or pit for the duration of the millennium (Rev 20:1–3). As Christ establishes his one-thousand-year reign on earth, the martyrs of the tribulation are raised from the dead in the "resurrection of the just" to rule with him, and saints raised and raptured before (Rev 20:4–6).[61] This is not, however, a second resurrection. For dispensationalists, the "first resurrection" encompasses both the resurrection of the righteous dead at the rapture and the remaining righteous dead now. The first resurrection, also known as "resurrection from the dead" (Phil 3:11), "better resurrection" (Heb 11:35), and the resurrection to life (John 5:29), involves a transformation of the body.[62] The idea of two resurrections comes from Revelation 20:4–6, 11–15, where dispensationalism sees separate resurrections for the righteous and the wicked.

> I saw thrones on which were seated those who had been given authority to judge. And I saw the souls of those who had been beheaded because of their testimony about Jesus and because of the word of God. They had not worshiped the beast or its image and had not received its mark on their foreheads or their hands. They came to life and reigned with Christ a thousand years. (The rest of the dead did not come to life until the thousand years were ended.) This is the *first resurrection.*

Blessed and holy are those who share in the *first resur-rection*. The second death has no power over them, but they will be priests of God and of Christ and will reign with him for a thousand years. (Rev 20:4–6)

This completes the company of believers who rule with Christ in the millennium.[63]

The millennium itself is a one-thousand-year period in which Christ and the saints rule an earth rehabilitated from the destructive effects of the tribulation and the battle of Armageddon. Dispensationalists imagine this world, drawing on many passages from the Old and New Testaments describing an idealized, even fantastic future existence incapable of having been fulfilled in Israel or the church's past. Thus, the restoration of Davidic rule (2 Sam 7:12–13; 22:51; Isa 9:6–7; Zeph 3:14–20; Luke 1:30–33), the miraculous transformation of the land (Isa 35:1–2, 6b–9; Zech 14:8–15) and of human existence (Isa 35:3–6a; Mic 4:1–5; Zech 8:4–8), the building of a new temple (Ezek 40–48), and the spiritual and moral regeneration of Israel and the nations (Jer 31:31–34; Zech 8:20–23; 14:16–21) are all examples.[64] Most poignantly,

> The wolf will live with the lamb,
>     the leopard will lie down with the goat,
> the calf and the lion and the yearling together;
>     and a little child will lead them.
> The cow will feed with the bear,
>     their young will lie down together,
> and the lion will eat straw like the ox.
> The infant will play near the cobra's den,
>     and the young child will put its hand into
>         the viper's nest.

> They will neither harm nor destroy
>     on all my holy mountain,
> for the earth will be filled with the knowledge
>     of the LORD
>     as the waters cover the sea. (Isa 11:6–9)

The reign of Christ and his saints over a renewed, physical earth,[65] however, is not the final destiny of the redeemed.

At the millennium's end, Satan is released from the abyss to do what he has always done—deceive. Again some from the nations rebel against Christ (Rev 20:7–9a). Although it is strange to think that after a thousand-year period of perfect, divine rule, any would rebel against Christ, many end-times teachers counter that these rebels are people who were born during the millennium and who had not adopted the faith of their parents.[66] Pentecost explains that Satan is released to demonstrate what has been evident in every other dispensation, namely, that "even when tested under the reign of the King and the revelation of His holiness, man is a failure," and "while those going into the millennium were saved, they were not perfected."[67] The rebellion is short lived; Satan is thrown into the lake of fire, joining the antichrist and the false prophet forever (Rev 19:20; 20:9–10).

Then comes the second resurrection. Unlike the two-stage resurrection of the righteous, this resurrection is of the wicked to judgment before God's great white throne and involves no transformation.[68]

> Then I saw a great white throne and him who was seated
> on it. The earth and the heavens fled from his presence,
> and there was no place for them. And I saw the dead,

great and small, standing before the throne, and books were opened. Another book was opened, which is the book of life. The dead were judged according to what they had done as recorded in the books. The sea gave up the dead that were in it, and death and Hades gave up the dead that were in them, and each person was judged according to what they had done. Then death and Hades were thrown into the lake of fire. The lake of fire is the second death. Anyone whose name was not found written in the book of life was thrown into the lake of fire. (Rev 20:11–15)

The wicked of all ages are now judged according to their deeds. Two books of reference are involved: an account of human deeds that provides the basis for judgment, and the book of life, in which are written the names of the faithful. Failure to have one's name recorded in the second book means the "second death" in the lake of fire, or "hell," a real, physical place to be distinguished from the Hades of the New Testament on the grounds that Hades is consigned to destruction in the lake of fire.[69]

Dispensationalism's two resurrections (see Rev 20:4–15) departs from the single resurrection of the Apostles' and Nicene Creeds. Accordingly, it reinterprets a number of New Testament passages that seem to point to a single resurrection of the dead, righteous and unrighteous. Thus, for example, John 5:28–29, "a time is coming when all who are in their graves will hear his voice and come out—those who have done what is good will rise to live, and those who have done what is evil will rise to be condemned," is regarded as at least consistent with the idea of separate resurrections and judgments of the good and the wicked.

## THE NEW HEAVEN, THE NEW EARTH,
## AND THE NEW JERUSALEM
### (Key Passages: 2 Pet 3:10–13; Rev 21–22)

With Satan, the antichrist, the false prophet, and the wicked consigned to the lake of fire, a total cosmic makeover takes place: the new heaven, new earth, and a new Jerusalem where God can live with his people for eternity (Rev 21–22). The presence of God and the Lamb in the city makes any temple superfluous. In place of a sanctuary stands God's throne, from which a life-giving river flows (Rev 21:22; 22:1–5). The light of God banishes night; the city's gates are never shut. The effects of the fall are so healed that there is no curse (Rev 22:3). Nothing impure, shameful, or deceitful is present (2 Pet 3:13; Rev 21:23–27).[70]

Spatially, this new city is a perfect cube of astounding size, with each edge measuring twelve thousand stadia (Rev 21:16), or 2,160 kilometers (1,342 miles).[71] Superimposed on a map of the United States, it would stretch from New York City to Dallas. In height, it would extend beyond the upper reaches of earth's atmosphere and well into space. Given their penchant for literal readings, many end-times teachers ponder the structural practicalities. Rhodes suggests that such a city could accommodate a population of twenty billion people. Wondering how residents would get around, he surmises that "our resurrection bodies will have amazing capabilities."[72]

Often missed is the more pressing similarity between this image and the square dimensions of the holy of holies of the temple (vertical dimensions are not given) and Jerusalem as described in Ezekiel's vision (Ezek 41:4; 48:16), and the cubic dimensions of the holy of holies of Solomon's temple (1 Kgs 6:20).[73] Given Revelation's well-known reliance on Ezekiel, it is more likely that the cubic shape of the new Jerusalem emphasizes it as the place where God and humans of all generations meet in perfect relationship. Entirely consistent with the rest of the imagery in Revelation 20–21, this profound theological point is lost if the new Jerusalem is approached literalistically. The new heaven and new earth is a wholesale recreation of the cosmos such that it is now God's fit abode: a new, single world where God and humans can dwell forever.[74]

If the details of this overview can be overlooked, two criticisms cannot. Dispensationalist eschatology tends to overlook the original biblical audiences and contexts. Instead of asking what Ezekiel, Daniel, or Revelation meant to their first readers or hearers, dispensationalist eschatology cherry-picks across the canon to shoehorn passages into our context. It presumes that we are really the first generation able to fully understand this material. God, apparently, plays a rather cruel joke on the original audiences, themselves undergoing oppression and persecution. Surely God intended immediate and tangible benefit from these texts for their first readers.

Second, the unrelenting focus on present fulfillment means that "literal interpretation" can be idiosyncratic and constantly shifting. While the framework for reading Daniel or Revelation might remain fixed, the identity of the characters changes. If you have been to the theater, you have probably had the experience of opening your playbill to find an insert reading, "Playing the role of so-and-so in tonight's performance is …" Current events are just that. World leaders and villains enter and exit the stage. End-times teachers both well-known and obscure come and go. As a result, the identities of the antichrist, Babylon the Great, or the fourth kingdom of Daniel are constantly under review. Just when you think you have understood everything there is to know, there's another book, a new idea, or a different end-times teacher. This is the nature of end-times teaching.

Thankfully, however, remaining up-to-date on the system's latest tweaks isn't necessary. It is far better to understand (1) the general dispensational picture and (2) how biblical prophecy and apocalyptic functions, and what to expect when reading each. In a later section of this book, therefore, we will look at the genres of prophecy and apocalyptic to see how and what they communicated and to note how this delivers different results from those derived from their use in dispensationalism. Before we venture there, however, we need to consider what dispensationalism means for how its adherents live in the world and what they might contribute to the life and work of the church.

# 4

## The Belief and Behavior of Dispensationalism

Why bother with theology? Perhaps the answer most relevant to the church is that what we believe affects how we behave. This chapter examines some of dispensationalism's distinctives and explores their effect on dispensationalists' actions. The goal is not criticism—which is readily available—but to observe both potential and demonstrable relationships between belief and behavior.

### LITERAL INTERPRETATION OF SCRIPTURE

We start with dispensationalism's commitment to read the Bible literally and its two corollaries: (1) the Bible is for everyone and (2) can be understood by anyone. Summarized in the motto of the church of Brian's youth, "The Bible as it is—for people as they are," this belief removes psychological barriers to engagement, understanding, and obedience. After all, if the Bible is highly symbolic, open only to experts, then some readers might lose confidence in their own ability to read and apply it. On the other hand, if the Bible "means what it says and says what it means," then its truths are self-evident, accessible, and relevant. Readers are less intimidated and more likely to read and apply the Bible independently.

At the same time, however, a commitment to "literalism" can blind readers to symbols and metaphors that biblical writers deliberately used. Consider the domestication of wild animals in Isaiah 11:6—"The wolf will live with the lamb, the leopard will lie down with the goat, the calf and the lion and the yearling together; and a little child will lead them"—and their removal from the roads in Isaiah 35:8–9. Dispensationalists believe that such as-yet-unrealized zoological camaraderie will be fulfilled in the coming millennium. Likewise, the natural renewal of Isaiah 35:1–2—"The desert and the parched land will be glad; the wilderness will rejoice and blossom. Like the crocus, it will burst into bloom; it will rejoice greatly and shout for joy. The glory of Lebanon will be given to it, the splendor of Carmel and Sharon; they will see the glory of the LORD, the splendor of our God"—is thought yet unfulfilled and so awaiting a millennial realization.

Reading in this way fails to appreciate the prophets' use of poetic speech to highlight and idealize a future event. When surveying Israel's moral landscape, a prophet would pronounce blessing or discipline using covenant language of blessings and curses (Lev 26; Deut 28). Above, Isaiah does just this to refer to Israel's post-exile blessings. Predators making peace with prey and playing with children means that the covenant curse on disobedience—wild animals dangerously dominating the countryside—will be removed when Israel returns in obedience to God (Lev 26:6, 22). Likewise, the blooming desert describes the removal of agricultural sterility and the renewal of the land in abundance (Lev 26:4–5, 19–20, 34; Deut 28:8, 11–12, 22–24).

Failure to recognize the blessing and cursing language of Leviticus 26 and Deuteronomy 28 is to seriously misread much of prophetic literature. What Dwight Pentecost marshals as Old Testament prophetic depictions of the millennium are poetic recollections of covenant blessing to be realized after the exile among God's returned, obedient people.[1] To miss the imagery is to miss the message of the text. By imagining a yet-future realization where none is intended, the preference for literal interpretation misreads and misapplies Scripture. Reducing interpretative barriers that keep people from confidently reading Scripture and acting on what they learn is not foolproof.

## DISPENSATIONS

The most basic tenet of dispensationalism as proposed by Darby and accepted by others is that God has related to human beings in varying ways across time. Each of these "dispensations" exhibits the same general pattern ending in judgment. What does this basic approach to Scripture mean for dispensationalists? A benefit has been an interest in personal Bible study. The dispensational breakdown of Scripture clarifies and reassures people intimidated by its size and scope, not knowing where to begin. In his *Rightly Dividing the Word of Truth*, C. I. Scofield presented a readily understood "dispensational" method permitting readers to study on their own. Scofield offered courses through his own correspondence school, the New York Night School of the Bible, if any needed more directive help. Indeed, a plethora of tools were produced to assist independent reading and study.

Founded on lay leadership and preaching and, as dissenters, now cut off from the theological colleges of the great universities, the Plymouth Brethren were especially active in the production of these resources. Through the nineteenth and early twentieth centuries, Plymouth Brethren scholars produced translations of the Septuagint, critical editions of the Greek New Testament, Hebrew lexicons and concordances, theological wordbooks, and Hebrew and Greek grammars. This tradition continues today through the Plymouth Brethren–sponsored Emmaus Bible School correspondence ministry; in its seventy-five-year history, it has distributed over forty million Bible courses in one hundred countries, in eighty languages. It is unsurprising that dispensationalists as a whole are ranked among the most biblically literate of Protestants. Referring to the ministry of C. I. Scofield, H. A. Ironside, and others, non-dispensationalist George Eldon Ladd asserted the following: "It is doubtful if there has been any other circle of men who have done more by their influence in preaching, teaching and writing to promote a love for Bible study, a hunger for the deeper spiritual life, a passion for evangelism and zeal for missions in the history of American Christianity."[2]

Dispensations can, nevertheless, be complicated. That they appear arbitrary is a commonly expressed concern, one bolstered by the existence of competing dispensational outlines. Darby taught that there were six dispensations. Most dispensationalists today (following Scofield) teach seven. More recently, a movement known as progressive dispensationalism has pared the number to four. If dispensationalists themselves cannot agree, we may ask whether the system is inherently biblical or something imposed on the text. The problem of imposition also arises when considering the inner-dispensational pattern. Is the structure "God relating to humans > human failure > preservation of a faithful remnant > judgment" embedded in Scripture, corresponding to different periods of God's working, simply read into the text? Further, are all elements of the pattern equally present across all supposed dispensations?

Scofield's age of the law provides an example of a dispensation being forced to fit. If law ends with the crucifixion of Christ (AD 33), then the judgment—that is, the destruction of Jerusalem and the Babylonian exile (586 BC)—is centuries premature. A third example relates to the current church age. Must it follow the same pattern as others? Darby answered yes. The current church age was already in the stage of failure, the church was "in ruins," and the faithful were called to come out of the organized denominations. This commitment to the pattern was counterproductive. Darby's ministry was subsequently marked by division and sectarianism that ultimately limited the effectiveness of his work. Thankfully, most dispensationalists have not followed Darby to this extreme.

Being able to approach Scripture through the sequence of dispensations has provided structure and predictability, lowering the barrier to entry and creating enthusiasm for Bible study among dispensationalists. The clouds of eisegesis and sectarianism, however, hang over the benefits offered.

## ISRAEL AND THE CHURCH

Dispensationalism's distinction between Israel and the church also has major ramifications for belief and practice. Most Christians have understood the church in some way to supplant Israel as the people of God. Apart from oft-cited New Testament passages, we can cite the second-century writer of the Epistle of Barnabas, who urges his readers to avoid the sin of assuming that the covenant belongs to both Israel and the church, declaring, "it is ours" (Epistle of Barnabas 4.6–7). At its worst, this orientation, combined with a vindictive reading of Matthew 27:24–25, gave rise to long-simmering animosity and charges of Jewish deicide that resulted in anti-Semitism and periodic violence, particularly during the Easter season. In contrast, traditional dispensationalism posits two distinct peoples of God—Israel as God's earthly people and the church as God's heavenly people.

The belief that Israel maintains a place in God's heart and plan, along with special heed to the promise God gave to Abram in Genesis 12:3 ("I will bless those who bless you, and whoever curses you I will curse"), has meant that anti-Semitism has had little chance of taking root in dispensationalist communities. In fact, North American dispensationalists often enjoy close relationships with Jewish groups, exemplified by the Christian Friends of the Magen David Adom (the Israeli paramedic service and equivalent of the Red Cross) and the International Fellowship of Christians and Jews. The 2012 death of Canadian end-times writer Grant Jeffrey was reported in the *Jewish Tribune* newspaper, and the president of B'nai Brith Canada delivered a eulogy at his funeral. Given dispensationalism's philo-Semitism, it is no surprise that many in the Messianic Jewish movement in North America and Israel have tended to be dispensational in their theological and eschatological outlook.

This same philo-Semitism has led many dispensationalists to embrace Christian Zionism. Besides the conviction that Jews have a right to some form of state in their ancient homeland, Christian Zionism often includes an uncritical and fulsome endorsement of the modern state of Israel and the settler movement. This stance can leave dispensational Christians out of touch with evangelical Palestinian Christians, who are their theological kin and who have suffered as the settler movement has expanded and gained political strength. Although dispensationalists have supported or sponsored education and service works such as Bethlehem Bible College and the Bethlehem School for the Blind, they have been slower to advocate for the human, political, and territorial rights of Palestinians.

The radical Israel/church distinction has also led (again) to an uneven approach in reading and interpreting Scripture. Darby, for example, held that since Israel was God's earthly people, the Old Testament, particularly its prophetic portions, applied literally only to them. If they applied to the church at all, it was only in a symbolic sense. Thus, the instructions in Exodus 25–30 for the building of the tabernacle were, for Israel, literal blueprints. For Christians, however, this same material could be interpreted spiritually as a complex set of symbols pointing to Christ. Confusingly, it is not always clear when a symbolic referent is permitted or ruled out. The distinction, further, does not limit itself to the Old Testament. Many dispensationalists maintain that since the Sermon on the Mount (Matt 5–7) was delivered to Jews prior to the crucifixion and the start of the church age, it does not apply primarily to Christians, but to Israel in the coming millennium—this despite the fact that the gospel in which it was preserved was written for Christians well within the church age.

To summarize, like the notion of dispensations, the sharp Israel/church distinction has both benefits and costs. On the one hand, it has inoculated dispensationalists to the contagions of anti-Judaism and anti-Semitism that have marked so much of Christian history. On the other, it has often led to an uncritical support of the modern state of Israel and a blindness to the suffering of Palestinians, especially Palestinian Christians. And like the dispensations, it also fosters idiosyncratic biblical interpretation. Just how does one discern whether a problematic passage applies only to Israel (whether in the past or in the millennial future) or, in a twin-track way, to both peoples of God?

## PRETRIBULATION RAPTURE
## AND PREMILLENNIALISM

While the notion of a premillennial return of Christ is rooted in the earliest expressions of Christian faith, it was revived by dispensationalism in the nineteenth century, which wedded it to the idea of a pretribulation rapture. In its modified, modern form, Christ will appear suddenly in the sky and remove all Christians to meet him in the air (1 Thess 4:13–18), sparing them from the seven years of great tribulation. Christ will then return to reign on earth itself for one thousand years. It is this conviction that has penetrated most deeply into popular evangelicalism, again with both positive and negative results.

More than in any other area, millennial convictions have had a profound positive influence on evangelism. In the nineteenth century, American evangelist D. L. Moody was among the first to use them as powerful evangelistic tools. That Christ could return at any moment sharpened the sense of immediacy that fit well with Moody's decision-oriented preaching and altar calls, and those of other nineteenth- and twentieth-century evangelists. They also injected a sense of urgency into the life and work of dispensationally minded churches, spurring domestic evangelism and international missionary activity. Consider the Southern Baptist Convention, the largest Protestant missionary sending denomination in the world, in which premillennial dispensationalism was an influential (if not official) eschatological view through the latter half of the twentieth century. In 2017, that group's International Mission Board had an operating budget of over $270 million and by the end of the year expected to have over thirty-six hundred missionaries and support workers serving abroad. Similarly, the much smaller Plymouth Brethren movement has nonetheless contributed in an outsized way to global missions. For example, the 2017 edition of *The Missionary Prayer Handbook*, a prayer guide listing missionaries sponsored by Open Brethren churches in the United States and Canada, totals the missionary families sent from the United States at 274. The nondispensationalist Presbyterian Church (USA), despite being more than ten times larger, sponsored only eighty missionary families that same year. The significance is clear.

Negatively, belief in future global deterioration followed by a pretribulation rapture may leave dispensational Christians pessimistic about and perhaps unconcerned with the world's state here and now. Dispensationalists have not been at the forefront of Christian work in creation care, global development, or social justice initiatives. Notable exceptions are medicine and education. Since the nineteenth century, much dispensationalist missionary work in the developing world has been coupled with education and medical services, sometimes providing the only schools or hospital care in many rural areas. In nineteenth-century Britain, dispensationalists George Muller and Thomas Bernardo were prominent in caring for orphans and vulnerable youth. Throughout the world, dispensationalists have been and remain a major source of charitable giving and activity. Such endeavors, however, are typically related to an interest in evangelism rather than springing solely from a desire to make the world a better place.

Dispensationalists are often similarly suspicious about world peace initiatives. Understanding the antichrist as one who promotes world peace and comes to dominate the period of the great tribulation has left some dispensationalists perpetually on alert when it comes to individuals or organizations that have promoted peace accords and global cooperation. Some dispensationalists have regarded figures such as Henry Kissinger, Mikhail Gorbachev, and Barack Obama—all winners of the Nobel Peace Prize—as the antichrist. Of course, like most people, dispensationalists would rather live free of war, illness, and pollution. At the same time, however, they are perhaps more likely to see activism as secondary and ultimately doomed to fail.

At this point, it is worth pausing to recall what we noted at this section's start—what we truly believe affects how we behave. Problems arise when any theological perspective is applied uncritically. Consider premillennialism's polar opposite. Postmillennialism holds optimistically that Christ will return following a prolonged period of peace and prosperity, something toward which the church should work. At the turn of the nineteenth–twentieth centuries, this was the eschatological framework of most North American liberal Protestants and social gospelers. The advance of Christianity could lead to a global tipping point, after which peace and good would create the millennium and lead to Christ's return. If one believes that the growth of the church and the spread of its influence will lead to the earthly triumph of good over evil and the return of Christ, then interest in global improvement is obvious. This is exactly what the social gospel movement set out to do through tireless promotion of labor rights, prison reform, universal suffrage, social welfare, and public health care.

But there was a dark side. The social gospel movement sought to achieve its aims by applying the best of human knowledge to the solution of social problems. In the late nineteenth century, when natural selection as the mechanism behind human evolution became clear, many in Europe and North America took the next logical step and asked, "How might the world be improved if humans directed their evolution through controlled, rather than natural, selection?" The result was the so called science of eugenics. In the early twentieth century, the expanding eugenics movement sought to promote reproduction of the fittest and discourage reproduction of those races, classes, and "feeble" judged unfit. In many jurisdictions, they succeeded in passing laws requiring engaged couples to have a certificate of medical and mental fitness before they could marry. They discouraged reproduction among races thought to be less desirable (i.e., African Americans and immigrants) by promoting birth control. The mentally "feeble" were segregated into residential institutions to separate them from society and prevent their reproduction. Many postmillennial Christians regarded these practices as promoting conditions consistent with the millennium and the return of Christ.[3]

## CONCLUSION

The point is this: there are potential dangers in any theological belief applied without reflection and consideration; the risk is not limited to "those people over there." For early twentieth-century postmillennialists and for contemporary premillennialists, tempering eschatological enthusiasm with the truth that all humans are created in the image of God would have provided a corrective for the unreflective exuberance of the former and the pessimistic detachment of the latter. Thankfully, both premillennial dispensationalists and postmillennial nondispensationalists seem to have learned from their past mistakes.

Furthermore, the risks ought not to derail the positives. Recall the picture of a dispensationalist church member appealing for more teaching on end times and a pastor's befuddled response. We wrote this book from the shared observation that too many pastors, unable to understand dispensationalist members of their congregations, write them off as a mild nuisance. This is to dismiss biblical knowledge, energy, and a passion for the gospel that can enliven and support the life and ministry of any congregation—dispensational or otherwise. To ignore such a resource is to miss out on the strengths that one part of the body of Christ can offer.

# PART 2

## THE WORLD OF PROPHECY
## AND APOCALYPTIC

# 5

## The World of Prophecy and Apocalyptic

Have you ever thought of how miraculous reading is? Easily taken for granted, reading is a wonder of human development. Slowly, a child learns the sounds of letters and syllables and then strings them together to form words and attach those words to objects and concepts. As time progresses, they learn to arrange those words into simple sentences that communicate meaning. The amazing brain development underlying reading, furthermore, does not end in childhood. Reading is a skill honed over a lifetime. As we encounter different kinds or genres of literature, we learn how they differ in style and purpose. We begin to recognize distinguishing features and how each conveys meaning.

As we read, we develop a kind of literary muscle memory. Eventually, we're able to identify a genre instantaneously and adjust our expectations accordingly. Think about a newspaper. A single broadsheet contains a multitude of different genres. The front page displays a banner headline introducing a story of national or international importance. The article describes an event that has taken place, including the times, dates, and people or issues involved. The headline's purpose is to sell copy; the article ought to inform. A headline may be humorous, dramatic, exaggerated, or even lurid; the article may in fact be a bore. Compare, for example the way in which the staid and sober *New York Times* and the flamboyant and populist *New York Post* each reported the elimination of the US men's soccer team from the 2010 World Cup. The *Times* announced the defeat with, "A Final Day of Chasing Ends the U.S. Run," while the *Post* blustered, "This Sport Is Stupid Anyway: USA Out of World Cup." Same story, different take. Knowing how to interpret the headline depends on preknowledge of the newspaper and its temperament.

Inside the paper, we find the op-ed section. Now the purpose is to state the opinion of the editorial board and to persuade. Editorials typically conform to the political stance of a newspaper, and the stances of papers vary. Over a page we find the obituaries. Like articles and editorials, an obituary provides details: it announces a person's death, summarizes their life, lists family members, and offers the time and location of the funeral. It tends to do so, however, while placing the deceased in the best possible light. An obituary is unlikely to mention that a person was a rude, disagreeable neighbor who annually cheated on their taxes. To browse through the newspaper is to shift from one genre to another easily. A lifetime of training has equipped us to recognize genre and attune expectations. A salacious headline precedes a sober article. An editorial then opines, and an obituary honors a person's life as much as it informs.

The Bible is also a collection of varied genres that convey meaning in different ways. Second Timothy 3:16 makes this clear when it declares, "All Scripture is God-breathed and is

useful for teaching, rebuking, correcting and training in righteousness." Note what Scripture does: teaching, exposing, correcting, training. The list is by no means exhaustive. The psalms,
for instance, comfort and inspire. A first step to unlocking a
piece of literature is determining its genre, and the Bible is no
exception.

Of course, the Bible is not as easy to "open" as the newspaper. Newspapers (whether print or electronic) are entirely present; the Bible is sequestered in sacred space and drawing from
a different world. With the Bible, it is much easier to miss how
and what the author was trying to communicate. For example,
approaching Old Testament narrative as if it were merely a collection of individual stories fit for bedtime can mean missing
the author's theological point unfolded through an entire book.
Chapters of arcane detail sometimes interrupt biblical story
lines. Here too, readers can puzzle over why such material was
preserved and how it should be understood. Consider the blueprints for building and outfitting the tabernacle (Exod 26–30).
Chapters of materials and measurements have led many to an
allegorical reading recognizable only in light of the incarnation,
unhappily imposing a message that would have been wholly
inaccessible to the original audience. That Christ "tabernacled
among us" (John 1:14) warrants a certain level of typological
reading; to see every measurement, color, and material as some
coded reference to Jesus is too much.

The opposite error is to ignore foreign material altogether, adopting a "that-was-then-this-is-now" stance. Not
only does this approach risk missing lessons that might have
been attained through thoughtful, patient study, but also it
easily avoids dealing with discomfiting passages. The end is
a Scripture that is made in our own image—able to comfort,
but never allowed to challenge or change. Second Timothy

3:16 is once again instructive—"all Scripture is God-breathed." The Scripture here mentioned is what we today would call the Old Testament. It is this Scripture that is profitable for rebuking and correcting us. When we ignore foreign or challenging genres or passages of the Bible, we distance ourselves from God's teaching and correction. If we read Scripture without regard to genre we can, despite the best of intentions, miss what God has to say to us.

## READING AND INTERPRETING
## PROPHECY AND APOCALYPTIC

The interplay between genre and understanding is especially relevant for our discussion so far. Specifically, older dispensationalism has tended to merge or blur the lines between prophetic and apocalyptic genres, often treating them as if they were one and the same. Thus, John Walvoord's commentary on Daniel bears the subtitle *The Key to Prophetic Revelation*, where most Old Testament scholars today would categorize Daniel as apocalyptic, not prophetic, literature. Likewise, Dwight Pentecost's substantial work, *Things to Come*, omits all mention of apocalyptic as a genre. Proponents of progressive dispensationalism have attempted to develop a more sensitive dispensational hermeneutic that engages with the genre of apocalyptic more deliberately. In fact, one of the best resources on interpreting and applying apocalyptic literature available today was written by a senior faculty member of Dallas Theological Seminary.[1]

And yet, the older error persists. If prophecy and apocalyptic differ, how is this so, and what happens when the genres are confused? This section takes up this question, exploring the differences between the genres, their contexts, and the different messages that each brought to its audience.

## WHEN DID PROPHECY FLOURISH?

Prophecy had a long history in ancient Israel, with prophets being found in multiple contexts in varying roles and relationships. All prophets, however, shared the conviction that they had received divine revelation from God to communicate to their audience, whether kings, commoners, or foreign nations. In the premonarchic era (pre-eleventh century BC), several prophets mediated the will of God to the nation. Although we think of Moses primarily as a lawgiver, he is also remembered as a prophet. As the one who met God atop Mount Sinai and continued to meet God face to face in the tent of meeting (Exod 19–32; Num 12:5–7), he remains the prophet par excellence. During the period of the judges, Deborah was a prophetess who judged legal disputes and who relayed God's will to Barak in time of national crisis (Judg 4:4–6).

The last of the judges, Samuel, himself a prophet and national leader (1 Sam 3:20–21), was also a transitional figure. In the early monarchic era (eleventh–tenth centuries BC), he interceded for the people and related the will of God (1 Sam 12:19–25), but also distanced the prophet from national leadership, pivoting toward a sort of divine adviser (1 Sam 10:17–27; 13:7–15; 15:10–35; 28:11–20). During the time of David, the prophet Nathan functioned similarly and was even more entrenched in court than was Samuel, acting as trusted royal adviser and conscience to David, and playing a role in royal succession (2 Sam 7:1–17; 12:1–25; 1 Kgs 1:22–27).

Prophets continued as royal advisers into the ninth century—the classical period of prophecy in Israel. Prominent figures such as Elijah and Elisha and lesser-known or anonymous prophets independently announced God's word and chastened the monarch (1 Kgs 17:1; 18:16–46) even as they sometimes appeared at court or with the army on campaign (1 Kgs 20:13, 22; 22:7–28;

2 Kgs 3:9–20). During the classical period we first encounter the so-called writing prophets—figures whose names are attached to preserved collections of prophetic material, many of which feature reference to covenant blessing and cursing, often in relation to threats from foreign foes. Such classical prophets as Jeremiah and Ezekiel carried their ministries into the exilic era (586–539 BC). It is prophetic material from this period and the exile that tends to find its way into the work of end-times teachers.

After the exile, as a province of the Persian Empire, the people of Judah were initially overseen by one of their own—a governor descended from the royal line of David through King Jehoiachin. In this postexilic era (538–333 BC) the prophets regarded the Persians as liberators. Cyrus the Great (559–530 BC) not only allowed the return but was identified as divinely anointed for that purpose (Isa 45:1; also 44:28; 45:13). As the people were safely resettled in the land, the issues that animate the postexilic prophets are more moral and spiritual than those of their predecessors. Haggai stresses the need to rebuild the temple of God in Jerusalem (Hag 1–2). Similarly, Zechariah encourages the returnees to rebuild the temple and live in obedience to God so that they might enjoy his presence there and attract the attention of the nations (Zech 1–8). With the temple rebuilt, however, both priests and people lapsed into disobedience, earning divine rebuke through Malachi, who warns of divine punishment should covenant unfaithfulness persist (Mal 1–4).

It thus appears that most prophecy is set in a context where Israel is in the land. It controls its own destiny—to some measure. This is not surprising: the covenant curses recorded in Leviticus 26 and Deuteronomy 28—drought, famine, wild animals, foreign attack, and exile—pertain to life in the land. Come the exile, these curses lose their persuasive effect. After all, once Israel has been expelled from the land, what is left to say?

The exile, however, did not end prophecy. It introduced a different context. Consider Ezekiel, active when Judah was in captivity in Babylon, unable to exercise independence. Apart from judgment pronounced remotely on those remaining in Jerusalem (Ezek 4–24), his message is for those outside the land. Ezekiel looks forward, not to covenant curse, but to a future of covenant blessing when an obedient people returns to the land (Ezek 33–48). Covenant curses crop up when the people are in the land, but risk expulsion because of disobedience or when their sin has made judgment unavoidable and imminent. Pronouncements of covenant blessing, on the other hand, can occur anywhere, often appearing alongside promises of restoration when the people are in exile.

## WHAT IS PROPHECY?

### ISRAEL AS GOD'S INTERMEDIARY

In their helpful book *How to Read the Bible for All Its Worth*, Gordon Fee and Douglas Stuart aptly describe prophets as "covenant enforcement" mediators.[2] Prediction of future events by no means exhausts the range of prophetic activities. Prophets were more like smoke detectors—Israel's theological early warning system. How did this work? The intermediary role of the prophets originated in Israel's own intermediary vocation. God's call to Abram made the patriarch an intermediary between God and the world: "All peoples on earth will be blessed through you" (Gen 12:3). With Abraham and his descendants singled out as a conduit of divine blessing to the world, the rest of Genesis then unfolds how this family fulfilled this role. Consider Joseph: in the midst of widespread famine, Joseph blessed the nations by advising Pharaoh and saving the Egyptians and others from starvation (Gen 41).

At Sinai, God expanded this intermediatory mandate to include the nation. Israel was to be a "kingdom of priests and a holy nation" (Exod 19:6). In the ancient world, a priest mediated between God and those who wished to approach God. His call to a higher state of purity allowed the priest to enter the sanctuary on the worshipers' behalf and also rendered God's holiness and character visible to them. The laws and regulations of the Sinai covenant placed Israel "between" God and the world in this priestly way. Among the many things the law or Torah embodied for ancient Israel, a large part was to order national life to reveal God's character to the nations. As God rested on the seventh day, so Israel was to rest on the seventh day; since God was holy, his people Israel was to aspire to holiness. Since God cared about society's most vulnerable, Israel was to make such people their concern also. By obeying Torah, Israel would disclose God's character and thus bless the nations.

Covenant blessings and curses were aids in fulfilling Israel's divine vocation. Prophets mediated words of divine blessing when Israel was living in obedience to God, and warnings when they strayed. Thus Ezekiel summarizes his call to be a "watchman": "Son of man, I have made you a watchman for the house of Israel; so hear the word I speak and give them warning from me" (Ezek 3:17; 33:7). While warnings often involved predictions, these were not inventions, but applications of well-understood and codified blessings and curses— or encouragements and warnings. To see how the prophets used covenant blessings and curses in prediction, let's take a closer look at the shorter of these two passages, Leviticus 26.

## COVENANT BLESSING AND CURSE

Leviticus 26, like its longer and more complicated counterpart Deuteronomy 28, is a list of covenant blessings and curses. It concludes a book offering divine instruction concerning worship, personal purity, and living. Its opening summary reduces the Ten Commandments to two. The first, "Do not make idols" (Lev 26:1), harkens to the second commandment (Exod 20:4–6; Deut 5:8–10). Idols are a covenantal deal-breaker to be avoided at all costs. In this regard, Israel blundered at the beginning when, at the foot of Sinai, they made golden calves (Exod 32). The result was immediate judgment and reschooling in the relevant parts of the covenant. Idolatry violated the essence of a covenant in which God alone was to be worshiped. The second, "Observe my Sabbaths and have reverence for my sanctuary. I am the LORD," restates the fourth commandment, reminding readers that Sinai's sign and substance are grounded in Yahweh's identity (Lev 26:2; also Exod 20:8–11; 31:13–17). Blessings and curses begin with a restatement of Sinai's essence, the identity of the one with whom the covenant was made, and a reminder of its most important sign.

The list then follows: blessings (Lev 26:3–13) and curses (vv. 14–39). Blessings flow from obedience (v. 3). Unlike the curses' repeated promise of sevenfold punishment for continued disobedience, there is no obvious segmentation or gradation for the blessings. They are experienced concurrently, not consecutively. Blessings are thus God's default setting in his relationship with Israel. They are not benefits dispensed piecemeal as Israel proves itself to be good enough.

*Blessings* (Lev 26:3–13): "If you follow my decrees and are careful to obey my commands, I will …"

- send rain

- grant peace

- make you fruitful

- dwell among you

*Curses* (Lev 26:14–39): "But if you will not listen to me and carry out all these commands … I will bring … "

- terror

- crop failure

- wild animals

- sword and plague

- exile

- punish/afflict seven times over (26:18, 21, 24, 27–28)

The first blessing is rain, leading to agricultural plenty, and consequently a life of security (Lev 26:4–5). Then God promises peace and an absence of fear: wild animals are removed and enemies defeated (Lev 26:6–8). Predators, whether animal or human, will neither attack nor plunder; the land will be open to God's people. Third, God promises fruitfulness in terms of population growth and agricultural bounty (Lev 26:9–10). Last, obedience will bring the ultimate blessing of divine presence as God dwells with his people (Lev 26:11–13). The blessings together guarantee a life of stability and prosperity in the land God had given them as a base for blessing the nations (Gen 12:1–3, 7).

The curses are a similarly arranged but horrible undoing of the blessings. After a short introduction that parallels Leviticus 26:3, they are presented in five consecutive sections, each separated by a warning formula (Lev 26:18, 21, 23, 27). Unlike the blessings, the curses are clearly structured to show that they do not occur simultaneously, but in stages of increasing severity. Were Israel to heed God's warning, the curse would cease and blessing resume.

First is the curse of terror—a fear brought on by disease, enemy raids, and defeat in battle (Lev 26:16–17). Then follows drought (Lev 26:18–20): affecting crops and seed stock, creating vulnerability lasting months or years. Should rebellion persist, then wild animals will return to prey upon Israel's children (Lev 26:21–22). Continued neglect of God's law will result in sword and plague sweeping through the land, cutting down the population (Lev 26:23–26). Finally, the ultimate covenant curse of siege, destruction, and exile will be applied to the refusal to repent (Lev 26:27–33).

## BLESSING AND CURSE IN THE COVENANT LIFE OF ANCIENT ISRAEL

Several considerations draw our attention. First, the curse's reality notwithstanding, blessings are to be the norm. This much is obvious from God's own summation in Deuteronomy. There, with the blessings and curses just described, God urges his people to "choose life."

This day I call the heavens and the earth as witnesses against you that I have set before you life and death,

blessings and curses. Now choose life, so that you and
your children may live and that you may love the LORD
your God, listen to his voice, and hold fast to him. For
the LORD is your life, and he will give you many years
in the land he swore to give to your fathers, Abraham,
Isaac and Jacob. (Deut 30:19–20)

Blessings are the norm because they equip Israel to live collec-
tively in the land from which it was to bless the nations. This
predisposition is entirely consistent with God's self-description
at Sinai: "The LORD, the LORD, [is] the compassionate and
gracious God, slow to anger, abounding in love and faithfulness, maintaining love to thousands, and forgiving wickedness,
rebellion and sin" (Exod 34:6–7). Blessing is God's default setting with his people. In covenant, God desires to bless Israel
as he blessed the first human couple with plenty and fertility
in the garden of Eden (Gen 1:26–29; 2:8–9, 16). God is love;
he desires to bless those who are his. Hence, his blessing is not
dispensed in increments. Curses, however, depart from the
norm. Each undoes a corresponding blessing: terror replaces
peace; drought, rain. Wild animals, the sword, and plague undo
fertility and fruitfulness. Finally, exile cuts Israel off from God's
land and temple. In each case, the character of the curses as
reversals shows that the blessing is primary.

Second, despite their harshness, the curses are clearly corrective, not merely punitive. Unlike the blessings that come all
together, the curses are arranged in order of increasing severity.
They are administered consecutively only if Israel has refused
to listen to earlier warnings, as evidenced by the repetition
of phrasing similar to that found in Leviticus 26:21, "If you
remain hostile toward me and refuse to listen to me, I will …"

This makes Israel's position in its relationship with God clear. It can be restored with renewed obedience.

Third, the ultimate curse of exile relates in part to Israel's mandate to be an intermediary (Exod 19:6) and stops Israel from bearing false witness about God's identity. If the law was so to order Israel's life that it reflected God's character to the nations, then persistent disobedience amounted to lying about God's character. Exile from the land would be God's final tool to preserve his reputation from continued damage. Even here, however, breach is not final. Exile heals the land too long denied its sabbath rest as Israel scorned Sinai's sign (Lev 26:34–35, 43a). If Israel repents, God will return them to the land (vv. 40–45).

This curse's corrective aspect, and particularly the way exile curtails false testimony, finds parallels in New Testament passages relating to church discipline (Matt 18:15–20; see 1 Cor 5; 2 Thess 3:14–15). Often misinterpreted and misapplied to justify shunning or removing a member who has confessed sin, these passages stress that, like Israel, the church is called to be God's priestly intermediary in the world (1 Pet 2:9; see Exod 19:6). In all three passages listed, the command to expel a believer and disassociate from them applies only to the persistently disobedient and unrepentant. It parallels the ultimate covenant curse of exile. If the church shares Israel's call to be a "royal priesthood" (1 Pet 2:9), it reflects God's character so that the world will know who God is. To claim to represent Christ while persistently disobeying his commands is to lie about who Christ is. Accordingly, disassociation or removal is, like exile, only to be invoked after persistent resistance to correction. The church must protect the integrity of its testimony by disassociating itself from that disobedient believer. As was the case for Israel, this state need not be permanent. In both contexts, there exists a path to restoration through repentance and renewed obedience.

## FOUR MISCONCEPTIONS ABOUT PROPHETS AND PROPHECY

Why spend so much time talking about covenant blessings and curses when our subject is prophecy? This is because they form the touchstone for most prophetic prediction in the Old Testament. This impinges significantly on how prophecy is read and applied. Before we move further, however, we must correct four common misconceptions about biblical prophecy. This will provide us with realistic expectations about this genre and prepare us to think about its use by end-times teachers.

### MISCONCEPTION 1: PROPHETIC PREDICTION INVOLVED THE FORETELLING OF SURPRISING OR UNEXPECTED EVENTS

If your primary prophetic resources are the headlines of the *National Enquirer*, then you might suppose that prophecy is all about stunning, surprising, and spectacular predictions. In fact, quite the opposite was true. Prophecy encouraged and warned. It was one way in which God drew a line between Israel's behavior and consequences. As such, prophecies were to lead the Israelites to a national "Aha!" moment. Their behavior had taken them to a dangerous place. The warnings were most often dramatically framed and delivered announcements of covenant curses of the kind found in Leviticus 26 and Deuteronomy 28. Think about a scene played out in countless television police dramas. A detective sits across from a suspect in a grimy interrogation room and says, "Look, I'd like to help you, but if you don't confess and this goes to trial, you're looking at twenty to life!" The detective has not consulted a crystal ball or pulled a prison sentence out of the blue. Working from a knowledge of the crime and its usual penalty, the detective hopes to induce cooperation. The prediction is real because it is grounded in a known standard. The prophets spoke to Israel like the detective. When Ezekiel or Jeremiah foretold destruction and exile, they announced a well-understood and recognizable covenant curse. Conversely, when they predicted a return to the land, a rebuilt temple, and renewed abundance, they invoked the language of covenant blessing. For contemporary readers, recognizing these predictions as announced blessings or curses can be hard because we don't see the dramatic or poetic way in which they have been reframed. But the audience receiving the prediction would have. These announcements of covenant blessing or curse diagnosed their present condition. Disobedience required correction; future obedience would result in blessing.

## MISCONCEPTION 2: MOST PROPHETIC PREDICTION INVOLVED FULFILLMENT IN THE DISTANT FUTURE

Pick up any popular end-times prophecy book and you'll likely find a section on the dependability of prophecy. The prophets foretold distant events with astonishing accuracy. Most prophets, however, actually aimed at the near future. This may surprise us, because we think so quickly of christological passages such as Isaiah 53 that are highlighted in the New Testament. These, however, are the exception rather than the rule. For the most part, prophetic prediction was near term—and for a good reason. Because prophecy as a genre intends to induce behavioral change, near-term consequences are more compelling than distant ones. If we told you, "If you keep driving that gas-guzzling monster truck to work each day, in three hundred years the world will run out of oil," would your driving habits alter? On the other hand, were we to say, "If you keep driving that gas-guzzling monster truck to work each day, your fuel costs will leave you bankrupt in three months," you'd more likely trade your truck for something smaller. Consequences that we are likely to experience are powerful motivators. Likewise, the prophets make predictions based on covenant curses that alert Israel to its guilt and hold out consequences in the near future.

## MISCONCEPTION 3: FALSE PROPHETS WERE THOSE WHO MADE INACCURATE PREDICTIONS

Although some end-times teachers stress the fate of death by stoning reserved for false prophets (Deut 18:20), the real issue was not a lack of accuracy, but a lack of integrity. Prophetic utterances frequently began with the source citation "this is what the LORD says"—what followed came directly from God. To knowingly mislead while attributing the message to God was both to lie (Exod 20:16; Deut 5:20) and to misuse the LORD's name (Exod 20:7). Thus Deuteronomy 18:20, "A prophet who presumes to speak in my name anything I have not commanded him to say, or a prophet who speaks in the name of other gods, must be put to death." The penalty was severe not only because the false prophet attributed a lie to God, but also because in so doing they turned God's people to destruction. Since the prophet was to awaken Israel to its true moral state to correct its behavior, to lie about that moral state was to keep Israel asleep in its sin. Jeremiah, whose warnings to Judah were frustrated by false prophets peddling a soothing but ultimately deadly message, saw the cost clearly.

> "Therefore," declares the LORD, "I am against the
> prophets who steal from one another words suppos-
> edly from me. Yes," declares the LORD, "I am against
> the prophets who wag their own tongues and yet
> declare, 'The LORD declares.' Indeed, I am against
> those who prophesy false dreams," declares the LORD.
> "They tell them and lead my people astray with their
> reckless lies, yet I did not send or appoint them. They
> do not benefit these people in the least," declares the
> LORD. (Jer 23:30–32)

False prophets were punished severely, therefore, not because
they erred, but because they willfully misrepresented God; they
lured Israel to death and destruction.

## MISCONCEPTION 4: EVERYTHING THAT HAS BEEN PROPHESIED EVENTUALLY WILL COME TO PASS

The fourth misconception about prophecy is found in most
end-times teaching. Watch a video or read a book on end
times, and you will encounter it. Here's an example from the
late Canadian author Grant Jeffrey: "Those prophecies of the
Bible, which have already been accomplished, were fulfilled to
the letter. Since this is true, why is it so difficult for some people
to believe that the prophecies regarding future events will also
be fulfilled literally?"[3] The statement sounds true. Nonetheless,
it overlooks an important caveat in biblical prophecy—conditional prediction.

Consider Jeremiah 18. God sends his prophet to a potter's
house to watch him work his clay. At one point, the craftsman
stops, examines the clay, re-forms it into a ball, and starts
over. The point? God never gives up his sovereignty. If God

pronounces judgment on a people (like Jonah's Ninevites) and that people repents, then he reserves the right to suspend the planned punishment (Jer 18:7–8; Jonah 4:10–11). Likewise, if God pronounces blessing on a people and they take that pronouncement as a license to sin, then God reserves the right to judge (Jer 18:9–10). Because God sovereignly restores the repentant and withdraws blessing from the wicked, some prophecies of blessing or judgment are not fulfilled and never will be. Many prophecies present God's people with an opportunity. How that prophecy is fulfilled blends divine sovereignty with human responsibility.

Dwight Pentecost acknowledges this biblical reality, but counters that prophecy of this sort requires clearly stated conditions.[4] This seems reasonable, but it's not true to the text. Often—most often, in fact—when a prophet announces God's intent to bless his people, he is announcing a covenant blessing that presumes ongoing obedience. The conditions may not be stated because the audience already understands them to be present based on "if this, then that" passages such as Leviticus 26 and Deuteronomy 28. Even the promise of action without conditions is still often conditional.

With a better sense of what to expect, let us examine how prophecy functioned in Israel.

## THE INTERPLAY BETWEEN PREDICTION AND COVENANT BLESSING AND CURSE

Success in school, business, or relationships often requires self-awareness and personal responsibility. Successful students know what they know, what they don't know, and how to bridge the gap. Successful employees enter a performance evaluation aware of their goals, their effort, and their team-work. People with thriving relationships know themselves and others, and own their actions. Awareness and respon-sibility were also vital for Israel's covenant relationship with God. The law God delivered at Sinai was to help God's people stay in relationship with him, setting a standard and provid-ing guidance so that Israel would know when it was straying. Ideally, when the Israelites lapsed, the law enabled them to self-diagnose and correct course. When this did not happen, the prophets spoke.

We have already observed that prophetic prediction fre-quently was grounded in covenant curse. Curses were framed as predictions with imminent expected fulfillment. This basic characteristic of prophecy is critical to interpretation. Is the prophetic passage in question already fulfilled or awaiting future fulfillment? Where much dispensational end-times teaching regards a great deal of prophecy as unfulfilled, we have countered above that it is actually related to the original audience's immediate future. The result is different interpre-tations and potentially dramatic consequences for how one views the future. To illustrate our position, we'll consider sev-eral passages from different prophetic books. We'll show that their shared specific vocabulary and highly descriptive language allude to the covenant curses of Leviticus and Deuteronomy, driving the audience to the realization that they have departed from God's teaching.

The following table (table 5.1), based on the blessings and curses found in Leviticus 26 and Deuteronomy 28, will help us recognize these curses where they appear in prophetic oracles and pronouncements.

| Leviticus 26 | |
| --- | --- |
| Blessings (vv. 3–13) | Curses (vv. 14–39) |
| rain leading to crops, fruit, grapes, security (vv. 4–5) | terror, wasting diseases, fever, defeat by enemies (vv. 16–17) |
| peace in the land, absence of fear, no threat from wild animals or the sword, enemies will be defeated (vv. 6–8) | lack of rain, soil and trees will not produce (vv. 19–20) |
| human fertility, bountiful harvest (vv. 9–10) | wild animals will appear and kill children and livestock (v. 22) |
| divine presence in sanctuary (vv. 11–12) | sword, plague, food supply cut off (vv. 25–26) |

| Deuteronomy 28 | |
| --- | --- |
| Blessings (vv. 2–14) | Curses (vv. 15–68) |
| your enemies defeated and scattered (v. 7) | curses, confusion, rebuke, destruction (v. 20) |
| your storehouses blessed (v. 28) | plague (v. 21) |
| you will be God's holy people, nations will fear you (vv. 9–10) | wasting disease, fever, inflammation, heat, drought, blight, mildew, plague, lack of rain (vv. 22–24) |
| fertility of humans, livestock, crops (v. 11) | defeat by enemies, lack of burial (vv. 25–26) |
| rain leading to abundance and wealth (v. 12) | boils of Egypt, tumors, sores, incurable itch (v. 27) |
| stature and power (v. 13) | madness; blindness; confusion of mind; oppression; being robbed; women raped; houses, vineyards, livestock stolen; children exiled; invaders will plunder and oppress (vv. 28–34) |

*Table 5.1. Covenant Blessing and Curse in Leviticus 26 and Deuteronomy 28*

## COVENANT BLESSING AND CURSE
## AND PROPHETIC PREDICTION

### AMOS

During the late eighth century BC, the prophet Amos was sent from Judah to Israel to warn the northern kingdom of its sin and the fate that awaited if it did not reform. At the time, Israel was still a prosperous, independent kingdom. An Israelite king ruled. Internationally, however, a resurgent kingdom of Assyria wanted to restore its former imperial glory. Soon, it would march west and south—straight to Israel. In chapter 4, Amos warns Israel: God had already visited covenant curses of drought, famine, plague, and armed attack on a people that had failed to listen:

> "I gave you empty stomachs in every city
>> and lack of bread in every town,
>> yet you have not returned to me,"
>> declares the LORD.
> "I also withheld rain from you
>> when the harvest was still three months away.
> I sent rain on one town,
>> but withheld it from another.
> One field had rain;
>> another had none and dried up.
> People staggered from town to town for water
>> but did not get enough to drink,
>> yet you have not returned to me,"
>> declares the LORD.
> "Many times I struck your gardens and vineyards,
>> destroying them with blight and mildew.

> Locusts devoured your fig and olive trees,
>> yet you have not returned to me,"
>> declares the LORD.
> "I sent plagues among you
>> as I did to Egypt.
> I killed your young men with the sword,
>> along with your captured horses.
> I filled your nostrils with the stench of your camps,
>> yet you have not returned to me,"
>> declares the LORD. (Amos 4:6–10)

"Bread," "rain," "plagues," and "sword"—drawn from Leviticus 26 and Deuteronomy 28, they unmistakably connect prophecy to covenant curse. The condemnation's impact is enhanced by the prophet's imagery and highly descriptive language by accentuating the formal connection established by the shared vocabulary. The formal curse of rain withheld is imaged in the people staggering from town to parched town looking for water, yet refusing obedience. To vocabulary and image, add the sequential and incremental structure. Amos's condemnation parallels the presentation of the curses in Leviticus 26.

Later, Amos vividly invokes the covenant punishment of Leviticus 26:22 of a land surrendered to wild animals. Describing the disaster that would fall on Israel on the day of the Lord, the prophet declares,

> It will be as though a man fled from a lion
>> only to meet a bear,
> as though he entered his house
>> and rested his hand on the wall
>> only to have a snake bite him. (Amos 5:19)

In this ancient "horror film," an Israelite Jamie Lee Curtis avoids a lion only to confront a bear. Somehow eluding the bear, she slams the door shut at home only to be bitten by a waiting snake. With this biblical jump-scare, the prophet points to the prophetic warning of Leviticus 26:22 and in a single verse paints a future of judgment for covenant disobedience.

## HOSEA

Hosea also combines specific vocabulary with poetic imagery. A contemporary of Amos and likewise addressing Israel, Hosea summarizes God's message simply: "Because you have rejected knowledge, I also reject you as my priests" (Hos 4:6; see Exod 19:6). As Hosea elaborates, it is clear that here too Israel's sin invites warnings about impending covenant curses. The curse of failed crops is dramatically described as God clawing back his blessing just as it was about to be enjoyed: "I will take away my grain when it ripens, and my new wine when it is ready" (Hos 2:9; see Lev 26:20). Flourishing vines and fig trees will soon be wilderness: "I will ruin her vines and her fig trees, which she said were her pay from her lovers; I will make them a thicket, and wild animals will devour them" (Hos 2:12). The description of wild animals as those who will inhabit this new, overgrown territory depicts the curse of predation (see Lev 26:22). Hosea goes on, however, to promise that this situation need not be God's last word. Israel can experience restored vineyards (Hos 2:15; see Lev 26:5; Deut 28:30, 39), removal of wild animals (Hos 2:18; see Lev 26:6, 22), and a return to peace (Hos 2:18; see Lev 26:6) and fertility (Hos 2:21–22; see Lev 26:4–5; Deut 28:12)—all recalling Torah's covenant blessings. Like Amos, Hosea's predictions invoke specifics from Leviticus 26 and Deuteronomy 28 while using poetic language to maximize their impact.

## EZEKIEL

Ezekiel, a priest and prophet whose life and ministry straddled the exile, likely spent his recorded public ministry in
Babylon, arriving there in 597 BC when King Jehoiachin
(598–597 BC) was deposed and taken captive. Even as they
and other Judeans were in Babylon, a Davidic heir, Zedekiah
(597–586 BC), still ruled in Jerusalem. Ezekiel's ministry thus
looks in two directions. Those in Jerusalem, he insists, are
still threatened by invasion, defeat, and exile (e.g., Ezek 4–7),
while those in Babylon should not find hope in Zedekiah's
reign for an imminent victory and return to the land. The
exiles, Ezekiel says, will return to Judah only after those
remaining in Judah join them in Babylon. Only when all God's
people are chastened and obedient will God restore them
(Ezek 11:16–25; 34; 36–37).

One of the oracles warning the "remainers" (Ezek 5:5–17)
begins by noting how God placed Jerusalem where all could see
how she lived—"in the center of the nations, with countries all
around her." Because Jerusalem turned to idols, however, God
determined to judge her (Ezek 5:5–9). The city's status as the
center of world attention and the charge of idolatry drew attention to Jerusalem's intermediary role. Her behavior reflected
God's character to the world (Exod 19:5–6). Accordingly, idolatry was the covenant deal-breaker (Lev 26:1). Subsequent
verses relate the form this judgment will take. Each announced
punishment corresponds to the covenant curses of Leviticus 26—
sometimes by allusion through described scenarios, at other
times by the very words used.

Jerusalem's idolatry violated an essential element of
the covenant (Ezek 5:8–9; see Lev 26:1). God's inevitable

condemnation highlights the horrors that occur before and after a military siege: the struggle to live will be marked by cannibalism within families (Ezek 5:10a), clearly imposed covenant curses of Leviticus 26:29 and Deuteronomy 28:53–57 (table 5.2). Survivors will then be scattered abroad (Ezek 5:10b)—described, using the precise vocabulary of Leviticus 26:33 and the warnings of exile of Deuteronomy 28:36–37, 63–65. In Ezekiel 5:11, the certainty of this fate is sealed with a divine oath and the promise of divine abandonment. God's covenant blessing, his turning his face upon his people (Lev 26:9), is revoked (Lev 26:17).

Systematic and complete, God's judgment combines several covenant curses. Inside the city, plague and famine will kill one-third of its inhabitants (Ezek 5:12a, 16–17; see Lev 26:16, 25–26); outside, another third will fall by the sword (Ezek 5:12b, also 17; see Lev 26:17, 25); the final third will be scattered (Ezek 5:12c; see Lev 26:33). Rather than being a shining example to the nations, Jerusalem will be a cautionary tale to all passers-by (Ezek 5:13–17). The culminating cluster of covenant-curse vocabulary in verse 17—famine, wild animals, plague, and sword—clarifies that, far from a minor setback, this is God's final judgment. The entire sequence culminates with "I the LORD have spoken," a statement of claim and self-identification paralleling Leviticus 26:2. Ezekiel's audience would have recognized the prophet's pronouncements of covenant curses as exposing their unfaithfulness to God and the Sinai covenant. Ezekiel's prophetic word was indeed predictive, but it was prediction rooted in the covenant. Ezekiel's audience connected the prophet's words about Jerusalem's future to their own deeds in the past.

| Ezekiel 5:8–17 | Covenant Curses |
|---|---|
| cannibalism (Ezek 5:10a) | Lev 26:29; Deut 28:53–57 |
| scattered (Ezek 5:10b) | Lev 26:33; Deut 28:36–37, 63–65 |
| divine abandonment (Ezek 5:11) | Lev 26:9, 17 |
| plague, famine (Ezek 5:12a, 16–17) | Lev 26:16, 25–26 |
| sword (Ezek 5:12b, 17) | Lev 26:17, 25 |
| scattering (Ezek 5:12c) | Lev 26:33 |
| famine, wild animals, plague, and sword (Ezek 5:17) | Lev 26:16–17, 22, 25–26, 33; Deut 28:36–37, 63–65 |

*Table 5.2. Covenant Curses in Ezekiel 5:8–17*

Turning to his fellow exiles, Ezekiel has a much different message. In Ezekiel 34:20–31, the mood dramatically shifts. The prophet relates God's promise of a good future for his audience. This oracle comes at a critical moment, for up until this point, they had placed their hope in a Judean king still ruling from Jerusalem. Then the Babylonians attacked Jerusalem and destroyed God's temple (586 BC).

The night before news of this disaster reached Ezekiel and the exiles (Ezek 33:21–22), he received six divine messages regarding Jerusalem's and Judah's future. Although the second (Ezek 34:1–16) castigates Judah's unfaithful leaders, this oracle culminates in covenant blessings and inverted curses, speaking of a day when a restored people will thrive in the land under a new Davidic prince (34:17–31). Replacing Judah's unfaithful shepherds, God promises a future under a new shepherd, a princely descendant of David (Ezek 34:20–24). God will even make a "new covenant" with Judah, undoing the curses (as described in Ezek 5:5–17) and reinstating blessing—"I will make a covenant of peace with them and rid the land of savage beasts so that they may live in the wilderness and sleep in the forests in safety" (Ezek 34:25). The blessing—removal of wild animals—allows the people to take full possession of the land and dwell in it in safety (Ezek 34:25, 28; see Lev 26:6). The assurance that God will "send down showers in season" (Ezek 34:26) is the covenant blessing of rain in Leviticus 26:4 and Deuteronomy 28:2. It ensures that famine is replaced with further covenant blessings of trees that yield their fruit and ground that yields its crops (Ezek 34:27, 29; see Lev 26:4–5). Such abundance climaxes in a life of security (Ezek 34:27; see Lev 26:5–6). God will rescue his people from their enslavers, breaking the "bars of their yoke" in keeping with his covenant promise (Ezek 34:27; see Lev 26:13). All these actions display God's covenant identity—"I am the LORD" (Ezek 34:27; see Lev 26:2).

The repeated promise of removal of wild animals, ensuring safety and freedom from fear (Ezek 34:28), announces the return to covenant blessing (Lev 26:5–6). The promise in Ezekiel 34:29 that the people will "no longer be victims of famine" (lit. "gatherers of famine") inverts the curse that disobedient Israel will "gather little" (Deut 28:38). The promise that the restored people will no longer "bear the scorn of the nations" (Ezek 34:29) transforms the curses in which Israel suffers at the hands of the nations or is scattered among them (Lev 26:38; Deut 28:36, 49, 50, 65). In this new era, a renewed knowledge of God prevails even as his presence is restored (Ezek 34:27, 30; see Lev 26:9a, 12). For Ezekiel's exiled audience, this vision of the future is the application of covenant blessings. All can be theirs if they return to God.

Once we understand that these and similar predictions are (1) the fulfillment of covenant blessings and curses, (2) presented in the elevated language of prophetic rhetoric, and

(3) dependent on the wholehearted obedience of Israel, then the power of a passage such as Ezekiel 34 is unlocked. It points the exiles to the abundant future awaiting at the exile's end. God will return for and to them. The blessing that awaits, however, requires that they truly seek after God once restored to the land.

## THE USE OF OLD TESTAMENT PROPHECY IN DISPENSATIONAL END-TIMES TEACHING

Failure to recognize the use of covenant blessing and inverted curse language, the elevated nature of prophetic speech, and the original context of passages such as Ezekiel 34 leads to serious misinterpretation. As we've seen, dispensationalism commits readers to "literal" interpretation and treats symbolic or allegorical readings of Scripture with suspicion. Unfairly caught up in this preference, however, is the elevated, sometimes supercharged prophetic language that expands and amplifies covenant language. This leads most dispensationalists to adopt a literalistic reading in place of a truly literary one, with significant consequences for interpretation: namely, a post-exilic oracle is wrongly transposed to the distant future, shoehorned into a highly detailed eschatological schema. Thus, *The New Scofield Reference Bible* and Dwight Pentecost insist that since the details of this passage have never been fulfilled, the events they describe must refer to a "future theocratic kingdom," the millennium, in which Christ rules from David's throne in Jerusalem.[5]

An overly literalistic approach to reading, the dispensationalist approach also often fails to consider the social setting and expectations of the original audience. If, for instance, Ezekiel's vision referred to a millennial kingdom thousands of years distant, then it would have offered no divine comfort to its first hearers or readers. Why would God entreat his exiled people to turn to him with the promise of blessing that they would never live to experience? Such an offer is cruelly disingenuous.

Misreading "into the future" as Pentecost and others do also ignores events that lay in the original audience's near future. How might readers have understood Ezekiel 34 after their return from exile just a few decades later? Cyrus's edict (538 BC) that saw the Judeans return to Jerusalem was a stunning departure from previous imperial practice. Conquering Assyrians and Babylonians exiled the leadership class of conquered populations to prevent rebellions and enrich the imperial administration with human capital. When Cyrus the Persian swallowed the Babylonian Empire, no one expected that he would resettle exiles in their homelands—and yet, that is exactly what happened. This was an act of God! Isaiah describes Cyrus as *māšîaḥ*, "messiah," one set apart by anointing for divine service (Isa 45:1). Combining the Judeans' return to their homeland with the rebuilding of their temple (Ezra 1:1–4), Cyrus's edict literally removed the covenant curse of exile. Returnees rebuilt towns and agricultural terraces. They planted and tended; the land produced its grain, oil, and wine. The promise of covenant blessing was kept. A Davidic "prince" who would be their "shepherd" (Ezek 34:20–24) arrived in the first Persian-appointed governor of the Persian province of Yehud. Sheshbazzar, descended from the exiled king Jehoiachin, is described in Ezra 1:8 as a "prince of Judah." Ezekiel's prediction was fulfilled.

Misreading rhetorical techniques and skipping the social and historical contexts means that dispensationalist end-times writers don't see the return from exile and the resettlement of the promised land as prophetic fulfilment. Most Old Testament passages that dispensationalists understand as speaking of the millennium point to, and are in fact fulfilled in, the exiles' return.

When the details of these passages are collated and projected into the future, what results is a complex series of expectations about a future millennial kingdom whose biblical foundations are shaky.

We've talked about genre in general and prophecy in particular. We move now to consider another: apocalyptic. We'll show that many dispensationalist end-times teachers incorrectly distinguish, or fail to distinguish, between prophecy and apocalyptic. Again, the result is the misinterpretation of Scripture.

## APOCALYPTIC LITERATURE

Have you ever come across a mushroom that has seemingly sprung up overnight? Did you ever wonder whether it was safe to eat? Unless you're an expert in mushrooms, you likely didn't give it more than a passing thought. To do otherwise would tempt fate. Outside the grocery store, most of us have no idea whether a mushroom is desirous or deadly. Sometimes similar appearances belie large differences. In literature, so in cuisine: similar texts, like similar mushrooms, require different handling rules. Apparently similar genres can be quite distinct, conveying meaning in unique ways and requiring a different approach. Such is the case with prophecy and apocalyptic.

So, what is apocalyptic? How does it compare to prophecy? Unlike prophecy, apocalyptic is not a genre of covenant warning and moral correction. Rather, it is about hope and encouragement. Apocalyptic can be found in the books of Revelation and Daniel, in parts of Ezekiel and Zechariah, and even in snippets of the Gospel of Matthew. When embedded in narrative, apocalyptic is easily recognized. Embedded within a prophetic book, apocalyptic is sometimes harder to discern, not least because it sometimes reuses prophetic language and images. Reading apocalyptic as if it were prophecy is like reading an obituary or film review through the lenses better associated with a hard news story.

"Apocalyptic" comes from the Greek *apokalypsis*, meaning "disclosure" or "revelation." (It should not be confused with the similar-sounding *apocrypha*. Meaning "hidden" or "secret," apocrypha refers to books not included in the Protestant canon of Scripture, but found in Roman Catholic and Orthodox Bibles.) Today, "apocalypse" popularly evokes terrifying, global disaster: "nuclear apocalypse" and "environmental apocalypse," even "zombie apocalypse." Apocalyptic, however, is not a biblical literature of despair but of hope. From around 250 BC to AD 250, Jewish and Christian groups produced apocalyptic literature in abundance.

How do we recognize the genre? Arriving at a definition is challenging. A good one accounts for similarities that mark external boundaries while allowing for individual textual variations. In the 1970s, this concern prompted members of the Society of Biblical Literature to assess Jewish, Christian, and related literature from late antiquity to develop a basic definition of apocalyptic as a literary genre along with a list of some of its common features. Since 1979, the definition provided by this group has proved extremely helpful, guiding a generation of scholars in their study and research. According to this definition, an "apocalypse" is "a genre of revelatory literature with a narrative framework, in which a revelation is mediated by an otherworldly being to a human recipient, disclosing a transcendent reality which is both temporal, insofar as it envisages eschatological salvation, and spatial insofar as it involves another, supernatural world."[6]

This definition not only includes entire books, but also encompasses smaller elements embedded within larger works of different genres. Daniel 7–12 is an example of the latter. In these chapters Daniel experiences dreams and visions, heavenly conflict, and the future deliverance of God's people from oppression. In the book's final form this apocalyptic material is paired with a series of so-called court tales (chs. 1–6). In the New Testament, the book of Revelation is an example of the former, helpfully declaring its genre from the outset (1:1). Even though it begins with a series of letters (Rev 1:4–3:22) and includes several short laments (Rev 18:2–3, 10, 16–17, 19–20), this is an *apokalypsis* all the way through.

Because literary conventions seldom remain static, a genre's features can change over time. Among works classified as apocalyptic, there can be much variation. Different authors address distinct audiences from and within various historical, geographical, social, and religious contexts. Consequently, apocalyptic works may differ (greatly) in their details. To the basic elements in our above definition, therefore, we now add several features commonly used in apocalyptic. Several are particularly relevant to dispensational end-times teaching.

## COMMON FEATURES OF
## APOCALYPTIC LITERATURE

Recent decades have seen academic and popular treatments of apocalyptic and associated biblical material proliferate. Without duplicating what is readily available elsewhere, we'll list only some common features of the genre and comment on those that have particular significance for dispensational readings of apocalyptic.

## DUALISM

Within apocalyptic literature, dualism refers to the text's juxtaposition of opposite forces or elements. The forces of light confront those of darkness; the faithful are assailed by the enemies of God; heavenly angels battle fallen angels. The book of Revelation's opening letters highlight earthly struggles that often seem to anticipate the supernatural or cosmic struggles that dominate its latter chapters. Throughout the book, God's faithful followers are oppressed by the antichrist and his allies. Such dualism is more than an aesthetic device. In an oppressive social context, the book's readers might be tempted to vacillate or compromise. Dualism presents their situation in stark, either-or terms so that the path forward can be seen with absolute clarity.

## VISIONS

In many apocalyptic works, the seer frequently receives revelation through visions, leaving him troubled, confused, and afraid (e.g., Dan 10:7–12; Rev 1:17–18). The use of visions in apocalyptic is likely related to the revelation's often otherworldly content. Prophecy is prompted by readily observed national behavior measured against Torah; its predictions are grounded in well-understood catalogues of covenant blessing and curse. There is little need for a heavenly mediator or the disclosing of mysteries through visions. The prophet connects the audience to the requirements and ramifications of God's law. In apocalyptic, the issue is not obedience to the law, but oppression at the hands of an enemy; the solution lies not in pointing the audience to Torah, but to a word from God specific to their situation. Visions make the heavenly knowledge accessible to the seer.

A common type of vision is the heavenly or otherworldly journey through which the seer witnesses the revelation first-hand. In Ezekiel, the prophet, based in Babylon, makes a vision-ary journey to Jerusalem. There he witnesses the iniquity that will lead to that city's downfall (Ezek 8–11). In Revelation, John, interned on the island of Patmos, is taken by vision to heaven, where he witnesses the goings-on in God's throne room (Rev 4–6). Visions, then, enable the writers of apocalyptic to access a wide range of heavenly mysteries firsthand and then share those mysteries in vivid and captivating detail.

### SYMBOLISM

Apocalyptic also uses elaborate symbolism and imagery to communicate the author's message. More than anything else, symbolism has "closed" books such as Revelation to all but an enlightened few. Ancient authors, however, did not use symbolism to obfuscate, but to inform. Rightly read, symbols and images simplify the presentation of complex or abstract concepts. We do something similar when we explain diffi-cult-to-understand ideas using illustrations. How often have we explained the mystery of the Trinity with an egg, apple, the three states of matter, the shamrock, triangle, triquetra, and so on? Quite apart from the merits (or not) of these symbols, each attempts to explain through image or symbol a challenging abstract concept. If contemporary readers find symbolic imag-ery in Ezekiel and Revelation indecipherable, it is because our symbols come from a different world of thoughts and images. Good readers bridge these symbolic worlds.

Consider the visions that Ezekiel experiences of the *merkābâ* or chariot-throne of God (Ezek 1; 10). In chapter 1, the prophet encounters this chariot-throne in exile by the Kebar River. In the first vision, Ezekiel spies a flashing and glowing cloud coming from the north (Ezek 1:4–28). In a second vision (ch. 10), Ezekiel is mystically transported to Jerusalem to witness the departure of the chariot-throne from the temple there. He describes the figures he sees first vaguely—"living creatures" (Ezek 1:4–5)—then more precisely as "cherubim" (Ezek 10:1–2). These bizarre, composite creatures resemble humans, but each has the legs of a calf, two sets of wings, and four faces—a human, a lion, an ox/cherub, and an eagle. Beneath the wings of each creature there protrude hands (Ezek 1:5–10; 10:8). Beside the feet of each stand "wheels within wheels" (Ezek 1:15–16; 10:9–10). Chapter 10 adds that the wheels, bodies, hands, and wings of each creature are covered with eyes (Ezek 1:18; 10:12). The wheels allow horizontal movement in any direction as com-manded by the "spirit" (Ezek 1:17; also 1:12). Above the heads of the creatures there stretched an "expanse." The word used here is *rāqîaʿ*, the same term that appears in Genesis 1:7, 14–18 to describe the barrier that holds back the heavenly sea and in which the sun, moon, and stars were fixed.

What on earth (or in heaven) does this mean? Consider first the context and the concerns of the prophet's audience. Exiled in Babylon, Ezekiel ministered to those deported from Judah by Nebuchadnezzar II (605–562 BC). Several questions weighed heavily on them. If Babylon had defeated Judah, did that mean that Marduk had defeated Yahweh, the God of Israel? If Yahweh was to be worshiped in his temple in Jerusalem, how could the exiles worship? If God was in Jerusalem, how could he be present in Babylon? If a Judean king still sat on the throne in Jerusalem, given God's promises to David, how long would the exile last (2 Sam 7:4–17)?

Ezekiel's visions address each of these concerns and the underlying crisis of faith. God is firmly ensconced on his fiery throne. God still reigns. The four faces of each of the living creatures correspond to the four chief Babylonian gods.[7] In this vision, however, they are reduced to servants, bearing the throne of the one true God. When the throne moves, it is at the direction of God's spirit. The issue of worship and the presence of God is addressed by the cherubim and their accessories. God's throne is not bolted to the ground. The wheels within wheels allow it to move in any direction horizontally. The creatures' wings mean that the throne can move in any direction vertically. The throne can go anywhere. The many eyes covering the cherubim's bodies and wheels mean that the occupant of this throne sees all. The departure of the throne from the temple represents the covenant curse of defeat. The exiles will not be returning to Jerusalem; those left in Jerusalem will soon be joining them. When the temple is eventually destroyed, the exiles will understand that national defeat was something God had actually overseen. Moreover, this image assures the exiles that God is present with them even in captivity. God's sovereignty endures; his ability to see is unimpaired; he is present in their dislocation. All of this is understandable by considering the geographical and cultural context of the audience, the images they understood, and the trauma they had experienced.

The meaning of Ezekiel's chariot-throne is unlocked by attention to the symbolic world of both author and audience. If a modern reader comes to the text without such awareness, the message of the text is lost. This, unfortunately, is precisely what happens in dispensationalist readings. Pentecost imposes the framework of the dispensations, seeing the departure of God's glory from the temple as marking the end of theocracy and the beginning of the "times of the gentiles." Accordingly, Pentecost misreads the passage as one of judgment, blind to Ezekiel's use of images to reassure and encourage his audience.[8]

Complicating matters further, dispensationalist preference for wooden literalism can also lead to misinterpretation of apocalyptic symbolism entirely. In Revelation 17, John "sees" a new enemy of the faithful and a supporter of the Beast. Named "Babylon the Great"—"the great prostitute, who sits by many waters" (Rev 17:1, 5)—she is dressed in purple and scarlet and adorned with gold, precious stones, and pearls; she holds "a golden cup in her hand, filled with abominable things and the filth of her adulteries" (Rev 17:4). In a manner unbecoming of one wearing royal colors, she is depicted as "drunk with the blood of God's holy people, the blood of those who bore testimony to Jesus" (Rev 17:6). John's angelic informant describes this murderous woman as straddling a beast with seven heads and seven horns, explaining the seven heads as representing seven hills (Rev 17:7–9). For John's first readers, this is Roma, the goddess of the Roman imperial state. On coinage from the time of Emperor Vespasian she was depicted as reclining on Rome's seven hills with Tiber, the river god, at her feet. While Rome portrayed itself as the author of the Pax Romana, this "peace" was won and maintained at the cost of anti-Christian violence. Like Ezekiel's demoted Babylonian gods, Roma is likened not to a queen or goddess, but to a drunken, murderous prostitute.

The dispensational understanding of this image has been markedly different. Most end-times interpreters identify Babylon with Rome; beyond this, however, this image is not read in the light of the initial audience's context, but according to their own experience. Rome, for older dispensationalists, is not the Roman Empire, but the Vatican and the Roman Catholic Church. In older works, this "whore of Babylon" was sometimes identified with the Roman Catholic Church itself.

For later end-times writers, the woman is an apostate global church somehow connected with Rome. Writing at the time of the First Gulf War, Dallas Theological Seminary professor Charles Dyer argued that Babylon the Great should be identified with Babylon—the Iraq of Saddam Hussein.[9] Each of these dispensational understandings falters because it ignores the iconographic thought-world of the original audience, inserting instead its own era and interests. With the text's original message lost, any word for today is also.

## REUSE OF IMAGES

Many years ago, I (Brian) recall, my wife and my sister-in-law (both artists) took my brother and me on a visit to our local art museum. Throughout the afternoon, we drifted from room to room, pausing to gaze at Henry Moore sculptures, paintings by the French impressionists, and one large fabric hamburger. Paying little attention to the route I was taking, I at one point found myself in a small side room staring at a 1950s-era refrigerator. For a moment I thought that I had mindlessly stumbled into the security guards' lunch nook, but when I saw that the appliance was perched atop a large safe, I quickly deduced that I was looking at something that fell into the category of "art with found objects." In such a piece, the artist takes objects from disparate areas of human experience and reuses them in a way that creates a new object with new meaning. Often, meaning in such a piece is conveyed by thinking about how the old contexts and the new might relate. In the case of the refrigerator atop the safe, I sensed a message about our need to protect those things we cherish—like leftover brisket and stock certificates. To my brother, it spoke of man's inhumanity to man—but he said that about everything that day. When ancient apocalyptic writers reused cultural or biblical images, they were creating art with found objects—taking something already meaning-filled and reshaping it to say something new.

Thus, Ezekiel combines images from Israelite temple iconography with ones from Babylonian religion to create a fantastic image of God's throne that speaks of divine sovereignty, presence, and attention. A more complex and extended example of such reuse is found in Revelation's final chapters, where the author draws on images from Genesis, Ezekiel, and elsewhere. A new scenario communicating God's love for us and his desire to be in eternal relationship with us emerges. To understand how, we must begin with Ezekiel.

Its first two sections (chs. 1–24; 25–32) announce judgment; the final one (chs. 33–48), however, offers a message of hope for the exiles' future. After explaining that Jerusalem will indeed be conquered, the land of Judah left desolate, and its inhabitants deported, the prophet entertains the prospect that these covenant curses might one day be replaced by covenant blessing. In Ezekiel 36:22–38, the prophet details how God will pluck his people from among the nations, return them to the land, and give them new hearts, replacing those of stone that once turned so readily to idolatry. In chapter 37, this national "resurrection" is pictured as a wide expanse of desiccated bones restored to life by the breath of God himself. Judah and Ephraim/Israel, long separated, rival kingdoms, conquered by different powers, would be restored and united under the rule of a Davidic prince (Ezek 37:24–28).

In this new era of obedience, holiness, and divine presence, even the most intimidating enemy will fail in their attempt to attack Israel. In chapters 38–39, the prophet receives a new vision in which God addresses a mysterious enemy from the north, declaring that he will compel them to launch a self-destructive attack against his people and will destroy them—all to demonstrate his power and holiness to the nations (Ezek 38:3–4, 23; 39:1–2, 21). At the battle's end, the bones of Israel's attackers will be strewn across a broad valley, recalling the earlier vision of the scattered Israel (Ezek 39:11–16; cf. 37:1–15). This campaign and its outcome will remind Israel of God's identity as their God and the nations of why Israel went into captivity in the first place (Ezek 39:22–24). The nations should not, therefore, deceive themselves into thinking that their power caused Israel's exile. Exile was God's judgment for Israel's infidelity. The divine promise to restore Israel from captivity announced in Ezekiel 36:16–38 is repeated in Ezekiel 39:25–29 in a way that frames the powerful depictions of Israel's national resurrection and reunification, and their subsequent national security in a way that shows all of these events to relate to the time when Ezekiel's audience is returned from captivity.

Beginning in chapter 40 and extending to the book's end, Ezekiel paints a vivid picture of the returnees' new life: a rebuilt temple with priests, sacrifices, and reinstituted festivals; rule by a "prince" rather than a "king." These are consistent with postexilic conditions, when Israel lived in the land under Persian rule. This is the new era in which Israel with its new heart will inhabit a land characterized by holiness. They will enjoy God's presence as never before. Since covenant unfaithfulness culminated in exile, Ezekiel emphasizes what maintains Israel's relationship with God. Thus details of the temple, its staff, rituals, God's presence there, and its centrality within the land dominate this section (Ezek 40–47).

Because God's people have been resurrected by divine breath and given a new heart, everything speaks to easier access to, and greater intimacy with, God. The outer temple courtyard was a massive square with sides of five hundred

cubits each (Ezek 42:20). While the new temple will contain an altar (Ezek 43:13–27), the ark of the covenant will be
replaced by the voice of God declaring, "This is the place of
my throne and the place for the soles of my feet. This is where
I will live among the Israelites forever" (Ezek 43:7). In this
new era, God will be present with his people in a way previously unexperienced. Granted land adjacent to the holy city,
the Davidic prince will play a prominent role in facilitating
worship (e.g., Ezek 44:3; 45:7–8, 17). Unlike previous rulers,
this prince will be a spiritual leader. He will not confiscate
others' property to enrich his own sons (Ezek 46:18). In a
nod to the garden of Eden (Gen 2:10–14), where God's relationship with humans began, a life-giving river will flow from
the threshold of the temple, descending toward the Dead Sea
and nourishing fruit trees, animals, and fish all along its course
(Ezek 47:1–12). The presence of God in the midst of his people
will transform the whole world from death to life. The idea of
newness and return to the land is emphasized once more: a
much-expanded territory is redivided among the tribes, not
in geographically prescribed plots, but in expansive east-west
swaths (Ezek 47:13–48:29). Recalling Joshua's division of land
after the conquest, Ezekiel depicts this new era as a national
reboot or do-over.

The book's conclusion describes Jerusalem to stress newness and restoration. Unlike Jerusalem of old, whose walls overlooked the wadis that defined the hills on which the city rested,
this city will be laid out as a massive square of forty-five hundred cubits to a side. As in Solomon's temple, Ezekiel's holy of
holies, the place where the high priest would appear before
God, will be a perfect square of twenty cubits by twenty cubits
(1 Kgs 6:20; 2 Chr 3:8; Ezek 41:4). The footprint of the old

Jerusalem (*yərûšālayim*) will be replaced with an expansive, square city, making it a holy place, as reflected in its new name, *Yahweh šammâ*—"The LORD is There" (Ezek 48:30–35). With Judah and Israel reunited and the city once more the center of national worship, there will be gates for each tribe.

For Ezekiel's chastened and exiled audience, living far from the promised land, a future restoration was an invitation to a new start and a new relationship with God, a wholesale reversal of the covenant curse of exile. The dominance of the temple and allusions to Eden accentuate new divine-human intimacy. The redivision of the land means a fresh start: just as if the exiles were entering the land for the first time. Ezekiel draws on earlier imagery and events, deploying prophetic rhetoric full force to present an expansive picture of new life in the land for a restored Israel, fully obedient and in relationship with God. The visions of chapters 37–48 affirm that the exiles' future depended on God, not human powers. The holy character of this restored land would also have heightened the realization of the need to live holy lives in the present if they were to occupy the revived and holy city in the future.

Ezekiel's picture of new life, holiness, and Israel's new home, when God ended the exile and returned to the land himself, is all over John's depiction of the new Jerusalem in the closing chapters of Revelation. From the outset, the theme of newness is established in God's opening address to John—"I am making everything new!" (Rev 21:5). As in Ezekiel, holiness and relationship are also in view as a new heaven and earth come into being and the "Holy City" descends from heaven "prepared as a bride beautifully dressed for her husband" (Rev 21:1–2). This new city is marked by holiness not only in name, but because the last of creation's evildoers—along with death and Hades—have already been consigned to the lake of fire (Rev 20:11–15; 21:6–8; see Ezek 39:21–29). Like Ezekiel's city, this one has twelve gates corresponding to the tribes of Israel (Rev 21:12–14; see Ezek 48:30–34). As in Ezekiel, an angelic figure with a measuring rod conveys the city's dimensions (Rev 21:15; see Ezek 40:3–4). John reuses Ezekiel's imagery to signal common themes.

But it is not mere repetition. John uses Ezekiel's material to say something more than his predecessor. Where Ezekiel's measurements are two-dimensional, those for John's new city are three-dimensional (Ezek 48:15–16, 30–35; Rev 21:16). Furthermore, John's new Jerusalem far outstrips what is presented in Ezekiel. It is a massive cube, twelve thousand stadia (or 1,342 miles) in width, length, and height (Rev 21:15–17). The description of the bejeweled foundation and walls of the city duplicates almost entirely Ezekiel's list of the riches contained in the garden of Eden, which also adorned the tunic of the high priest who served in the tabernacle, which itself was adorned to recall the garden of Eden (Rev 21:18–21; see Exod 28:17–20; Ezek 28:13). Both the cubic dimensions of the city and its adornment recall both the cubic holy of holies of the tabernacle and temple and the garden of Eden writ large. This city symbolically expresses relationship with God as it was intended in Eden. There is no need of a temple (Rev 21:22)— God and his people dwell together at last.

In chapter 22 again biblical images are reimagined to emphasize a new, complete relationship with God. In Genesis, a river flows from the garden of Eden to nourish the earth (Gen 2:10–14). In Ezekiel, a river flows eastward from the temple, healing and restoring life and fruitfulness to a parched land (Ezek 47:1–12). In the templeless city of Revelation, the river flows from the throne of God and the Lamb (Rev 22:1). Reusing more imagery from Genesis, a "tree of life" grows on each bank, producing leaves to heal the nations. Mentioned alongside this is that there is no longer any curse (Rev 22:1–3). The river and the trees recall Eden's tree of life, reminding readers that the potential for life and relationship predates the sin that precipitated the fall and the curse (Gen 2:9; 3:14–19). No intermediaries will be needed; all will be priests. The declaration "They will see his face, and his name will be on their foreheads" (Rev 22:4) reminds us that no one was able to look upon the face of God and live, along with the inscription on the headdress of the high priest who entered the holy of holies, "Holy to Yahweh" (Exod 28:36–38; 33:20). John picks up images from various parts of the Old Testament and reapplies them to stress that this new place is one where God and humans can enjoy unimpeded relationship, as it was intended from the start. He creates his own piece of theological "art from found objects" to communicate a new message to his audience.

Once again, cultural distance, wooden literalism, and an inattention to context have meant that apocalyptic reuse of images has gone unrecognized and interpretation has been impoverished. In Ezekiel, this has led most dispensationalists to see the final section of the book as looking forward, not to the time of the return from exile, but to a time far removed from that of the original audience. The resurrection of the nation from the dead and the binding of the two sticks do not speak restoration and hope to an exiled people but predict the establishment of the modern state of Israel. The invasion of Gog is not a promise of God's covenant protection over a transformed people but predicts a future invasion of Israel by Russia and its allies. The temple and its staff, along with the "prince," is not a vision of how true holiness must define life for the restored community; it is projected to the end of time, depicting designs and plans to be literally and precisely realized in the millennium. In each case, failure to recognize the prophet's context and rhetorical approach, including his reuse of images, has limited the ability of dispensationalists and others to recognize the profound theological message that the writer was trying to communicate.

Similar problems arise with John's vision of the new Jerusalem. Many dispensationalists simply miss the allusions and images by which John has pictured the fully realized, eternal divine-human intimacy longed for since creation. Wooden literalism predisposes most dispensationalist interpreters to evaluate John's description in terms of engineering, with most imagining the city to be a cube, some a pyramid, and others a crystal sphere suspended in space. Others wonder about the city's capacity and the practicalities of travel within its confines. Despite the clear textual association of the constellation of precious metals and stones that adorn the city with the garden of Eden, dispensationalists' analysis rarely moves beyond the realm of aesthetic appreciation. Instead of recognizing reuse, some interpreters conclude from the spectrum of similarities between Ezekiel 40–48 and Revelation 21–22 that both passages depict the same millennial state. Rare are the dispensationalists who eschew literalism and see the new Jerusalem as mystical or symbolic.

## MESSIANISM

Messianism comes from the Hebrew term *māšîaḥ* and its derived English word, "messiah." In Greek, the term is *christos*, as in Jesus, the "Christ." The word *māšîaḥ* simply means "anointed." Prophets, priests, and kings were all anointed with oil as a sign that they were commissioned to act as an agent of God in this world; the term came to mean "set apart by God." As we've seen, even a gentile king could be a messiah. Cyrus, whose actions favored God's people and conformed to prophetic expectation, was deemed to have acted at God's direction (Isa 44:27–28; 45:1–4, 13). In the Old Testament, the "anointed" ideal was David, who took Israel from civil war to empire, established Israel's capital in Jerusalem, aspired to build Yahweh's temple there, and who—despite his many failings—never strayed into idolatry. When the monarchy ended, prophecy ceased, and Israel fell under foreign domination, Davidic qualities of faithfulness to Yahweh and victory over Israel's enemies transformed the concept of "messiah" from a general term to the title of a specific, expected individual. In popular understanding, God would someday deliver his people from their suffering by intruding into history through a divinely appointed human agent: "the Messiah."

In the first century AD, after a century of independence under the Jewish Hasmonean monarchs had given way to Roman rule, messianic expectations ran high. Many charismatic figures emerged to lead Israel in rebellion against Rome. After the first revolt against Rome (AD 66–70) ended in crushing defeat and the destruction of the temple in Jerusalem, the hopes of some waned; for others, though, they intensified. After all, if God was indeed to rescue his people in their darkest hour, surely the massacre of his people and the destruction of his temple would signal that his intervention was nigh. Only a few decades later, rebellion broke out once more against Rome (ca. AD 132–135), the charismatic Simon bar Kosiba at its head. He was known also as Bar Kokhba (son of a star), and his clear sense of messianic identity was supported by no less an authority than Rabbi Akiva.

## SYMBOLIC TELLING AND PORTRAYAL OF HISTORY
## AND THE FUTURE; "PROPHECY AFTER THE FACT"

A rhetorical device appearing in some ancient apocalyptic presents history through symbolism. In Scripture, this technique is found in Nebuchadnezzar's dream of the statue and Daniel's retelling and interpretation (Dan 2:31–45), and again in Daniel's vision of four beasts and its angelic interpretation (Dan 7). Outside the Bible, it is found in 1 Enoch 85–90, where biblical history is allegorized using a menagerie of animals. On occasion, surveys of history can be organized using a symbolic framework. Following the Animal Apocalypse, 1 Enoch documents events, moving from history into the future, using ten "weeks" (1 Enoch 91:12–17; 93:1–10). Similarly, Jubilees, a Jewish work produced around the mid-second century BC, divides history from creation to exodus into forty-nine periods (or "jubilees") of forty-nine years each.

Closely associated with these reviews of history is a device known as *vaticinium ex eventu*, or "prophecy from the event." Descriptions of already-past events are recounted as if they were predictions of the future. Dispensationalists, and conservative Christians in general, find this aspect of apocalyptic literature to be one of the genre's most problematic characteristics because it seems to rob a book like Daniel of all prophetic authority. Its remarkable predictions are suddenly reduced to reportage deceptively framed as prediction. *Vaticinium ex eventu* is, therefore, one reason why so many dispensationalists avoid the genre category "apocalyptic" altogether and insist on classifying Daniel as prophetic literature.

Were all the symbolic portrayals of events in biblical literature cases of "prophecy after the fact," then audiences would have cause to be concerned. This is not the case. One way apocalyptic conveys hope to a discouraged audience is narration of events, mixing history with prediction for the initial audience. If Ezekiel or Daniel refer primarily to our era (unraveling the geopolitics of the modern Middle East), as many end-times teachers maintain—then all of their distant-future promises were irrelevant to the original audience, thus raising the question, "What relevance could such promises possibly have had for that original audience?" None whatsoever. It brings no hope to an oppressed audience to say that thousands of years hence God will intervene. Almost all dispensationalist teachers argue, for example, that Daniel was composed in the sixth century BC by the man Daniel and that he predicts events from our day. If so, then it is difficult to see how this would encourage a group of oppressed Judeans in the sixth century BC.

Think about a sports team routinely described as "hapless." For us, the NHL's Toronto Maple Leafs come to mind. Once a hockey powerhouse with thirteen Stanley Cup wins, and despite enthusiastic fans and a perpetually sold-out arena, the Leafs have not won an NHL championship since 1967. If World Cup Football is your passion, there's England, which hasn't won the FIFA title since 1966. Imagine sitting with a Leafs goalie or an English midfielder and saying, "Hey pal, don't be discouraged! God has told me that two thousand years from now, your team is going to win the championship!" Would you respond with joy or enthusiasm? Telling you that the problem will be rectified long after you are dead brings no hope at all.

In order to speak hope into the lives of the persecuted, the author of Daniel put a new spin on an older prophetic approach. Earlier prophets often emphasized God's faithfulness by recounting his mighty acts in history on Israel's behalf. Amos, for example, uses a condensed review of God's acts to contrast his faithfulness with Israel's sin. God's people turned away from him, despite his rescue of Israel out of Egypt, his guidance through the wilderness, his gift of the land of the Amorites, and his guidance through the prophets and Nazirites (Amos 2:9–11). God's track record is displayed so Amos's audience can assess their current situation or behavior. Likewise, the writer of Daniel combines history and prediction into a single time-line of events, placing his audience in its midst. To understand this literary technique, we must first distinguish the writer of Daniel (the literary author) from the figure of Daniel (the designated author). The latter is a character set in the events of the book's opening half (the sixth century BC). While most biblical scholars today agree that the book of Daniel contains earlier material, the literary author wrote in the second century BC. His original audience was composed of Judeans persecuted by the Hellenistic king Antiochus (IV) Epiphanes (175–163 BC).

To this discouraged and persecuted people, the literary author takes events in the past, from his audience's perspective, and places them in the designated author's mouth (fig. 5.1). Sixth-century Daniel thus unfolds the future in the literary setting of the book. The literary author likely chose the historical Daniel as the designated author because of his great example of faithfulness thorough oppression. Historical Daniel experienced, endured, and triumphed through exactly the experiences that the book's audience was currently undergoing. As the designated author related story after story of divine deliverance from oppression, the original audience would have quickly recognized events from Israel's past when God's people had suffered past oppression similar to their own. As the episodes proceeded, however, the audience would have recognized that the designated author spoke to their present. As the narrative passed to events they didn't recognize, the audience would have recognized a depiction of their future. Past, present, and prediction mixed to bring the audience hope, allowing them to compare their present situation with similar past events in which God had rescued his people.

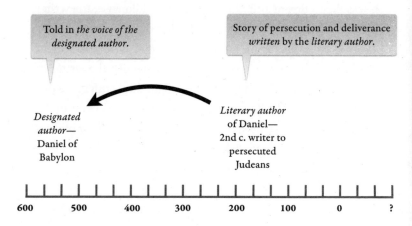

Told in *the voice of the designated author.*

Story of persecution and deliverance *written* by the *literary author.*

*Designated author*— Daniel of Babylon

*Literary author* of Daniel— 2nd c. writer to persecuted Judeans

600    500    400    300    200    100    0    ?

*Fig. 5.1. Daniel as a second-century composition speaking of the near future*

Had the author simply announced, "Don't worry, God will intervene to destroy your oppressors and rescue you," his words would likely have fallen flat: "Why should we believe you?" Placing a genuine prediction of deliverance in the context of an unbroken stream of God's miraculous interventions, however, demonstrates God's track record of rescuing the faithful. Emphasizing what God has previously done and what he will do helped the audience receive the present message. This is the secret of Daniel's symbols. Consider the vision in Daniel 8. A charging, two-horned ram is defeated by a shaggy goat. The goat has a single horn, which, when broken off, gives rise to four; one of these claims equality with the prince of the heavenly host and defiles the temple. The ram's horns are the kings of Media and Persia, the goat is Greece, and its single horn,

Alexander the Great. The four other horns are Alexander's successors, the Diadochi, and the final one, Antiochus IV Epiphanes (175–163 BC), who was currently persecuting God's people. This deft use of symbolism helped the audience recall how God's people had been preserved in past persecutions. Antiochus IV Epiphanes was the latest in a long line of declared enemies whom God would defeat.

Far from being deceitful, framing history as prophecy using a designated author grants the original audience a perspective on their present in the light of their past, so that they can receive God's promises for their future. As such, it is a profoundly pastoral tool that serves to encourage and strengthen the faith of those who are suffering.

## UNIVERSALISM

As we've seen, a defining feature of prophecy is its focus on Israel, its covenant relationship with God, and the pronouncement of the blessings and curses intended to correct its national behavior. Even God's interest in the nations is centered on Israel. From the beginning, Abraham was called to be a conduit of blessing to the nations (Gen 12:3). Likewise, as the missional successor to Abraham, the nation of Israel was to be a light to the nations (Isa 49:6; 60:3), with the result that someday the nations would stream to Jerusalem to worship the God of Israel (Zech 8:20–23). The entire book of Jonah is given over to the story of how Israel's God graciously gives a foreign power an opportunity to repent and avoid judgment. Periodically in prophetic writings, oracles against other nations are used to emphasize God's sovereignty or his right to judge Israel (e.g., Jer 46–51; Ezek 25–32; Amos 1:3–2:3).

Apocalyptic literature, however, turns from the national to the universal or even cosmic. The period in which it flourished coincided with one in which Israel no longer controlled its own destiny and God's people were no longer connected to the land. Sizable Jewish communities now existed outside the land of Israel in places such as Alexandria, Rome, Asia Minor, and Mesopotamia. The land-centered message of the preexilic prophets was, for dispersed Jewish communities, difficult to apply. It is no surprise, then, that the themes and emphases of the earlier prophets disappear from this point on. In its place, apocalyptic literature deals with the entire world. The scope and interest of apocalyptic writing frequently breaks the constraints of Israel as a nation and addresses the nations, the world, and even the cosmos.

### PSEUDONYMITY

Finally, pseudonymity is a literary strategy that was common in the ancient world in which authorship of a work was attributed to a "designated author." This figure stood in as the human recipient of the apocalyptic revelation. In Jewish and Christian apocalyptic literature, the designated author is usually a hero from Israel's past. In Second Temple Jewish and early Christian literature, for instance, we find Adam, Enoch, Abraham, Moses, Solomon, and Elijah. We drew attention to an example of such above.

Pseudonymity has worried dispensationalists and conservative Christians generally since the rise of historical criticism in the nineteenth century. For many Christians at that time, textual authority was closely tied to the identity of the inspired author. As critical scholarship began to propose theories that added to or discounted altogether the canonical and traditional attributions of authorship, many conservative scholars took this as an attack on the authority of the text and its message. The conservative response was apologetic, with members of the Old Princeton school, authors of *The Fundamentals*, and others defending the traditional authorship of books such as Genesis–Deuteronomy, Isaiah, and Daniel. In the case of Daniel, the suggestion that the sixth-century figure Daniel was not the author of the Old Testament book of Daniel, and that the book was likely written in the second century BC, smacked of an author's attempt to deceive and undermined the book's value as predictive prophecy.

We have already suggested, however, that ancient authors used pseudonymity not to claim authority through deception, but to serve the overall message through a device well-known to the audience. Designated authors were deliberately selected to fit the message's material or the audience's needs. Who better than the antediluvian Enoch to go on several heavenly excursions and be given detailed revelation regarding the workings of the cosmos (1 Enoch)? Unlike other humans, he did not die and descend to Sheol. So close was he to God that he was taken to heaven instead (Gen 5:21–24). Enoch's holy character and heavenly home make him well-suited to receive and pass on the heavenly realms' mysteries. Similarly, Daniel is a well-chosen spokesperson to encourage faithful Jews suffering under the hand of the Seleucid monarchs. The court narratives of Daniel 1–6 situate Daniel as one who well understood what it meant to live faithfully in a foreign empire that sometimes persecuted God's people. The narrative's sixth-century BC setting closely parallels the second-century BC audience's context. An unfortunate consequence of continuing to insist on an early date for Daniel's composition is that the author's rhetorical strategy and its implications for understanding the message of the book have gone largely unrecognized.

## THE CONTEXT OF APOCALYPTIC LITERATURE

Looking at those times when apocalyptic flourished, its differences from the prophetic become obvious. Old Testament prophecy tended to appear when Israel was in the land and (even though crisis might be looming or present) had some autonomy or control of its own destiny. Prophecy's moral thrust intended to provoke a change in Israel's behavior. The common prophetic ultimatum that "If you obey, you will stay in the land; if you don't, you will be thrown out" is one that can be given either when Israel is living in the land and has some measure of political autonomy or when it is conceivable that obedience will lead to a return to the land and covenant blessing there. What happens, however, when the people are driven into exile, the people reform, and a return doesn't take place? Or what happens when, living faithfully in the land, they are nonetheless under foreign rule and even experience violent persecution? Israel has repented, but nothing has changed—the expected covenant blessings haven't appeared. In fact, faithfulness might even be leading to persecution.

In these settings apocalyptic brings the hope of salvation, reminding people that

1. God remains Lord of history.

2. Faithful believers have his support in the present oppression.

3. God will someday intervene to usher in a better age.

How the genre of apocalyptic conveys hope is something we will explore next as we examine the biblical books of Ezekiel, Daniel, and Revelation.

# PART 3

## THE MEANING OF
## BIBLICAL APOCALYPTIC

# 6

## EZEKIEL

The real estate mantra, "Location, location, location!" was first attested in a 1926 ad in the *Chicago Tribune*. Now ubiquitous, it emphasizes that a key consideration when purchasing a residence or business is whether the location combines critical qualities such as proximity to shops or customers, public transit or highways, parks, schools, and more. While the specifics vary, much of what contributes to a successful purchase is bound up in where one starts.

Success in biblical exegesis is not that different; the comparable mantra is "Context, context, context!" Between the Bible's contemporary readers and ancient authors is a literary, historical, and cultural gap at least two millennia old. If we are to read well, we must narrow that gap by attending to a passage's original setting, even so far as to imagine ourselves into the original cultural mindset. We are thus more likely to detect the authors' intent and content and the genres employed to deliver them. Finally, and most critically, we must pay attention to the literary flow of the whole biblical book to discover the overall issues that gave rise both to the book and to the author's use of literary techniques and strategies.

Dispensational writing on biblical books related to end times lacks this kind of foundational inquiry. Instead we find a highly selective sampling of key verses simplistically pasted to related verses in other biblical books or applied directly to contemporary global events. Consider the way Walvoord's *Armageddon, Oil and the Middle East Crisis* easily moves from a few verses in Ezekiel 38 to a detailed analysis of Russian plans for the modern Middle East or from a single number in Revelation 9:16 to commentary on military intervention by the People's Republic of China.[1] Likewise, in Walvoord's commentary on Daniel, historical context and literary genre barely figure in the seventeen-page introduction, while in the commentary itself the vision of the fourth beast of Daniel 7:23–25 is understood without any appeal to original context, but rests entirely on an intertextual reading of the book of Revelation.[2]

The remaining chapters propose a different route. Looking at the books Ezekiel, Daniel, and Revelation, we'll assume that they were relevant to and readily understood by their original audiences. We'll look at the historical and cultural context and the genre of each book, asking how the original audiences might have understood them. We begin with the earliest, attributed to the exiled priest and prophet Ezekiel.

## THE SETTING OF EZEKIEL

Ezekiel's priestly and prophetic life and work straddled the final years of the kingdom of Judah and the first of the exile. During the late seventh century BC, Judah had been emboldened by the nationalistic reforms of the energetic young king Josiah. He undertook a religious renewal and extended the kingdom's territory (2 Kgs 23:1–25). This national confidence survived Josiah's battlefield death in 609 BC and frustrated attempts by prophets such as Jeremiah to warn the nation of impending peril. People came to believe that Jerusalem, home of Yahweh's temple, would never fall, a view bolstered by Jerusalem's deliverance a century earlier when, under King

Hezekiah (729–687/6 BC), the Assyrians had besieged but did not conquer the city (2 Kgs 18:13–19:37). Between Hezekiah and Josiah, Assyria declined. After its fall, Egypt briefly dominated the weaker Judah. In a series of campaigns from 605 to 601 BC, however, Nebuchadnezzar, the king of Babylon, came south and brought all of Palestine under Babylonian control.[3]

With Babylon growing in power and Egypt pressing Judah to rebel, the final Judean kings vacillated between submitting to Babylonian rule and asserting their independence. Always doomed to failure, however, each rebellion led to Babylonian reprisals. Portions of the population were exiled in 605, 597, and 586 BC. At this time, the kings of Judah shifted loyalties and reigned only briefly. In 609 BC, Pharaoh Neco II (609–593 BC) led a large Egyptian army along the coastal plain toward Carchemish on the Upper Euphrates River. He hoped to aid the king of Assyria in preventing the advance of the Babylonians. A former enemy, the Egyptians now wanted to preserve Assyria as a buffer state between them and Babylon. For Josiah of Judah, however, Egypt threatened Judean sovereignty. With his army, he set out to challenge Neco. Judah and Egypt clashed at Megiddo on the edge of the Jezreel Valley, where Josiah was defeated and mortally wounded. His son and successor, Jehoahaz (609 BC), reigned only for as long as it took Pharaoh Neco II to resume the march north and join his Assyrian allies. On the return journey, the victorious Neco detoured to Jerusalem. There he deposed and exiled Jehoahaz, and appointed his half-brother Eliakim to the throne. To display his power, Neco renamed Eliakim "Jehoiakim" (609–598 BC); the king of Judah was now a vassal to the Egyptian pharaoh. David's sons still ruled Judah, but they now pledged loyalty and paid taxes to Egypt. This new arrangement, however, was short-lived. In the same year, Nebuchadnezzar II campaigned through the region, taking captives from Jerusalem back to Mesopotamia (Dan 1:1).

Conquerors took captives for several reasons. First, exile created social disruption that discouraged further insurrection. Although both royals and commoners were exiled, removing the ruling class left insurrectionists without leaders and gave victors hostages to discourage any elites who might have been left behind. Second, captives were a valuable resource. Literate and well educated, members of the elite class could be placed into the imperial administration of the conquering power; craftspeople could be used in building projects and royal workshops; able-bodied men and women could become servants, builders, and agricultural laborers. Thus Daniel and his companions were pressed into service in the Babylonian administration (Dan 1:3–7). Enough able-bodied and skilled people were left behind to ensure the land's continued productivity so that taxes could be paid.

Neco II, however, did not give up easily. Egyptian promises of support likely encouraged Jehoiakim to rebel against Babylon in 601 BC. The Babylonians unleashed their other regional vassals against Judah, and a few years later (598 BC) Nebuchadnezzar's army arrived to finish the job. About this time (the circumstances are unclear), Jehoiakim died. His son Jehoiachin (598–597 BC) ruled only three months before he too was carried off to Babylon. His puppet replacement, Zedekiah (597–586 BC; son of Josiah, brother to Jehoiakim), also eventually rebelled. Their patience exhausted, the Babylonian army arrived in 586 BC, killed Zedekiah, deported many of the people, destroyed the temple, and placed the land under a governor. Under Josiah and in the years following, Judah seems to have been confident about its ability to stand against its enemies. Three successive Judean kings rebelled against the

Babylonians; three times they experienced military defeat and partial exile.

Ezekiel himself was exiled to Babylon in the second of these deportations.[4] Thus, while the prophet Jeremiah preached to those who remained in Judah, Ezekiel preached to the Babylonian exiles. Both prophets had a difficult task. In Judah, Jeremiah had to contend with the message and legacy of the great Isaiah. A century earlier, when the Assyrians were threatening Jerusalem (701 BC), Isaiah instructed Hezekiah to resist the enemy and wait for God's victory. Now, Jeremiah was given a different message to proclaim to the king—"you have sinned, God is punishing you, you should surrender to Nebuchadnezzar" (Jer 25:8–11; 38:1–2, 14–28). The message proved unpopular, and soon Jeremiah was languishing in prison (Jer 37:11–21). Ezekiel fared no better, having been forcibly removed from his homeland and facing the task of ministering to his fellow exiles.

Babylon was not a hopeful setting for the Judeans. By 586 BC, the year of the final Babylonian assault on Jerusalem, some Judeans had been living in captivity for almost two decades. One can imagine that these captives had long since repented of the idolatry and other covenant violations that had sent them there; many might reasonably have expected the restoration of covenant blessings and return to the land. The exiles looked back at those left in Judah as the remnant that Yahweh had preserved. Soon, they felt, Yahweh would defeat the Babylonians, and they would return to Jerusalem.

Ezekiel countered this expectation in two ways. First, he described what was actually going on in Jerusalem. The people there were hardly a righteous remnant; God was about to judge and exile them, too. The exiles, in turn, were to see Babylon as their sanctuary.[5] *They*, declared Ezekiel, were God's true remnant; those left in Judah would soon join *them* in captivity. Second, he announced that God's plan for Judah extended beyond captivity to a future return to the land. And he used both prophetic and apocalyptic styles to do so.

## THE STRUCTURE AND MESSAGE OF EZEKIEL

In its final form, the book of Ezekiel has three clearly discernible sections. In the first section (chs. 1–24), the prophet declares that God has judged Jerusalem and Judah. The city and kingdom will be destroyed; those still living in Judah will soon join the exiles. This is achieved through a series of vividly symbolic visions (1:1–28; 10:1–22) and some bizarre symbolic acts (4:1–5:17; 12:1–16; 24:1–27). The second section (chs. 25–32) consists of oracles against seven of Judah's neighbors: Ammon, Moab, Edom, Philistia, Tyre, Sidon, and Egypt (25:1–32:32). If the exiles think that Judah's defeat means that God's power is limited, that he cannot care for them, then the prophet counters that God's rule is universal. He does not allow sin to go unpunished. Through a series of nocturnal sermons (33:21–39:29) and visions (chs. 40–48), the book's third section (chs. 33–48) looks forward in hope to the end of exile portrayed as a new conquest and settlement. Physically and spiritually, these chapters depict a physical and spiritual do-over for God's people in which the land will be re-allotted and the people will receive a new heart that will allow them to follow God's law.

Parts of Ezekiel—which combine both prophetic and apocalyptic genres—have provided fruitful ground for end-times speculation. In our next section we will look at the way in which popular prophecy writers have used the material at the end of the book in their reconstruction of end-time events and how this same material likely spoke to those who first received it.

## HOW SYMBOLISM SPEAKS

EZEKIEL 36–37: THE VALLEY OF DRY BONES (OR, IS THE
BIRTH OF MODERN ISRAEL FOUND IN PROPHECY?)

The vision of the valley of dry bones (chs. 36–37) figures prominently in end-times teaching. Many dispensationalist writers rightly note the use of imagery and appreciate the passage's inherent symbolism. Reading the passage literalistically would leave one nonsensically ransacking the past for, or projecting into the future, an account of a mass of human bones in a specific geographical location being brought back to life. The correct interpretative instinct is to see this as an image of a restored nation of Israel. But this leaves the question of time unanswered: past or future? Consider the historical and literary context of the passage. In 36:1, Ezekiel prophesies not to the people, but to the "mountains of Israel." Sin and exile have left the land desolate. This was a common idea in the ancient world; we find a similar story from the city of Ugarit, on the coast of what today is Syria. In the tale of Aqhat, a prince is murdered, and as a consequence the land suffers famine. In an effort to revive the land, the murdered prince's father travels his realm, kneeling down, embracing, and kissing its withered vegetation and interceding on behalf of the land.[6] In the Bible, after the fall, the earth no longer produces food the way it had before (Gen 3:17–19); Abel's blood cries out to God from the land (Gen 4:10); the land vomits out sinful Israel (Lev 18:25, 28); and creation groans as it waits for its redemption (Rom 8:22). The land has feelings too. Here, Israel's sin has left the land desolate and caused it to suffer the ridicule of the nations (Ezek 36:6–8). Now Ezekiel consoles an empty land and prophesies about a future in which it will once again be full of people.

In chapter 37, Ezekiel paints two pictures. In the first, he is transported to a broad valley full of bones. There the prophet is told to prophesy to the bones, and as he does, they rise up, become covered with flesh, and return to life. Interpreters are unanimous in seeing the picture as depicting a revived Israel. In the second picture, the prophet is commanded to take two sticks, write "Judah" on one and "Israel" on the other, and then tie them together (37:15–17). The interpretation is given in the passage itself. God will bring Israel and Judah back from captivity, return them to the land, and make them one nation (37:19–21). They will at last put away their idols and be ruled by David (37:23–28).

Both the vision and the prophetic act speak of the restoration of Israel from exile to nationhood. For many end-times teachers, this chapter had its fulfillment in 1948, when Israel once again became a political entity with borders and a capital in Palestine.[7] For most dispensationalist end-times teachers, Ezekiel 37 represents a long-term prophecy and the events of 1948 its astounding fulfillment. This equation may seem bizarre for many contemporary readers, but as we have seen, understanding this conclusion is easier when one considers the context of 1948, when the Israeli War of Independence took place. In the years following World War II and the Holocaust, thousands of European Jews attempting to run the British blockade and enter Palestine found themselves again behind barbed wire, this time in British camps in Cyprus. Imagine how beaten and hopeless such people must have felt! Imagine too, however, how deliriously elated many felt in 1948 when that downtrodden remnant could see that they were a nation once more. For dispensationalist Christians watching from the sidelines, this was nothing less than the hand of God and a direct fulfillment of the words of Ezekiel 37—Israel had truly been raised from the dead. This restoration of Israel to the land in 1948 was understood to be a prerequisite to the return of Christ. Hal Lindsey describes it as "the paramount prophetic sign."[8]

But is this a sound interpretation of Ezekiel's vision? Let's start with the original audience's context. Does it make any sense that God would seek to bring hope to a group of people languishing in exile by promising something that would never be fulfilled in their lifetime? Second, consider the wider cultural context. For ancient Israel and its neighbors, the dead had to be buried quickly and properly (e.g., 1 Sam 31:11–13; 1 Kgs 13:27–32). Placing a family member's body in a tomb, providing grave goods, and ongoing acts of ritual feeding ensured enduring remembrance and a comfortable time in the afterlife. Bones being left exposed to the elements, to be picked over by animals, was a catastrophe and disgrace (e.g., 1 Sam 17:45–47; 2 Sam 21:7–14; 1 Kgs 21:23–24; Ps 79:1–4). The picture here, then, is of an Israel defeated and disgraced by its enemies—precisely what is laid out in Ezekiel 36. How could a nation possibly recover from such a thoroughgoing destruction and humiliation?

This is what Ezekiel has to mentally reckon with when God shows him an entire valley strewn with bones and asks, "Can these bones live?" (37:3). Ezekiel defers to God, who in response tells the prophet to prophesy to the bones. That Ezekiel is the one told to prophesy tells us that the bones represent his contemporaries—the exiles of Israel and Judah. God then speaks to the bones and tells them that he will bring them back to life so that "you will know that I am Yahweh" (37:6). For an exiled people wondering whether the gods of Babylon had defeated the God of Israel, this kind of demonstration was an important proof. Yahweh was alive and powerful and would soon restore them to the promised land. It was exactly the message of hope that the exiles needed to hear.

Ezekiel prophesied to a people suffering in captivity, hoping to be restored to their homeland. His audience would have understood the revived and reunited nation (ch. 37) as describing their immediate, hoped-for future. And, as we've seen above, that's precisely what happened following the edict of Cyrus in 538 BC. The action of Cyrus in releasing captive peoples was an unprecedented event. Nothing like this had ever happened before. The exiles were, so to speak, brought back from the dead. While a Davidic king never reigned over Israel again, it was nonetheless the case that the first governors the Persians appointed to rule the new province of Yehud (as the new Persian province was called) were direct descendants of the exiled king Jehoiachin.[9] Given all of the above, the idea that chapter 37 applies to 1948 represents a massive leap across time that is nowhere supported by the text. When end-times teachers take this same material to refer to the establishment of the modern state of Israel, they are ignoring the more immediate and obvious context of that prophecy—the edict of Cyrus, king of Persia, and the sixth-century BC return of the Judeans from captivity.

## EZEKIEL 38–39: THE ATTACK OF GOG
## (OR, WILL RUSSIA ATTACK ISRAEL?)

In chapters 38 and 39, Ezekiel describes an attack on the land of Israel by a nation or person named "Gog, of the land of Magog." From the far north, Gog assembles a group of allies who attack God's chosen people who have returned to live peacefully in the land. God intervenes, however, and the foreign invaders are destroyed. Their corpses would fill an entire valley, and the leftover weapons would provide enough kindling for seven years!

As we have noted already, many dispensationalist end-times teachers maintain that Gog is a biblical codename for modern Russia and that Ezekiel 38–39 predicts a future Russian attack on Israel. At the height of the battle, God will intervene to destroy the invaders and rescue his people. The prospect of Russia attacking Israel may seem like an exceedingly remote possibility today, but again, consider the context in which books like *The Late Great Planet Earth* were written. We have already seen how the sudden and unlikely founding of the state of Israel in 1948 seemed to many like a clear case of prophetic fulfilment. Hal Lindsey, the author of *The Late Great Planet Earth*, attended Dallas Theological Seminary in the 1960s, when the Soviet Union controlled Eastern Europe and had established itself as a nation with global ambitions, fomenting communist insurgencies as far away as Southeast Asia. At home, America had just emerged from the hysteria of McCarthyism and the nuclear brinksmanship of the Cuban missile crisis. The Cold War was in full swing. Communism seemed everywhere on the move. In this context, if it was understood that the revived Israel of Ezekiel 37 was the modern state of Israel, then who could be the fearsome enemy from the north who would attack her in chapters 38–39? Given previous interpretation and the geopolitical context of the day, Russia seemed a likely possibility.

As we have seen, this idea was bolstered from what such prophecy teachers regarded as clues within the text itself.[10] Gog leads a vast multinational force against Israel (38:1–6), and many end-times writers then and now have mined the groups mentioned in this list in an effort to identify their modern-day counterparts. To do so, these interpreters followed the Greek version of the Old Testament, the Septuagint (LXX), to read verse 2 as "Gog of the land of Magog, Rosh, prince of Meshech and Tubal." From this, using a series of now-discredited correlations, they identified Rosh-Gog-Magog with "Russia," Meshech with "Moscow," Tubal with "Tubolsk," and Gomer with the then–"East Germany." They then went further to identify other nations in the passage with modern-day states. With these identifications in place, the whole passage then becomes a prophecy involving a Russian-led invasion of Israel in the last days. Suggested motivation for this attack varies, but one most commonly proposed is a desire to control Middle East oil.[11] Once these authors had identified this invader from the "far north" with Russia, then this identification could be applied in other places in Scripture where a northern invader is in view (e.g., Isa 10:12; 30:31–33; 31:8–9; Dan 11:40; Joel 2:1–27).

What to do with this passage? We have noted that the identification of *rosh* with Russia, and Meshech and Tubal with Moscow and Tubolsk, rested on old, incomplete data and has been discredited for over a century. What, then, did this passage say to its original audience? These two chapters are acknowledged to be among the most difficult in all of Ezekiel. Still, it remains good practice to start with the overall context in which the passage appears. How does this passage fit within the flow of the Ezekiel's thought? To answer, let's back up a little. Beginning in 37:15, Ezekiel "sees" the people of Israel reunited in the land in a way that returns them to their original covenant purpose and blessings and once again makes them a beacon of God's holiness to the nations:

> I will make a *covenant of peace* with them; it will be an everlasting covenant. I will establish them and increase their numbers, and I will put my sanctuary among them forever. My dwelling place will be with them; *I will be their God, and they will be my people.* Then the *nations will know that I the* LORD *make Israel holy*, when my sanctuary is among them forever. (37:26–28; see Exod 19:6)

For exiles hoping to return home, these verses address an important, nagging question: "Once we return from exile, what will prevent a repeat of the catastrophe we've endured?" The Babylonian attack of 586 BC was an act of judgment on Israel for its sin. In this new era, God himself will make his restored people holy. This is the same reunification and new covenant that Ezekiel's contemporary, Jeremiah, speaks of in Jeremiah 31:27–40. There God declares, "'This is the covenant I will make with the people of Israel after that time,' declares the LORD. 'I will put my law in their minds and write it on their hearts. I will be their God, and they will be my people'" (Jer 31:33). Israel's new heart and imputed holiness will preclude the need for a foreign power to come as an instrument of God's judgment. Gog and Magog, then, appear to assure the exiles of what kind of life they can expect to live when God restores them to the promised land.

Ezekiel 38 and 39 provide an illustration of what this means for Israel. Judah had gone into exile at the hands of the Babylonians because of its sin. Now God rolls the tape forward to show his people a time when Babylon itself is no more. The restoration will be in the distant past; God's people will have long been in the land, enjoying covenant blessing. In this future, God will summon a fearsome coalition against Israel from far and wide, representing territory even greater than the Assyrian Empire had reached at its peak.[12] These nations will march out boastfully, thinking that they are acting according to their own design (38:11–13), but they are being lured into a trap to be destroyed (38:17–23). The destruction of this great force will assure Israel of God's protection and demonstrate to the nations that their sin will be judged, just as Israel's was (39:21–24). Just as Israel's earlier exile had occurred not because of Yahweh's weakness, but because of his holiness, so now her miraculous protection will emphasize the greatness and holiness of God (36:22; 37:28; 38:23; 39:27). Just as Yahweh had earlier judged

Israel and left her as a valley of uninterred skeletons (37:1–3), so will the nations one day be judged and their corpses strewn across a valley (39:11–17). While God will have revived Israel, however, the corpses of the nations will be gathered and buried, never to rise again.

The account ends by returning to the question of Judah's return from captivity. God's character is compassion; the shame of the exiles' past will be forgotten. Having returned, they will know why they went into exile in the first place and by whose power they had been restored. In this new era, God will show his face to them and pour out his spirit upon them so that they can be in relationship with him in the land (39:25–29). Ezekiel 38 and 39, then, do not comfort God's people by assuring them that an enemy will be destroyed, but bring comfort by assuring them that they will return to the land. In a new covenant relationship with God, they will experience his spirit and holiness in a new way, with the result that they will live in obedience, free from the idolatry and backsliding that brought them under judgment in the first place (37:23). What lies before them is life with God, free from fear.

## EZEKIEL 40–48: ISRAEL RETURNS TO THE LAND (OR, GOD'S MILLENNIUM PLAN?)

In chapters 40–48, Ezekiel sketches what postexilic life will be like. Chapters 40–44 describe a rebuilt temple, reconsecrated priests and Levites, and God's returned glory. Chapters 45–46 reintroduce liturgical festivals, and chapter 47 describes a river flowing from the threshold of the temple to bring life and prosperity back to the land and its people. Finally, chapter 48 details how the land will be redivided equally among the tribes. Not remotely resembling the distribution according to the book of Joshua (Josh 13:8–21:45), Ezekiel's description lays

out the ideal future for God's restored people. The literary tool
by which he accomplishes this is hyperbole. God is giving his
people a completely fresh start. The restoration will be just
as if they were entering the promised land for the first time, a
complete spiritual do-over.

Most end-times teachers use Ezekiel 40–48 to depict life in
the millennium, when the curse will be rolled back, the temple
restored, and Christ will rule on earth. First, the flow of Ezekiel
fits quite well with what dispensationalists believe about the
last days. If chapter 37 and the valley of dry bones that come
to life and the two sticks that are bound together represent
the birth of the modern state of Israel in 1948, then the attack
of Gog described in chapters 38–39 fits nicely with the Battle
of Armageddon that follows this. Then Christ sets up his one-
thousand-year reign on earth, so chapters 40–48 must describe
a future millennial reign of Christ over his earthly people Israel.
Second, the specific measurements for the temple given in chapters 40–42 do not conform to those of the Solomonic, postexilic,
or Herodian temples; they must therefore refer to some future
structure.[13] Third, as noted above, the conditions these chapters
describe are unlike anything in Israel's prior experience and
await fulfilment in the yet-to-be-realized era of Christ's rule.[14]

Again, the critical question is that of the original audience.
What would they have understood? Dispensationalist readings
would have made no sense to Ezekiel's audience and brought
them no hope. On the other hand, it is easy to see how a group
of exiles would have seen this material as pointing to their forthcoming return to the land, something fulfilled with the edict of
Cyrus (538 BC). They also fail to see Ezekiel's use of hyperbole, symbolism, and allusion in the passage, and how this
would have been understood by the original audience, a problem exponentially compounded when many end-times teachers

make flawed interpretative intertextual connections between this material and passages in Revelation.

Intertextuality names another challenge to following and understanding the work of end-times teachers. Rather than working through a paragraph, section, chapter, or book on its own and only then reading within the canon, they dart from one biblical passage to another, haphazardly making connections between snippets of verses and entire chapters from one end of Scripture to another. This makes a book such as *The Late Great Planet Earth* difficult to follow. On television, the rapid-fire Scripture-quoting of Jack Van Impe, a man who, to his credit, had memorized vast swaths of Scripture, is simply overwhelming. It is thus common for these teachers to connect the depiction of the city and land in Ezekiel 40–48 with similar material in Revelation 21–22 and assume that both point to the same places and events.

Is such a reading warranted? We don't think so. While we can see Ezekiel in Revelation (we'll explore this further in chapter 9), it does not follow that we can read Revelation back into Ezekiel, or that both are seeing some third, extrabiblical reality. Again, it is more likely that Ezekiel's vision spoke to his immediate exiled audience. Ezekiel prepares his audience for a new start with God in the land. He heralds the reinitiation of institutions and practices that the exile had put on hiatus. The return from exile will be marked by the building of a new temple complex to ensure that worship is revived and at the heart of the community (Ezek 40–43). The temple offerings and pilgrimage festivals (Ezek 45:13–46:24; see Lev 23; Num 28–29; Deut 16) will be reintroduced. The river flows east from the threshold of the temple to the Dead Sea, making it teem with new life (Ezek 47:8–11). Fruit trees grow on either side, providing a fresh crop each month (Ezek 47:7, 12). The land will be even more fruitful than God first promised. It will even be redivided in a way that cut across the old tribal boundaries (Ezek 47:13–48:29; see Josh 13–21). In all of this, what Ezekiel is telling the exiles is that in returning his people to the promised land, God will give them a new start. It will be better than as if they were under Joshua, setting foot in the land for the first time.

## CONCLUSION

But what can Ezekiel possibly have to do with us? Here are some initial thoughts. We have already seen how the vision of the mobile, all-seeing throne of God declared that God was with the Judeans in their exile. Such unchanging divine character reminds us that in a world of personal failure, alienation, and loneliness, we are never out of God's sight or care. What Ezekiel conveys symbolically, the apostle Paul affirms directly: "Neither death nor life, neither angels nor demons, neither the present nor the future, nor any powers, neither height nor depth, nor anything else in all creation, will be able to separate us from the love of God that is in Christ Jesus our Lord" (Rom 8:38–39). As with Israel, the vision of the desiccated bones restored to life reminds us that ours is a God of second chances. In a cancel-culture world where "wrongdoers" are hunted down and destroyed with glee, this vision is a reminder of how grace and redemption lie at the heart of the Christian faith. Our sin and failure are not the end of the story. God is ready to lift up the repentant and restore them to life and purpose. Chapters 38 to the end of the book declare to Israel and us that ongoing life and purpose is possible because of God's holiness written on our hearts. The covenant blessing enjoyed by the restored community is God's default setting toward us. This is not the gratuitous material blessing imagined by prosperity-gospel preachers, but a promise of abundant equipping that enables us to live and serve God in the world. For Israel, this enabled a life of testimony in a promised land at the crossroads of the ancient world. For followers of God today, it will be something different.

# 7

# Daniel

## CONTEXT AND SETTING, DISPENSATIONAL USE

### CRITICAL CONFLICTS OVER DANIEL

Since the nineteenth century, scholarship has divided over two fundamental issues regarding the book of Daniel—genre and dating. Until then, most believed Daniel to be a prophet who lived during the sixth-century BC Babylonian exile. The birth of archaeology and historical criticism, however, led scholars to question the previous consensus. Eventually, two camps emerged; the first, largely conservative Jewish and Christian scholars and laypeople, retained the traditional view. The second, mostly secular and Christian critical scholars, saw Daniel as an apocalyptic work dating from the second century BC.[1]

Committed to reading the Bible as if it were any other book, the second group detected elements that gave them doubts about the long-accepted views of Daniel's authorship and setting. As prophets came to be understood not as foretellers of future events, but as social critics and champions of ethical monotheism,[2] Daniel's lack of genre fit became clearer. That the

Hebrew canon placed Daniel in the Writings rather than the Prophets supported this growing awareness. With the growth of form criticism—a critical approach that analyzes and classifies elements of literature according to their genre and pre-literary use—most critical scholars came to identify Daniel as an example of apocalyptic literature.

With regard to the dating of the book, many scholars looked askance at Daniel's detailed predictions. Appearing too good to be true, they came to be regarded as *vaticinium ex eventu* or "prophecy from the event." Their accuracy was attributable to the fact that they were written after the event (thus reintroducing a criticism first made in the third century AD by the Tyrian Neoplatonic philosopher Porphyry [ca. AD 234–305]).[3] The accurate predictions of the wars between the Ptolemies of Egypt and the Seleucids of Syria (chs. 11–12) were possible because the material was composed *after* the events had already happened. These scholars saw the book as having been composed at the point where the predictions become *less* specific, that is, the time of Antiochus IV Epiphanes.[4]

They further maintained that historical errors existed in the book that were understandable in a work written long after its purported context. Many argued, for example, that the date formula in 1:1 linking the third year of King Jehoiachim with the arrival of Nebuchadnezzar to besiege Jerusalem was incorrect. Not only did Daniel's Aramaic reflect a second-century BC variety, but the presence of Persian and Greek loanwords therein clearly pointed to the Hellenistic era, when Greek was widely used throughout the Near East.[5] By the second decade of the twentieth century, Daniel was widely regarded as a pseudepigraphic, apocalyptic work designed to encourage the Jews of Palestine, who were facing persecution at the hands of the Seleucid emperor Antiochus IV.

Conservative Christians, who saw the doctrines of biblical authority and inspiration battered by the nineteenth-century tide of higher-critical theories, defended Daniel's predictive prophecy. Locating inspiration in the *person* of the prophet, they perceived a crisis when critical scholars challenged Daniel's traditional *authorship*. If Daniel didn't write Daniel, then the book's authority was undermined—someone was trying to trick the original audience. Jesus himself, who in Matthew 24:15 states that "the prophet Daniel" predicted the coming desecration of the Jerusalem temple, was often quoted. Daniel, these scholars insisted, should be taken at face value: a first-person account clearly dated to the Babylonian and Persian eras. Not only had this always been the view among Jewish interpreters, but Daniel's Aramaic sections also strongly resembled the Imperial Aramaic of traditional date.[6] Even as conservative Christians differed as to the predicted events, they agreed that Daniel is predictive prophecy written during the exile.

As the nineteenth century progressed, however, more and more scholars became convinced of Daniel's late date. Through his popular *An Introduction to the Literature of the Old Testament* (1891), English churchman and scholar S. R. Driver (1846–1914) made these critical views accessible to a lay audience. Even in the United States, where democratizing tendencies and the absence of a state church made the dominance of a single and novel view more difficult to establish, the critical view gradually came to dominate, particularly in secular colleges and many mainline Protestant institutions.

Among the Bible colleges and seminaries associated with the independent and more evangelical denominations, the traditional view often persists. The last mainline Protestant conservative holdout was Princeton Seminary, where scholars such as William Henry Green (1825–1900), Robert Dick

Wilson (1856–1930), and Oswald T. Allis (1880–1973) contended not only for Daniel, but also for the Mosaic authorship of the Pentateuch and the eighth-century prophet Isaiah as author of the book of Isaiah until their ouster in 1929. Today, the sixth-century BC dating of Daniel and its designation as prophecy is seldom defended. In 1979, a popular book, *Prophecy, Fact or Fiction? Daniel in the Critics Den,* by evangelical youth speaker and apologist Josh McDowell, collated evidence for the traditional view.[7] It, along with R. K. Harrison's *Introduction to the Old Testament,* handily distills the conservative arguments. Within evangelical scholarship, however, the critical stance on the genre and dating of Daniel is increasingly common with slight modifications.[8]

### DANIEL AMONG THE DISPENSATIONALISTS

Unsurprisingly, dispensationalists adhere to the early date and the prophetic designation. Unlike other conservatives, however, dispensationalists read Daniel as a road map to the future and the end of the world. Where the Old Princetonians, for example, understood Daniel to predict the Hellenistic period, dispensationalists see predictions of the future.

Dispensationalists uniquely read the apocalyptic portions of Daniel through the book of Revelation. Consider, for example, the vision of the seventy weeks found in chapter 9. Daniel, remember, writing in the sixth century BC, is told, "Seventy 'sevens' are decreed for your people and your holy city to finish transgression, to put an end to sin, to atone for wickedness, to bring in everlasting righteousness," and, "From the time the word goes out to restore and rebuild Jerusalem until the Anointed One, the ruler, comes, there will be seven 'sevens,' and sixty-two 'sevens'" (Dan 9:24–25). After sixty-nine weeks (7 + 62), however, the Anointed One will be "cut off" or killed, and the people of a future ruler will enter Jerusalem and destroy the sanctuary (Dan 9:26).

While it's natural to date the climax of week 69 to Christ's death, the math to justify it is complicated, and multiple proposals have been advanced, each one tweaking a previous suggestion. Grant Jeffrey's proposal, offered below, leans heavily on the work of Sir Robert Anderson, a nineteenth-century Plymouth Brethren writer and onetime Assistant Commissioner of Scotland Yard.[9] If a "week" is seven years, and the count to sixty-nine begins with the 445 BC command to rebuild the city given to Nehemiah (Neh 2:1), then sixty-nine weeks leads to AD 38, too late for the crucifixion. But what if a solar year is not the type of year the author intended? If we follow the reckoning of months in the flood account in Genesis 7:11–24; 8:3–4 and in Esther 1:4, then one week per year is only 360 days.[10] When this is done, it is possible to take the 476 solar years between 445 BC and AD 30 and convert them to days (the result being 173,740). To this is added 119 days to account for leap years plus 29 days between March 14 (AD 30) and April 2 (AD 30),[11] for a total of 173,879. This is divided by the "prophetic year" of 360 days so that Daniel's sixty-nine weeks runs out on April 2, AD 30, when Jesus rode into Jerusalem on his way to the cross.[12]

The obvious next question is, How does one account for the now-two-millennia gap between the end of the sixty-ninth week (the death of Christ) and the descriptions of war, "the end," and desolations that will mark the seventieth week (Dan 9:26)? Since the church was first announced by Jesus in Matthew 16:18, it was unknown to Old Testament writers such as Daniel and Ezekiel. Jesus himself posits the gap—the church age or dispensation of the church.[13] Daniel's seventieth week begins when the church age ends (fig. 7.1). This still-future seven-year period is known as the "great tribulation," in which the saints will be oppressed and the sanctuary defiled. The reference to the "sanctuary" in this verse has convinced dispensationalists from Darby on that during this future period Israel will be in the land and the Jerusalem temple will have been rebuilt.

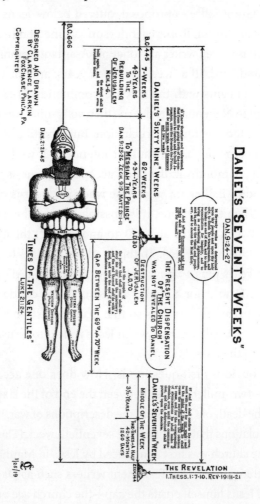

*Fig. 7.1. Daniel's seventy weeks and the gap of the church age (Larkin)*

In chapter 2, Daniel is asked to recall and interpret for King Nebuchadnezzar a dream the king had experienced. Daniel then describes the statue the king had seen—one with a head of gold, chest and arms of silver, stomach and thighs of bronze, legs of iron, and feet of iron and clay. Without warning, the statue is smashed by a giant rock not made of human hands (Dan 2:31–35). Daniel then says that the head of gold is Nebuchadnezzar, king of Babylon, and the other parts of the statue are the kingdoms that will follow Babylon. They are not, however, specifically identified. Most end-times writers identify the chest and arms of silver with the Medes and Persians; the stomach and thighs of bronze with the empire of Alexander and his successors; and the legs of iron as Rome. Some, such as Larkin (fig. 7.2), are more elaborate: the thighs are the old Roman Empire, while the calves are the eastern and western divisions of the established church. This era of iron is understood to fall within the gap between the sixty-ninth and seventieth weeks of Daniel 9. The iron-and-clay composite feet resemble the legs but are weaker. Most dispensationalists read them as a future "revived" Roman Empire, emerging immediately prior to the tribulation era, Daniel's seventieth week. These feet are finally smashed by a divinely quarried rock: the final intervention of God at the battle of Armageddon, which ends the tribulation and begins the millennial reign of Christ.

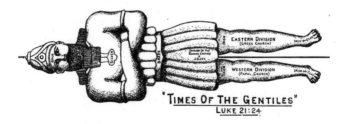

*Fig. 7.2. Nebuchadnezzar's statue (Daniel 2) and world history (Larkin)*

This material relates also to the visions of the four beasts in chapter 7 and the ram and the he-goat in chapter 8. Chapter 7's fourth, terrifying, beast with the ten horns, which supplants all the preceding beasts is, like the legs of iron above, identified with the Roman Empire. Among this beast's horns there grows an additional horn (Dan 7:8). This is the antichrist, who will lead the revived Roman Empire and persecute the faithful during the tribulation. While dispensationalists vary on the details—particularly when it comes to the relationship between the rapture and the tribulation, and the question of the church's presence during this period—this is the general picture of the future that they see in Daniel.

Following the establishment of the state of Israel in 1948, the rebuilding of the "sanctuary" presumed in Daniel's visions became a possibility. The floodgates of speculation opened wide. Two key questions revolved around the identity of the antichrist and the revived Roman Empire. If, as many end-times teachers concluded, Israel's creation placed the world on the cusp of Christ's return, then many of the actors in the final end-times drama were already living. It would be foolhardy *not* to try to identify them. If Scripture is being played out in world affairs today, further, one ought to model television programs and podcasts as news and current-affairs shows—because Scripture really is "tomorrow's news, today."

But is this how the first readers of Daniel understood this material, and is this the meaning that these words and images hold for us today? What is found when we read it first on its own terms—as a whole literary work and without reference to a later book such as Revelation? This is the task we will undertake next.

## SHAPE AND MEANING

### INTRODUCTION

To begin, let's recall the problem of apocalyptic literature's "two worlds." One is the physical realm that we experience every day. We are tempted to believe this is the only one that matters or exists. Apocalyptic adds another, unseen world that is just as real, but is usually hidden. The unseen spiritual realm impinges on our lives in profound ways for good and for ill. These two worlds figure prominently in the book of Job. On earth, Job experiences unimaginable suffering and loss and is verbally assailed by his so-called friends (Job 1–31). He knows that he has been faithful, however, and this makes his lot more difficult for him to understand. Hidden to Job, but opened to the reader, is the parallel heavenly drama. Satan challenges God: far from loving God, Job does what he must to manipulate God into giving him things (Job 1:6–12). God disagrees. Satan is freed to destroy Job's riches, and even to harm him physically, so that the truth of Job's commitment will be made clear. While Job never sees the heavenly drama, the author's point is clear: what goes on in this world is fully understandable only once the spiritual realm is seen.

On rare occasions, the curtain is drawn aside to reveal activity that God is constantly undertaking on believers' behalf. Consider the story of Jacob (Gen 28:10–17). Jacob, a scoundrel and a cheat, a manipulator of people and circumstances has, by Genesis 28, robbed his brother of his inheritance and deceived his father into giving him the deathbed blessing. Now he is running for his life, alone in an empty, unnamed place, bedding down beneath the stars. As Jacob sleeps, he dreams of a stairway linking earth with heaven, packed with angels moving back and forth between the physical and spiritual realms. When he awakes, a stunned Jacob proclaims, "Surely the LORD is in this place, and I was not aware of it" (Gen 28:16). The dream shows Jacob that God is at work. In the light of God's power and activity, all Jacob's scheming is redundant.

At a time when the persecuted might easily conclude that the powers that dominate them are permanent and unassailable, apocalyptic insists that there is an unseen spiritual realm where God's reign is better seen. God rules over both worlds and will ultimately deal with those in power. Apocalyptic literature shows us what really matters and who ultimately wins. What happens when we read Daniel with this as our primary orientation?

Old Testament scholar Stanley Walters observes that Daniel is a practical book. It chronicles what it means to live as the people of God through times of openness and persecution.[14] We'll take that assumption as basic in what follows.

## THE OVERALL SHAPE OF DANIEL

While we tend to read in bits and pieces, ancient authors wrote expecting audiences to read whole books. They had an overarching purpose; individual parts were chosen and arranged with that one purpose in view. As a result, understanding the structure of an entire book helps us grasp its meaning. The book of Daniel is no exception. End-times teachers often become so bogged down in the details of this or that vision or verse, how passages here match with passages elsewhere, that they miss Daniel's larger concerns.

In terms of language and genre, Daniel is a composite text. Six chapters of narrative written in Aramaic are surrounded by an introduction and a series of visions written in Hebrew (fig. 7.3). The narratives emphasize that there is an unseen kingdom with an omnipotent ruler who exercises authority even over the greatest kings of the earth. In this relatively open setting, the faithful are able to engage culture with only periodic threat from the temporal powers. When the faithful are threatened, the power of God intrudes to rescue them and humble their oppressors. The visions reckon with the fact that despite this divine authority, wickedness sometimes seems to advance unrestrained. While the attacks of the wicked go largely unanswered, that this persecution is disclosed in advance shows that its days have been numbered by God.

## The Structure of Daniel

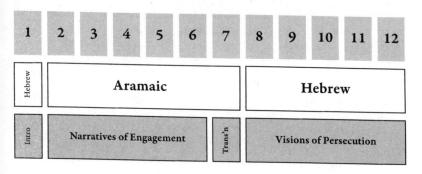

Fig. 7.3. Outline of Daniel

### NARRATIVES OF ENGAGEMENT

Daniel 1 introduces the collections of stories and visions that comprise the book,[15] supplying a historical and social setting, explaining the prominence of the Judahites, and establishing the theme. In Babylonian captivity, four Judean nobles are entirely stripped of control. Their inability to determine things so basic as their names or diet (Dan 1:5–7) introduces the book's theme. They may lack power; God, however, remains in control.

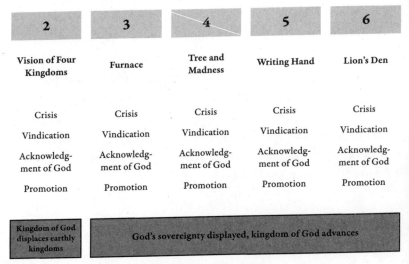

Fig. 7.4. Daniel 2–6 and narratives of engagement

Working invisibly, God *controls the mind* of the Babylonian official[16] so that he risks royal sanction and allows Daniel and his companions to set their own diet (Dan 1:9–10). From its outset, therefore, Daniel is going to be a story of faithful living in a foreign world, with God working both visibly and invisibly for his people.

Chapter 2 narrows the focus to the book's first half. Nebuchadnezzar's dream provides a framework for the narratives running from chapters 2–6. They all follow a pattern of *crisis > vindication > royal acknowledgment of God > promotion* (fig. 7.4).

The originating *crisis* is Nebuchadnezzar's demand that his advisers both relate and interpret his dream (fig. 7.5). The task stuns his astrologers: "No one can reveal it to the king except the gods, and they do not live among humans" (2:11). Daniel's *vindication* comes that night, when the king's dream and its meaning are revealed to him. The Judean prince then acknowledges God's sovereignty in a short hymn, declaring that God "deposes kings and raises up others" (2:21). Public vindication follows when Daniel successfully relates the dream and its interpretation to the king's satisfaction (2:27–45). Nebuchadnezzar's *acknowledgment of God* comes in 2:46–47, when he falls prostrate before Daniel, orders offerings to be made to the Judean, and affirms Daniel's god as "the God of gods and the Lord of kings" (2:47). This is a far-from-perfect expression of theological orthodoxy: sacrifices are made, for example, to Daniel and not to Yahweh. It is a natural, but naive, response to Daniel's success. The astrologers are right: only a god could reveal the dream (2:11).[17] Nebuchadnezzar's declaration that Daniel's god is "the God of gods and the Lord of kings" (2:47) mirrors Daniel's earlier affirmation that God "deposes kings and raises up others" (2:21). The substance of the chapter is summarized in the king's acknowledgment that the god of Daniel is the "revealer of mysteries" (2:47). Finally, Daniel and his friends are *promoted* to positions of authority and power within the kingdom. By the end of this first cycle, it is clear that even in hostile settings, God *does* live among humans and rules over earthly kings.

Two elements of this passage stand out for all that follows. First, Daniel's brief hymn of praise lists key attributes of God that will be on display throughout the rest of the book—"wisdom and power are his. He changes times and seasons; he deposes kings and raises up others" (2:20–21). In other words, *God is sovereign*, and those who reign do so at his pleasure. *God also establishes the patterns by which the world operates*; those who attempt to change these are attempting to take the place of God himself and will be dealt with accordingly. Second is the dream/vision itself. Without warning, a divinely hewn rock[18] strikes the feet of Nebuchadnezzar's statue, destroying it, and then grows to become a huge mountain that fills the earth.[19] Daniel's interpretation (2:36–45) clarifies that the rock is a kingdom God will establish among humans. While it strikes the last of the earthly kingdoms, it destroys and displaces them all (2:35, 44–45).

---

### 2

# Vision of Four Kingdoms

Crisis: Nebuchadnezzar's demand

Vindication: Daniel interprets dream

Acknowledgment of God: Daniel worshiped;
God reveals

Promotion: Daniel & friends

---

**Kingdom of God displaces earthly kingdoms:
God alone sets up kings and deposes them**

---

*Fig. 7.5. Daniel 2*

The remaining narratives of chapters 2–6 develop the kingdom's reality and the manner of its growth. Rulers are judged to the extent that they recognize both the kingdom and its Ruler. In this way, the narratives of the first half of Daniel demonstrate how the faithful engage a foreign and sometimes hostile realm that gradually gives ground to the expanding kingdom of God.

## 3

# Furnace

Crisis: Worship the statue

Vindication: Three Judeans are rescued

Acknowledgment of God: Praises God;
he delivers; no disrespect

Promotion: Daniel's friends

Quiet advance of the kingdom of God

*Fig. 7.6. Daniel 3*

In chapter 3, the cycle of *crisis* through to *promotion* begins again. Here too, it signals the presence and growth of the invisible kingdom of God (fig. 7.6). The *crisis* is the royal command to worship a colossal golden statue of the king and the refusal of Shadrach, Meshach, and Abednego to comply (3:1–23). They are condemned to death in the "fiery furnace," and *vindication* comes when God rescues the three. In the furnace, they withstand the fire, eventually walking out under their own power (3:24–27). In response, Nebuchadnezzar once again *acknowledges* the hand of God. Now, however, he goes further, offering an appropriately directed expression of praise ("Blessed be the God of Shadrach, Meshach, and Abednego, who has sent his angel and rescued his servants! They trusted in him"; 3:28). The king's affirmation is further expressed negatively by the threat he issues to those who would denigrate the God of the

Judeans (3:29). Last, the three Judeans are *promoted* within the province of Babylon (3:30). Again, the words of the Babylonian king show that even in a hostile setting, God is present and powerful, and can rescue the faithful:

> Then Nebuchadnezzar said, "Praise be to the God of Shadrach, Meshach and Abednego, who has sent his angel and rescued his servants! They trusted in him and defied the king's command and were willing to give up their lives rather than serve or worship any god except their own God. Therefore I decree that the people of any nation or language who say anything against the God of Shadrach, Meshach and Abednego be cut into pieces and their houses be turned into piles of rubble, for no other god can save in this way." (3:28–29)

The reappearance of Daniel the dream interpreter (fig. 7.7) is a culmination of sorts. The entirety of chapter 4 is framed as a *royal acknowledgment* of God's authority with the expected crisis-promotion cycle embedded within. The progression of God's kingdom and the positive influence of the faithful are immediately made clear. There is *no crisis* or threat to the safety of the faithful. Rather, King Nebuchadnezzar experiences the *crisis*, once again in a dream. A massive tree that provides shelter and sustenance for a vast array of animal life is suddenly and inexplicably destroyed by divine decree.[20] The dream then interprets itself: the events that befall Nebuchadnezzar will reveal the sovereignty of God, who appoints human monarchs at will (4:17; Heb. 4:14). Further, Nebuchadnezzar's *vindication* is achieved not by any action on his own part, but by the fulfillment of the divine prediction that his madness will run its course.[21] The subsequent royal acknowledgment of God both concludes the episode and frames the entire narrative.[22] The

## 4

# Tree & Madness

Acknowledgment of God: Eternal kingdom

Crisis: King

Vindication: Three Judaeans are rescued

Acknowledgment of God: Eternal kingdom;
praises God; he is right, just

Promotion: Nebuchadnezzar

Quiet advance of the kingdom of God

*Fig. 7.7. Daniel 4*

narrative opens with Nebuchadnezzar's candid acknowledgment
of the existence of God's eternal kingdom and authority (4:3;
Heb. 3:33); it ends with the most thorough acknowledgment of
God to this point, including a hymn declaring the eternal nature
of God's kingdom and his sovereignty over heaven and earth:

At the end of that time, I, Nebuchadnezzar, raised my
eyes toward heaven, and my sanity was restored. Then
I praised the Most High; I honored and glorified him
who lives forever.

His dominion is an eternal dominion;
    his kingdom endures from generation to generation.
All the peoples of the earth
    are regarded as nothing.

He does as he pleases
> with the powers of heaven
> and the peoples of the earth.
No one can hold back his hand
> or say to him: "What have you done?" (4:34–35;
> Heb. 4:31–32).

The king also acknowledges God's righteousness and his own subservient status (4:37; Heb. 4:34). The appearance of *promotion* parallels the earlier element of crisis. Nebuchadnezzar has his sanity and throne restored (4:36b; Heb. 4:33b). By the narrative's end, it is clear that God's kingdom is present in the world and that human kings do well to acknowledge the authority of the one who establishes and deposes them at will.

Chapter 5, the story of Belshazzar's fall (fig. 7.8), is a counterpoint to chapter 4, strategically altering the pattern of *crisis* through *promotion*. Again, crisis confronts not the follower of God, but the Babylonian monarch. Hosting a banquet, Belshazzar issues a drunken command that the vessels pillaged from the Jerusalem temple be brought and distributed among the guests. Whereas Belshazzar's predecessor had readily acknowledged the sovereignty of God, now drunken revelers praise idols even as they drink from cups once dedicated to the God of Israel. God then intrudes into the human realm. The fingers of a hand appear and begin to write on the wall (Dan 5:5). Once again, Daniel is summoned. Before he interprets the miracle, Daniel informs Belshazzar that his father, Nebuchadnezzar, reigned only at the pleasure of the Most High God. Moreover, he had humbly recognized that appointment (5:18–21):

> Your Majesty, the Most High God gave your father
> Nebuchadnezzar sovereignty and greatness and glory
> and splendor. Because of the high position he gave him,

## 5

# Writing Hand

Crisis: King

Vindication: None

Acknowledgment of God: None;
did not honor God

Promotion: Daniel; Demotion: Belshazzar

Quiet advance of the kingdom of God

*Fig. 7.8. Daniel 5*

all the peoples and nations and men of every language
dreaded and feared him. Those the king wanted to put
to death, he put to death; those he wanted to spare, he
spared; those he wanted to promote, he promoted; and
those he wanted to humble, he humbled. But when his
heart became arrogant and hardened with pride, he was
deposed from his royal throne and stripped of his glory.
He was driven away from people and given the mind of
an animal; he lived with the wild donkeys and ate grass
like the ox; and his body was drenched with the dew of
heaven, until he acknowledged that the Most High God
is sovereign over all kingdoms on earth and sets over
them anyone he wishes.

Unlike his father, Belshazzar has not humbled himself. He has
desecrated God's property, using his vessels in the praise of

idols (5:22–24). The miraculous writing announces that there will be no *vindication*. Belshazzar's reign is ended. In the Old Testament, idolatry is the ultimate deal breaker. Thus, replacing the expected *acknowledgment of God* is only Daniel's chastisement. Belshazzar had *failed* to acknowledge God (5:22–24). The narrative ends with *promotion* for Daniel (5:29) and the ultimate *demotion*—overthrow and death—for Belshazzar (5:30). The dramatic, physical intrusion of the disembodied hand marks the *increasing* way in which the authority of God's kingdom is making itself felt in the human realm. Daniel's God, who reinstated a penitent Nebuchadnezzar in chapter 4, can as easily depose an arrogant Belshazzar.

The final narrative provides the clearest evidence of the growth of God's kingdom, displacing and influencing this-worldly powers. God has swept Belshazzar and the Babylonians aside, replacing them with Darius, and the cycle of *crisis > vindication > royal acknowledgment of God > promotion* reverts to its expected form (fig. 7.9). Once again serving in the royal administration, Daniel, despite his integrity and competence, is victimized by scheming rivals. A sympathetic Darius is duped by his own officials and forced to sentence Daniel to be devoured by lions (6:6–16). When Daniel is rescued (i.e., *vindicated* [6:17–24]), the king *acknowledges God*. Going well beyond Nebuchadnezzar's previous three attestations, Darius not only declares God's sovereignty and saving, but also commands the people of *all* nations to fear him (6:25–27):

> Then King Darius wrote to all the peoples, nations and men of every language throughout the land:
>
> "May you prosper greatly!
>
> "I issue a decree that in every part of my kingdom people must fear and reverence the God of Daniel.

"For he is the living God
and he endures forever;
his kingdom will not be destroyed,
his dominion will never end.
He rescues and he saves;
he performs signs and wonders
in the heavens and on the earth.
He has rescued Daniel
from the power of the lions."

Finally, Daniel is once again *promoted* (6:28). In this clearest example of the advancing presence of the divine kingdom, the rulers of the earth not only recognize the authority of God, but also enjoin their subjects to do the same.

## 6

# Lion's Den

Crisis: Daniel's enemies conspire

Vindication: God shuts lion's mouths

Acknowledgment of God: All should fear God;
imperishable kingdom; he rescues

Promotion: Daniel

**Quiet advance of the kingdom of God**

*Fig. 7.9. Daniel 6*

VISIONS OF PERSECUTION

As a vision presented in Aramaic, chapter 7 mirrors much of the material in chapter 2 and closes the book's first half (fig. 7.10). Daniel receives a vision of four kingdoms (7:2–14), paralleling the four kingdoms of Nebuchadnezzar's statue (2:31–35). In both chapters, the final kingdom is destroyed and all are displaced by the kingdom of God. Specific phraseology connects the two sections.[23]

The present form and language of chapter 7 also suggests a transitional function. While written in Aramaic, like the preceding narratives, this terrifying vision of bestial empires that persecute the faithful has neither vindication nor promotion. The kingdom of God seems absent.

Packed into the vision are many features that will unfold in the book's second half, features found in apocalyptic literature generally.[24] Four "beastly" kingdoms devour and destroy before any divine action takes place. Only when the fourth successfully wages war against the saints and challenges divine authority by attempting to change the *"times and the seasons"*[25] does the heavenly court decree the beast's destruction (7:25). God ordained the times and seasons at creation (Gen 1:14); any attempt to change them presumes upon divine authority. Earlier, Nebuchadnezzar recognized that only God could do this (2:21). While the faithful are ultimately vindicated, this final part stresses that rescue will not always come quickly. While God is present and his kingdom is real, earthly kingdoms will sometimes claim divine authority and war against God's followers. Thus, this chapter prepares the reader for the visions to come and an era of ongoing persecution and justice delayed.

The era is unpacked in three visions that comprise Daniel's second half (chs. 8–12). The eighth chapter's abrupt shift in

## 7

# Vision of Four Beasts

Arrogant enemy dominates

Faithful are killed

God intervenes and judges

---

Kingdom of God overcomes earthly kingdoms &
would-be gods (God alone has authority & eternal
dominion, vv. 14, 27)

---

*Fig. 7.10. Daniel 7*

language and content signals a new direction. Aramaic yields
to Hebrew, and simple narratives to complex visions. Daniel
is no longer the confident wise man who had ably served
Babylon and Persia but is now a bewildered recipient of terrifying visions.

In the first of these, Daniel sees a two-horned ram, a goat,
and finally a horn. The Medes and the Persians (fig. 7.11) are the
ram. The goat is the Greek Empire; its single, prominent horn
is Alexander the Great, and its four later horns Alexander's
inheritors, the Diadochi. The Greeks supplant the Persians
even as the goat replaces the ram (Dan 8:3–8). The emergent
fifth horn defies God, attacking the saints, appropriating the
sacrifices, destroying the sanctuary, and throwing "truth to the
ground" (8:11–12). He is destroyed by the hand of God.[26]

## 8

# Ram & Goat

Arrogant enemy dominates

Faithful killed

God intervenes & judges

Quiet advance of the kingdom of God

*Fig. 7.11. Daniel 8*

The knowledge that the suffering of the faithful is a consequence of their rebellion (8:12) spurs Daniel to penitence. Thus, the next section opens with his fasting and pleading with God on behalf of his people (9:3–19; see fig. 7.12). His words reflect the specific vocabulary of the previous vision, in which the heavenly messengers discuss the sanctuary's desolation (8:13).[27] The interpretation the angel Gabriel gives to Daniel also parallels in part that of the previous vision. The faithful are delivered only after great persecution; while the end of the desolation has been decreed, much violence and suffering must first occur (9:24–27). Again, the enemy will defy God, defile his temple, and persecute the faithful. God will eventually intervene.

# 9

# 70 Sevens

Faithful suffer as a result of their past sin

Arrogant enemy dominates

Faithful killed

God intervenes & judges

Quiet advance of the kingdom of God

*Fig. 7.12. Daniel 9*

The book's final vision continues to show how earthly powers will challenge God and his kingdom, kill the faithful, and ultimately be judged by God (fig. 7.13). It begins with the notation that it concerns a "great conflict" (*wəṣābāʾ gādôl*, 10:1)—a fact that sends Daniel into a three-week period of mourning.[28] Gabriel reveals that the heavenly powers have been engaged in a difficult, unseen battle against earthly kingdoms (10:13, 20). He details a story of kingdoms, alliances, and warfare that will result in a king from the north occupying "the Beautiful Land" (i.e., Judea). He will be empowered to destroy it (11:16).[29] His successor will oppose the "holy covenant," desecrate the temple, and end regular sacrifices (11:28, 31). The truly faithful will oppose him only at enormous cost. They will "fall by the sword or be burned or captured or plundered" (11:33). When the king of the north comes again to invade the "Beautiful Land," Michael, the angelic protector of Israel, will rescue God's people. In short, even though an enemy will challenge God's authority and kill the faithful, God remains sovereign and has limited the suffering of his people. Divine rescue will eventually come.

## 10–12

# Kings of North & South

Arrogant enemy dominates

Faithful killed

God intervenes & judges

Quiet advance of the kingdom of God

*Fig. 7.13. Daniel 10–12*

Most scholars agree that Daniel's original audience were Jews in Judea suffering persecution under the Seleucid emperor Antiochus IV Epiphanes. This northern king enforced the hellenization of the Jewish population and desecrated the temple of Yahweh in Jerusalem. For them, Daniel brought a message of reassurance. The first half of the book reminded this audience that they were not the first to experience abuse. Even in such situations, God is present and his kingdom can grow. This divine track record of faithfulness was important, for the same audience experienced the second half of the book as a grim reality. Even when oppression led to martyrdom, they could remain true to God because they had been reminded, by Daniel's experience and their own history, of the promise of divine rescue.

## CONCLUSION

The book of Daniel was not written *to* us; nonetheless, it bears a message *for* us—namely, how God's people ought to navigate a world that is foreign and not naturally inclined toward the will of God. While God's kingdom and power are always present and active, *they are not always seen to be so*. According to the book's first half, in some times and places, the faithful will find that they are able to engage an essentially alien and sometimes hostile culture, advance in it, and even witness to the influence of God over it. At other times, however, the kingdoms of the earth will be so hostile and unreceptive that engagement is impossible. It may even be the case that these kingdoms will actively war against God and his followers. In such circumstances, the book's second half reminds God's followers to remain faithful, that God's unseen kingdom does exist, and that God will someday make his power felt.

Daniel invites Christians to think deeply about our times, giving us a clarifying reality check. The kingdom of God is present even when it does not seem to be visible; its existence does not entail freedom from persecution. Daniel reminds those of us living in liberal democracies and elsewhere in the developed world that our context is *engagement*, not *martyrdom*. Danger may still be present; a system founded on values other than God's will always be *potentially* dangerous. Livelihoods and reputations of those who fail to affirm the latest ideology can be destroyed by a cancel culture with frightening speed and ferocity. On the whole, however, followers of Jesus continue to engage society without fear of persecution unto death. We err, in other words, if we see Daniel 7/8–12 as depicting our situation. While Christians find themselves increasingly out of step with contemporary mores, Western nations remain cultures of engagement. For good or ill, some countries in Europe retain a state church. The separation of church and state notwithstanding, US presidents still seek the "churchy" photo op, Bible in hand. In North America, Christian radio and televisions stations flourish. Christian churches and organizations are free to lobby government, and faith-based nongovernmental organizations such as World Vision regularly take on development contracts in partnership with federal governments. Western democracies, and the United States of America especially, remain places where God's people are safe and able to participate in civil society. Despite living in a world where persecution is present, we ought to be thankful that our culture does not (yet) resemble that of Daniel 7/8–12.

Still, Daniel 2–6 reminds us that we cannot completely identify even with an open society. The title of the spiritual "This World Is Not My Home, I'm Just a-Passing Through" gets it right—ultimately, our citizenship is elsewhere. The more deeply churches identify with the powers of this world, the more likely they are to be co-opted. The North American social gospel movement of the late nineteenth and early twentieth centuries supported and promoted the evil of eugenics. Canadian churches readily lined up to establish government-funded residential schools that harmed generations of indigenous peoples.[30] More recently, a significant swath of American evangelicals have identified much of the Republican Party platform with "God's agenda." In engaging with the world, the warning of Jesus in Matthew 10:16 is "I am sending you out like sheep among wolves. Therefore be as shrewd as snakes and as innocent as doves."

Should churches participate fully in civil society? Of course! But Daniel and his friends remind us that danger is never absent.

Daniel's two halves also invite thought about the situation of Christians in other parts of the world. Many Global South Christians more reasonably identify with the world of Daniel 7/8–12 than we do. They live as minorities in societies where government and civil harassment, antiblasphemy laws, consistent denial of rights, and family honor can mean persecution and death. The persecution index published annually by the Christian mission organization Open Doors offers a well-researched and troubling picture. In China (number 27 on the list in 2019), a recent law prohibiting children from being exposed to religious teaching has resulted in the closure of nursery and Sunday schools and summer camps, and has forced churches to post signs prohibiting entry to anyone under eighteen years of age. In Egypt, number 16 on the index and home to the largest population of Christians in the Middle East, churches are regularly harassed and attacked, and Christian girls are often kidnapped and forcibly married to Muslim men— all with little to no intervention on the part of authorities. In Pakistan, the antiblasphemy law introduced by the late president Zia-ul-Haq carries a possible sentence of death and has been used to threaten Christians.[31] We may not live under such second-half-of-Daniel threat, but many of our brothers and sisters do. Living among the wealthiest and most influential strata of the world's population, we can help those Christians who truly are being persecuted unto death in many places throughout the developing world. In the second half of Daniel we hear the cry of the persecuted global church. For those who live in safety, it is a summons to intercede on their behalf.

Daniel tells us that there has never been only one way to live out our status as members of the kingdom of God. What is critical is that we are constantly reflective regarding ourselves and society and are careful in thinking about how we should act out our identity as members of God's kingdom. To misread the culture may lead to ineffectiveness in engaging culture or to unwarranted pessimism when imagining the church's future. If we read Daniel as a roadmap to yet-future events, we must concede that it made scant sense to its initial audience and offers little instruction and encouragement for how we are to live in the present. Rightly understood culturally and historically, however, its message addresses its first readers and continues to challenge and sustain the church today.

# 8

# REVELATION

## APPROACHES TO REVELATION

Since their earliest days, Christians have used the book of Revelation to unravel the mysteries of the return of Christ and the end of the age. After all, it opens declaring that it is a revelation and prophecy (Rev 1:1–2) and ends pleading for Christ's soon return (Rev 22:20). Between these two statements, however, the material has admitted to multiple readings: Symbolic or literal events? Past or future? Since Revelation combines several genres (e.g., letters and prophecy in chs. 1–3; apocalyptic in chs. 4–22), further, some interpreters adopt different approaches for different sections. Typically, interpretative approaches have been divided into four: historicist, futurist, preterist, and idealist.[1] Let's take each in turn.

### HISTORICIST

Historicists understand Revelation to predict events in human history from the time of the original author up to the end-time return of Jesus. Most of those events, however, are to be found in the past. They are history to the modern reader (fig. 8.1). Some dispensationalists apply this approach to the letters to the seven churches at the beginning of the book (chs. 1–3; see fig. 8.2), while adopting a futurist take on the rest of the book.[2]

Others have applied it more extensively, even to the whole book. Among the Reformers, historicism was the dominant approach. Martin Luther, for example, identified the great harlot Babylon of chapter 17 with the Roman Catholic Church and the pope; Gog was the Turks, who in his day were threatening Christian Europe.[3] Another notable historicist, Sir Isaac Newton, provided a light treatment of Revelation at the end of a long work focusing mainly on Daniel.[4]

## Historicist View

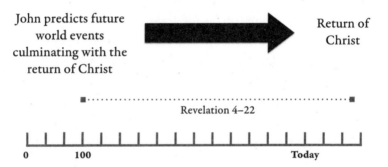

*Fig. 8.1. Historicist approach to Revelation*

This perspective invites readers to see the sovereignty of God displayed across the broad canvas of history. The contemporary reader can retrospectively see both prediction and fulfillment in major historical events. A serious problem, however, is one we've run into before: it abandons the original audience; only those who see in hindsight what God has done are rewarded. Furthermore, it is geographically limited. God is decidedly Mediterranean and Eurocentric in his interests; much of the world is simply omitted from prediction and fulfilment. Finally,

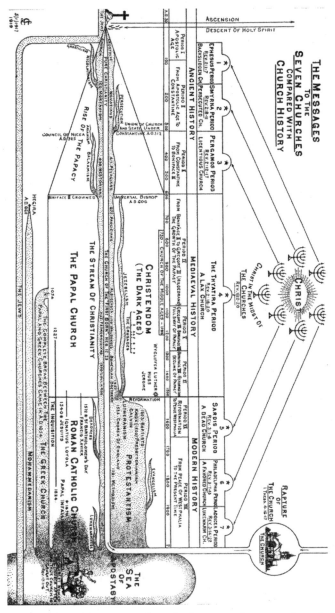

Fig. 8.2. Historicist approach to the letters to the seven churches
(Larkin)

historicism-as-hindsight results in wholesale revisions as subsequent generations of interpreters read the book from their own historical vantage point. The result? Disagreement over what events Revelation actually predicts.

Historicism enjoys the support of few today. Adherents are found primarily among Seventh Day Adventists and Jehovah's Witnesses, who retain William Miller's broad hermeneutical outlines, from whom both groups trace their descent. Outside these denominations, one will search in vain for a recently published commentary from this perspective.[5]

## FUTURIST

As the name implies, the futurist view sees Revelation as a road map to the future. Revelation is unfulfilled prophecy; to understand it is to understand God's plan for the end times. Although it is usually associated with dispensationalist end-times teachers we've critiqued in this book, it is not limited to them. In the sixteenth century, partly responding to the Reformers' anti-Catholic historicist interpretations, Jesuit scholar Jesuit Francisco Ribera (1537–1591) wrote a commentary on Revelation from a futurist perspective.[6] Since the time of Ribera, the futurist approach has tended to understand Revelation 4–22 to refer to events that immediately precede the return of Christ to earth. Consequently, futurism reads Revelation as describing the *modern* reader's future. Moreover, this future is *imminent*. Futurists spend a great deal of energy analyzing current events for occurrences that might correspond to Revelation's predictions. Positively, futurism takes Revelation seriously, seeing its warnings as for today's world and a tool for evangelism. Negatively, however, futurism shares historicism's fatal flaw. The original audience would have found little that spoke to their immediate situation.

# Futurist View

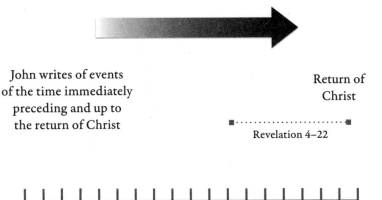

John writes of events
of the time immediately
preceding and up to
the return of Christ

Return of
Christ

Revelation 4–22

0          100                              Today

*Fig. 8.3. Futurist approach to Revelation*

Commentaries from the futurist perspective are uncommon among academic writers today. Its best expositors remain older dispensationalist authors.[7]

### PRETERIST

Preterism reads Revelation assuming the primacy of the original audience entirely. Its symbols and predictions apply to the literal Roman Empire of the late first century and the experience of the early church within it (fig. 8.4). First systematically proposed by a Jesuit named Luis de Alcazar (1554–1613), preterism was a response to the Reformers' penchant for historicism and its attendant anti-Catholic bias.[8] Preterism often dates Revelation's composition to the time of Nero (54–68) and identifies the great tribulation with the first revolt against Rome in AD 70. Some preterists further understand the return

# Preterist View

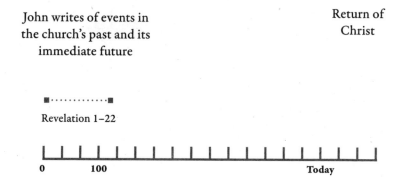

John writes of events in the church's past and its immediate future

Return of Christ

Revelation 1–22

0          100                                    Today

*Fig. 8.4. Preterist approach to Revelation*

of Christ and the resurrection of the saints as spiritual events that took place around the time.[9] This fully realized form of preterism has never achieved wide acceptance. Its placing of the return of Christ in the distant past is fundamentally at odds with the creeds of the church and reduces the parousia to a cosmically underwhelming event. Today, a modified form, "partial preterism," sees most of Revelation as speaking of the original audience's immediate past and near future, with perhaps the final three chapters referring to the end of time.

Partial preterism takes the opening words of Revelation 1:1 seriously. "The revelation from Jesus Christ, which God gave him to show his servants what *must soon take place*." As something that applied directly to the time of the original audience, the preterist approach sees the book as having had relevance for those who first received it. As those who see the book of Revelation as having been largely fulfilled in the first century, preterists often view the millennium as overlapping with the era of the church.

The tension between strict preterism and the creeds is not its only perceived problem. If historicism and futurism ignore the original audience, some have argued that preterism's preoccupation with it renders the book silent for the contemporary reader. If so, however, such a criticism would apply to most of the prophetic books of the Old Testament, whose predictions came to be in the life of ancient Israel. If the prophets can be read beneficially by believers today, then the same must hold true for the book of Revelation even if read from a preterist perspective.

The focus on the context of the original audience means that preterist commentaries often include much helpful information on the social, political, and religious context of the first-century Christian community. Although not widely held, preterism has found enthusiastic support among Christian reconstructionists or dominion-theology adherents who share its postmillennial stance.[10]

### IDEALIST

Last, idealism regards Revelation as a symbolic representation of the church's struggles with evil and its suffering at all times in the world (fig. 8.5). Thus, the harlot Babylon of Revelation 17 is not a specific person in the past or future but figures all the religious and political opposition that the church consistently faces. Idealism frees the text from historical and contextual constraint, making it available for ready application in the struggle against evil regardless of where and when the interpreter might be located.

On the positive side, by focusing on spiritual interpretation, idealists see Revelation as an abidingly relevant book that communicates spiritual truths applicable across time. They further claim a deep affinity with patristic methods of allegorical interpretation. Their critics counter that allegory is a slippery slope; divorced from historical and social contexts, Revelation becomes a wax nose, bending any which way. Lacking the hermeneutical constraints that come with paying proper attention to social, historical, and literary context, idealists tend to overlook the significance of *apocalyptic* as a genre and admit a wide range of possible meanings. The relatively unfettered way in which idealism can move from text to application has meant that the idealist approach has been employed by a wide range of interpreters, including social gospelers, feminists, and evangelicals.[11]

# Idealist View

(John writes symbolically of the struggles facing all believers at all times)

Return of Christ

0     100     Today

*Fig. 8.5. Idealist approach to Revelation*

### ECLECTIC

This book does not follow any of these approaches exclusively. Rather, it proceeds from the assumption adopted already in connection with the treatment of Ezekiel and Daniel: Revelation meant something to its original audience. Much of the book had to be understandable and immediately relevant for those who first encountered its message (partial preterism). Another factor is in play, however. Throughout the book, repeated appeals to

oft-seen biblical numbers and images from the Old Testament
suggest that the author is heavily invested in communicating his
message through symbolism (idealism and historicism). The
final chapters of the book, with their full and utter destruction
of Satan, death, and Hades, and the translation of the faithful
to a new heaven and new earth, suggest that part of Revelation
awaits fulfillment at the end of time (futurism). When it comes
to reading Revelation, we adopt an eclectic approach, and in
this we're in good company. Many recent commentaries recognize that no single hermeneutical approach entirely delivers
when it comes to understanding this complex book.[12]

## COMPOSITION AND DATING OF REVELATION

Theories of the dating of Revelation typically revolve around
three issues: (1) early Christian testimony, (2) known Roman
persecutions of Christians in the first two centuries AD, and
(3) internal evidence. Early Christian testimony is divided. Some
of the earliest and most important authorities place John's exile
to Patmos or the book itself sometime in the reign of the emperor
Domitian (AD 81–96). This was the view of Irenaeus of Lyons
(ca. 130–202; see *Against Heresies* 5.30.3), Eusebius of Caesarea
(ca. 263–ca. 339; see *Ecclesiastical History* 3.18.3), Victorinus
of Pettau (d. ca. 303; see *Commentary on the Apocalypse* 10.11),
Jerome (340–420; see *On Illustrious Men* 9), and Sulpicius
Severus (363–420; see *Chronicle* 2.31). Another leading con-
tender for the one who exiled the author of Revelation to Patmos
is the emperor Nero (AD 54–68). Some scholars have taken this
also to be implied in the writings of Clement of Alexandria (ca.
150–ca. 215) and Tertullian (ca. 155–ca. 240).[13] Many note that
the prologue to editions of the Syriac version of Revelation sets
the book in the time of Nero, but Revelation is among the latest
New Testament books added to the Syriac text, and the earliest

editions featuring this attestation hail from the sixth and seventh centuries.[14] Epiphanius (ca. 310–403), bishop of Salamis in Cyprus, dates the book's composition even earlier: to the reign of Tiberius Claudius (AD 41–54; see Epiphanius, *Panarion* 1.12.2; 1.33.9). Dorotheus of Gaza (505–565), on the other hand, locates it in the reign of Trajan (AD 98–117), but acknowledges that some in his day believed that John's exile to Patmos occurred during the time of Domitian.[15]

The broad range of dates above is understandable. Persecution was sporadic, but common until the fourth century. Nero persecuted Christians in Rome for starting the great fire of AD 63 (Tacitus [ca. 56–ca. 120], *Annals* 15.44). Roman historian Suetonius (ca. 69–ca. 122?) says nothing of the fire but libels Christians as "a new and mischievous superstition" (*Nero* 16.2). Church historian Eusebius of Caesarea recorded that both Peter and Paul were killed during this time (*Ecclesiastical History* 2.25.1–8). Problematically, Revelation addresses churches in Asia Minor (Rev 1–3), while Nero's persecution seems to have been limited to the vicinity of Rome itself.

How about Domitian? Eusebius cites Hegesippus (ca. 110–ca. 180), Tertullian, and Melito of Sardis (d. ca. 180) as accusing Domitian of killing the descendants of David, exhibiting cruelty, and slandering Christians (Eusebius, *Ecclesiastical History* 3.19–20; 3.20.9; 4.26.9). He maintains that Domitian followed in the footsteps of Nero as a persecutor of the church (Eusebius, *Ecclesiastical History* 3.17). Recent studies, however, have questioned whether Domitian oversaw an organized and severe persecution, noting that no ancient non-Christian historians make reference to any such program.[16] Trajan (AD 98–117) did authorize occasional persecutions of Christians and others whose loyalty to Rome was suspect. A remarkable correspondence between the emperor and his governor of Bithynia, Pliny the Younger (61–113), reveals something of a "don't ask, don't tell" policy in which Christians were not actively sought out, but were tried and executed if uncovered (Pliny the Younger, *Letters* 10.96–97). According to Eusebius, Ignatius of Antioch was one of those killed during this time (Eusebius, *Ecclesiastical History* 4.33–36). Hadrian (AD 117–138) continued Trajan's policy.

The latest possible date is the reign of Marcus Aurelius (AD 161–180), a Stoic whose view of the innate goodness of humans and the nature of the divine was at odds with Christianity. In the late second century, when bouts of plague and other natural disasters threatened parts of the empire, the emperor encouraged the population to turn to the traditional gods. It is likely that it was the refusal of Christians to engage in such worship rather than a specific edict targeting them for their faith that left them open to persecution.[17]

Even if Domitian's persecution is exaggerated and "official" persecutions were few, this does not mean that no persecutions—whether mob or state-sanctioned—took place. Today, for example, there is no official policy of persecution of Christians in India, Indonesia, Pakistan, Afghanistan, Egypt, Iraq, Nigeria, and scores of other countries in what evangelical missiologists call the 10–40 window (the area between 10° N and 40° N latitude). Yet harassment, displacement, destruction of property, forced marriage, and murder of Christians are well documented.[18] In many jurisdictions, governments and local officials tacitly allow attacks on Christians to proceed, mildly intervening once the damage is done. In Egypt, it is not uncommon for Christian girls to be kidnapped and forced into marriage outside their faith. In such circumstances, when parents appeal to authorities they are often told that the woman is now married and that this is a matter for her husband's family to sort out. In places such as Egypt and Indonesia, mobs have attacked and burned churches with no intervention from local police. All these violent acts have occurred without state sponsorship. Even in the age of social media and digital communication, they are little known in the west.

Absence of evidence is not evidence of absence. The lack of ancient non-Christian documentation does not mean there were no persecutions. For example, what is clear from Acts 19:23–41 and the account of the public riot against Paul and his colleagues at Ephesus is that spontaneous, uncontrolled public attacks against Christians sometimes did occur, which public officials struggled to contain. The New Testament evidence also suggests that persecution proceeded with the connivance of the authorities, if not with the official sanction of the state. What seems clear from Acts 16:12–24 and the attack on Paul and Silas at Philippi is that mob attacks on Christians could occur at random and involve the *cooperation* of the authorities even in the absence of an official program targeting Christians. The absence of official Roman persecution does not mean, then, that persecution did not take place or that Roman authorities did not give their approval to spontaneous, popular persecution. With regard to the dating of Revelation, comparison with the reality of persecution of Christians in the world today means that the dating of the book does not hinge on the existence of an official state policy of persecution.

If the external evidence is ambivalent, so is the internal evidence. Supporters of a Neronic date can point to several factors. Chief among these is the command to John to "go and measure the temple of God and the altar, with its worshipers" (Rev 11:1). Seemingly presupposing the existence of the temple in Jerusalem, this suggests a date prior to AD 70. Still, this chapter is part of a visionary experience, and the temple in question may not be a physical one. The Neronic date is also supported by Revelation 17:10, where the writer refers to seven kings, five of whom had "fallen" and "one who is." If the first king is Julius Caesar (100–44 BC), the first acknowledged emperor of Rome, then the sixth king is Nero. Julius Caesar, however, is not the only starting point. One could count from the beginning of the Julio-Claudian dynasty, making Nero the fifth emperor and his successor, Galba (June 68–January 69), the sixth. Furthermore, if one starts after the demise of the Julio-Claudian dynasty and begins with the four emperors of the year 69 and the Flavian dynasty, which followed, then the sixth king becomes Domitian. Finally, if one considers the term "fallen" of Revelation 17:10 to refer to death at the hands of another, then counting only those emperors who were murdered, the sixth king could be Domitian, who also died a violent death.[19]

## "NERO CAESAR"

666

*Fig. 8.6. Numerical value of the title "Nero Caesar"*

Another thread of evidence revolves around the perennially fascinating question of the identity of "the beast," identified only with the cryptic word that his number is "666" (Rev 13:18). An untold number of proposals continue to be advanced with regularity even today. It is likely, however that the author had Nero in mind (fig. 8.6). If one transcribes the title of Nero into

Aramaic—the language of many first-century Christians and Jews—then by one reckoning, it adds up to 666.[20] Revelation also speaks of the beast's healed fatal wound (Rev 13:3), a detail that might have in mind the *Nero redivivus* myth and any one of the three known Neronic pretenders that arose following the death of Nero in AD 68. The last of these "revived Neros" appeared in the time of Domitian. Thus, while the number 666 points to Nero, his "resurrection" might extend the identification beyond Nero himself. This may be supported by the fact that in each of its digits, 666 falls one short of seven, a number associated in Scripture with deity, fullness, and perfection. This "shortcoming" is consistent with the identity of the beast as one who lays claim to divine status but falls short and so might apply to all who, like Nero, claim deity and sit on the throne of the Roman Empire.

The number associated with the beast clearly shows that the figure of Nero loomed large for the author of Revelation. It does not, however, preclude the possibility that this number could also have been associated with subsequent emperors. This is especially the case if Revelation 13:3, 12 alludes to the *Nero redivivus* myth. The identity of the sixth king in Revelation 17:10 is similarly open to question. Depending on with whom one begins and how one interprets the word "fallen," the sixth king could be Nero or Domitian.

Most modern interpreters divide over Nero and Domitian to date the book, with Domitian in a slight lead.[21] Straddling the debate, one scholar has argued that Revelation took its initial shape in the time of Nero and its final form during the reign of Trajan.[22] Fortunately, little hangs on precision here. Within the three-decade span that separates the most likely periods of composition, there was no significant change in Christian beliefs or in Roman attitudes. In both the time of

Nero and Domitian, Christians were the worshipers of Jesus of
Nazareth, the one true God, who was crucified and rose from
the dead. Rome remained a global empire founded on poly-
theism and submission to an all-powerful emperor. In both
contexts, Christians could not engage in many of the practices
that marked one as a good citizen, and this left them vulnerable to discrimination and attack, whether through official edict
or whispered innuendo.

## THE DISPENSATIONALIST VIEW OF REVELATION

Dispensationalists see the bulk of chapters 6–19 of Revelation—
the majority of the book and easily its most densely symbolic
part—as referring to the seven years of the great tribulation,
placing them firmly in the futurist camp.[23] The book begins,
however, not with bizarre symbolism, but with letters to
seven churches in the Roman province of Asia Minor. Here
Pentecost speaks for many dispensationalists in adopting three
interpretative approaches simultaneously. Historically, the letters are pastoral missives to first-century churches. Spiritually,
they represent true and false Christians throughout the ages.
Prophetically, they foretell eras of church history.[24] Of these
three the latter dominates. Interpreters understand the churches
as seven historical epochs and thus view this part of the book,
at least, through a historicist lens. Those taking this approach
generally see 4:1 as a point of transition and regard what follows
as referring to the future from the perspective of the contemporary reader: "After this I looked, and there before me was a
door standing open in heaven. And the voice I had first heard
speaking to me like a trumpet said, 'Come up here, and I will
show you *what must take place after this.*'"

If this is the case, then how does one get from the time of
the original audience to our future? Historicists see the letters

to the churches as describing epochs of history that bridge that gap between the context of the audience and last days. Specific identifications differ, but a common schema identifies Ephesus with the apostolic age; Smyrna with the persecutions under Nero, Diocletian, and Maximillian; Pergamum with the legalization of Christianity under Constantine; Thyatira with the papacy; Sardis with the Western post-Enlightenment church; Philadelphia with the Great Awakening and the missionary work of the English-speaking countries; and Laodicea with the uncommitted and lukewarm church of the modern Western world.[25]

As noted already, in historicism, God restricts his attention to Europe and the Mediterranean basin to the exclusion of parts of the world such as Africa and South America, which today are home to the majority of the world's Christians. More fundamentally, however, this approach to Revelation 1–3 fails on the grounds that there is no evidence at all in the text that suggests taking this material as anything other than it claims to be, namely, a series of letters to churches in Asia Minor in the time of John that were facing multiple challenges.

While dispensationalists differ on the details, there is wide agreement that Revelation 4–19 refers to the seventieth week of Daniel, or the tribulation. This is related to the description of troubles or tribulations that are found in Jesus's words in Matthew 24:3–51, "Nation will rise against nation, and kingdom against kingdom. There will be famines and earthquakes in various places" (Matt 24:7). The Matthew passage has all the elements that one finds in Revelation 4–19—war, betrayal, martyrdom, false Christs, and more—all of which culminate in the return of Christ himself.

End-times teachers debate among themselves whether the events of the seals (6:1–8:5), trumpets (8:6–11:19), and bowls (15:1–16:21) are sequential or whether there is some overlap between them. Tim LaHaye regards these things as a sequential description of events during the tribulation.[26] Dwight Pentecost agrees that the events of Revelation 4–19 fall into the seventieth week of Daniel and the great tribulation, but sees some overlap within this material. According to his view, chapters 4–11 depict Daniel's seventieth week and culminate with the return of Christ in 11:15–18.

> The seventh angel sounded his trumpet, and there were
>> loud voices in heaven, which said:
> "The kingdom of the world has become
>> the kingdom of our Lord and of his Messiah,
>> and he will reign for ever and ever."
> And the twenty-four elders, who were seated on their
>> thrones before God, fell on their faces and worshiped
>> God, saying:
> "We give thanks to you, Lord God Almighty,
>> the One who is and who was,
> because you have taken your great power
>> and have begun to reign.
> The nations were angry,
>> and your wrath has come.
> The time has come for judging the dead,
>> and for rewarding your servants the prophets
> and your people who revere your name,
>> both small and great—
> and for destroying those who destroy the earth."

According to this view, the seals that are loosed in 6:1–8:5 represent the events of the first 3.5 years of the tribulation, and the trumpets of 8:7–11:19 correspond to the second 3.5 years. Chapters 12–19, with the figures of chapters 11–12, the judgments of the bowls (chs. 15–16), and the judgments against

Babylon (chs. 17–18), represent a second survey of the events of the entire tribulation (cf. 10:11), at the end of which comes the victorious return of Christ (ch. 19).[27]

After the return of Christ and the battle of Armageddon in chapter 19, there follows the marriage supper of the Lamb, in which the church is presented to the returned Christ as a bride to her husband (19:6–9).[28] Following this, Christ reigns on earth for one thousand years. Faithful Jewish people figure prominently at this time, and the antichrist and Satan are incarcerated (20:2–6).[29] After this period, these two enemies of God are released and attempt to lead a rebellion against God. They are defeated and are finally and ultimately destroyed in the lake of fire (20:10–15), after which the world is recreated and God and the faithful live together forever.[30]

But is this a sound reading? What happens if our orienting question is not "What does this mean for us?" but "What did it mean to the original readers?" Let's examine the difficult world of power and persecution in which those early Christians lived first.

## LIFE IN ROMAN ASIA,
### THE LETTERS TO THE SEVEN CHURCHES

For Trans-Canada Highway travelers, the town of Wawa, Ontario, comes as a blessed relief from the rugged north shore of Lake Superior. An oasis in an unending expanse of granite and boreal forest, Wawa owes its prosperity to the highway that brings travelers to its door. With the completion in 1960 of the strip of asphalt linking Wawa to the outside world, the town imagined a soaring monument at the highway exit that would entice weary travelers to pause and enjoy all that Wawa had to offer. Thus was born the famous "Wawa Goose." At twenty-eight feet tall and boasting an impressive wingspan of twenty feet, the Wawa Goose holds the distinction of being the largest metal roadside waterfowl sculpture in Canada—if not the world. While not in quite the same league as Mount Rushmore or Niagara Falls, the Wawa Goose has done its job, annually diverting hundreds of thousands of travelers into the nearby downtown, where they are deftly parted from their dollars before resuming their journey.

Civic pride and local boosterism are not modern innovations. In the Roman province of Asia, cities competed for honors and status that enhanced the local reputation and enriched the economy. Among these, the most sought-after was the title of *neōkoros* or "temple warden." Deriving from a term referring to one who swept a temple precinct, by the first century AD it was an honor granted by the senate or emperor in Rome to select cities that had built shrines dedicated to the emperor. Far more prestigious than any modern roadside attraction, this title was a major source of local pride, and through the pilgrim trade to the associated temples it was also a major source of revenue for cities to which it was granted. The status of *neōkoros* was celebrated in inscriptions and on coins, and all good citizens embraced it as a sign of municipal achievement.[31] For the early Christians of Asia, the status of *neōkoros* and the emperor worship associated with it was one of many facts of life that placed them in a potentially perilous relationship with societal norms and the expectations of their neighbors.

This is one small snapshot of the world inhabited by Revelation's first readers. If God inspired John to write to a group of Christians living in this world, then it's reasonable to assume that it addresses their situation and concerns first. We propose, therefore, to read Revelation in the same way as we have Ezekiel and Daniel above. Starting here makes possible a series of questions. What was the world inhabited by those early Christians to whom John addresses his book? In what kind of world did they live? What were its values? And how did that world and values create challenges for those whose chose to follow Jesus?

Let's start with life in the Roman province of Asia Minor. You can accuse the Romans of a lot of things, but certainly not low self-esteem. Revelation was written at the height of Roman power: by the second century's end, the empire extended from Britain in the west to the Persian Gulf in the east, and from Germany in the north to North Africa in the south. Look at the map of the world below (fig. 8.7). Produced by Marcus Vipsanius Agrippa (ca. 64–12 BC), the right-hand man to Caesar Augustus (27–14 BC), it visually declared to everyone the global extent of Roman power.[32] The map shows the Mediterranean Sea and Rome at its center, with the rest of the world curving around it: Rome was the center of the world, and its power was unstoppable.

The center of this vast empire was the city of Rome and the emperor himself. An all-powerful entity to whom loyalty and devotion must be given, Rome was personified as a *deity*, the goddess Roma—often referred to as "Roma Aeterna" (Eternal Rome). The earliest evidence for Roma's cult comes not from Rome itself, but Smyrna (ca. 195 BC), home to one of the churches to which Revelation is addressed.[33] Several decades later, Attalus III (ca. 170–130 BC), the king of Pergamum, died without a male heir. An ally of the Roman state, he bequeathed his people and kingdom to Rome in his will. Thus Attalus's kingdom became the Roman province of Asia, and the cult of Roma in particular flourished. Roma was depicted as a beautiful woman dressed in a white robe and is often shown seated with helmet, shield, and spear. Among other things, Roma conveyed that the state was militarily powerful and required the devotion and submission of all. Modern depictions of "Britannia" are modeled on Roma (see fig. 8.8).

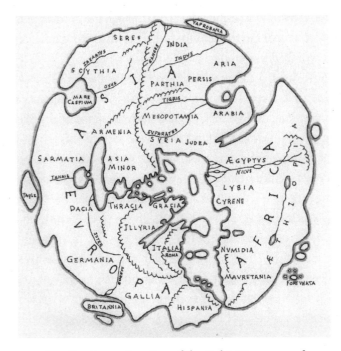

Fig. 8.7. Reconstruction of the Orbis Terrarum of
Marcus Agrippa (ca. AD 20)

Fig. 8.8. Britannia (left) and
the goddess Roma (right)

In addition to worshiping the state through the goddess Roma, those who lived in the empire (whether citizens or not) could also worship the emperor. The practice began slowly; in its earliest days, a deceased emperor could be declared to be divine by the senate. Later, worshiping a living emperor was also possible, though this seems to have been more popular in Asia than in Rome itself, where it was seen as unseemly and created potential conflict with the power of the senate. Asia's Hellenistic cultural heritage, however, meant that worship of a living monarch was not at all novel. For example, the Seleucid king Antiochus IV (r. 175–163 BC), who figures in the book of Daniel, adopted the epithet "Epiphanes," or "god manifest." Worship of the Roman emperor seems to have been enthusiastically embraced by all strata of society in the province of Asia.[34] In Rome, a few emperors took the unusual step of declaring themselves to be gods and demanding worship during their lifetimes. For the study of Revelation, the most important of these were Nero (AD 54–68) and Domitian (AD 81–96).

Cities striving for the title of *neōkoros* could erect a temple dedicated to the emperor. The right to display this title was a matter of civic pride, and so refusal to worship the emperor on the part of Jews and Christians put both groups in a difficult position. Unlike Christians, however, Jews had an established history within the empire, and an accommodation to their religion was made that allowed them to sacrifice in the temple in Jerusalem *on behalf* of, rather than to, the emperor. After the destruction of the temple in AD 70, however, this was no longer possible. Even so, an exemption for Jews was maintained for the practical reason that they were numerous, prosperous, well connected throughout the empire, and known as monotheists. Given this, it didn't make sense to antagonize them.

This does not mean that Jewish life was uncomplicated. Josephus records how in the late third century BC, the Seleucid king Antiochus III transferred two thousand Jewish families to western Asia Minor to quell unrest in the recently conquered region, granting them land, provisions, and tax exemptions (Josephus, *Jewish Antiquities* 12.148–53). Following the Treaty of Apamea and the transfer of this territory to the local Attalid dynasty, however, the lot of these Jews suddenly became precarious. How would the newly empowered local inhabitants view the foreign interlopers who had been brought in to keep them under control? Even in the first century AD, a people with such a history would have been keen to keep a low profile and to be seen as good citizens.

Promoters of the gospel such as the apostle Paul unhelpfully raised that profile. The synagogue was always his first stop when he was evangelizing (Acts 17:2; 18:19; 19:8). Even with their special status, Jews in Asia strove to avoid anything that might harm their relationships in society and with the state. That Christians followed a man executed by the Roman state for sedition, declaring that man to be their one true king and god, tested the Jewish population's clear interest in keeping the peace and being good citizens. As much as the Jewish population of Asia might have seen a kinship with the followers of Jesus who were now in the synagogue, they were also keen to avoid guilt by association. Given this, there was always the potential for conflict between the two groups (Rev 2:9; 3:9).

Early Christians of the province of Asia thus lived in a potentially dangerous world. As followers of the crucified and risen Christ, the universal King, they placed themselves on a path that led to potential conflict with their Jewish and gentile neighbors. The former did not want controversy; the latter enthusiastically embraced the worship of both state and emperor. To follow Jesus meant denying things that made you a good citizen. You weren't a good neighbor. The letters to the seven churches of Asia laud and warn the followers of Jesus to encourage them to live faithful and watchful lives in this milieu. Now, how did the book of Revelation address their situation? Let's begin with a bird's-eye view of the book itself.

## THE SHAPE AND MEANING OF REVELATION

### THE STRUCTURE AND MESSAGE OF
### THE BOOK OF REVELATION

Based on an examination of literary genre and transitional phrases, Revelation falls into three sections: an *introduction* (1:1–3:22), followed by a *body* (4:1–20:15), and finally a *conclusion* (21:1–22:21).

The introduction opens by declaring that what follows is a "revelation" (or unveiling) of the risen Christ, who has observed the suffering of the faithful and will now communicate what will soon happen (1:1–20). This is followed by a series of short, formulaic letters addressed to seven churches in Asia Minor (2:1–3:22). Revelation 4:1 announces a temporal shift with the phrase "after this." The text's genre also shifts from epistle to the apocalyptic language of visions. Interpreters differ on what constitutes the conclusion to the book. We place it at 21:1 because of the major shift of locale from the extant world to the new heaven and the new earth.

Although it happens in different ways in different genres, most biblical books signal what the book is going to be about and what themes and motifs to look for right at the beginning. If there are motifs and thematic elements that are emphasized in the introduction to a book, then it makes sense to see whether they are developed and resolved through the rest of the book. While persecution is a huge part of Revelation and figures prominently in the letters to the seven churches, these letters are not *all* about physical persecution. They tell of a *range* of challenges that the followers of Jesus face, including being too comfortable in society (2:20; 3:15–16). Each of the churches Christ addresses bears its own unique set of burdens—some more obvious than others. As a whole, this introductory material functions much like the overture to an opera, setting the tone and theme for the rest of the work. Elements introduced in this section in the context of the here-and-now struggles of the seven churches will recur in various forms in the visionary materials that form the main part of the book and will often appear in the conclusion to the book.

## INTRODUCTION (REV 1–3)

### *The Initial Vision (Rev 1)*

The initial chapter of Revelation prepares the reader for the content to come by establishing three key truths. First, verses 4–5 reassure readers at the outset that the heavenly Father and Son are in control and that victory is theirs. Then John answers two critical questions of identity: Who is Jesus? and, Who are we? Jesus, he says, is the "ruler of the kings of the earth"— immediately displacing Rome—and we, according to verse 6, are a "kingdom and priests." Identity as a kingdom marks us as ruled by Christ (not Rome or any earthly power). As priests, we are intermediaries and witnesses on earth to God. What some would ascribe to Rome—namely, "glory and power"— actually belong to God. Third, verse 9 establishes the author as not merely a contemporary, but also a co-sufferer with his audience in all that they are undergoing and will experience in the future. Far from a detached observer free from harm, he has already experienced arrest and banishment.

In verse 10, John hears a voice like the sound of a trumpet that calls him to write to the churches. In ancient Israel, trumpets called to worship or to battle, and warned people of an approaching enemy. In Second Temple Jerusalem (the time of Jesus), an inscription marked the spot at the southwest corner of the temple precinct from which the priest blew the trumpet to mark the start of the Sabbath.[35] John notes the occasion of this trumpet blast. The vision comes to John on the *tē kyriakē hēmera*, rendered by most translations as "the Lord's Day," and this is probably the intended meaning here. To contemporary ears, this brings to mind Sunday and worship. Elsewhere in the New Testament, however, the day of Christian worship was referred to as the "first day of the week" (Matt 28:1; Mark 16:2, 9; John 20:1, 19; Acts 20:7; 1 Cor 16:2). Throughout the Old Testament, these words, albeit in the opposite order (*hēmeras Kyriou*), refer to the "day of the Lord," that moment in history when God intervenes to bring judgment. This ambiguity is fitting, for the remainder of the book will alternate between acts of worship and judgment.

In Revelation 1:12–15, Christ appears ablaze, in a guise that is reminiscent of the picture of the enthroned Yahweh seen by Ezekiel in Ezekiel 1: "Above the vault over their heads was what looked like a throne of lapis lazuli, and high above on the throne was a figure like that of a man. I saw that from what appeared to be his waist up he looked like glowing metal, as if full of fire, and that from there down he looked like fire; and brilliant light surrounded him" (Ezek 1:26–27). Drawing on Ezekiel at this point makes clear the *deity* of Christ and his *authority*. In both settings, the image is of a figure awesome and ablaze against whom no one can stand. Christ is the one who is living and active in the world and who will achieve victory.

In Revelation 1:16, we see the means by which the risen Christ will act. Holding "seven stars" in his right hand and a sword in his mouth is not what is expected. Normally, the weapon is in the right hand. The image of gods and kings wielding weapons in their upraised right hand is common in ancient Near Eastern iconography. Placed here, this image shows at the outset that despite their current persecution, the fundamental identity of the seven churches is not one of victim, but as those who are key agents in the plans of the risen Christ. That the angels attached to the churches are in his right hand suggests that the churches are an important part of Christ's plans for the world. The churches have an important role to play in the battle against the evil one.

In verse 17, we have Jesus's second words in the book, in which he describes himself as "the First and the Last." This is another claim of deity in that these words quote the self-description of Yahweh in Isaiah 44:6 and 48:12:

> This is what the LORD says—
>     Israel's King and Redeemer, the LORD Almighty:
> I am the first and I am the last;
>     apart from me there is no God. (Isa 44:6)
> Listen to me, O Jacob,
>     Israel, whom I have called:
> I am he;
>     I am the first and I am the last. (Isa 48:12)

Jesus affirms his divine identity—to the *exclusion* of all others. For those living in the cosmopolitan, polytheistic world that was the Roman Empire, this statement girded the followers of Jesus against the temptation to worship other deities on the grounds that there were *many* pathways to God. Jesus's words testify to his sufficiency and his power. It is because he is God that he has the power to deliver, which he will exercise through the book.

Furthermore, as he is "the First and the Last," nothing comes before or after Jesus. He has the final word—a fact that robs death of any real or imagined authority. In Revelation 1:18, then—here at the beginning of the book—we have the idea clearly expressed that Christ has power over death and Hades. This gives hope through what is to follow and provides an *inclusio* (or a literary bookend) to what happens at the close of Revelation, where Christ raises the dead and sends others to the second death. Verse 19 carries on with what to expect— what John writes relates to his present and his future.

In verse 20, Jesus stands among seven lampstands, items symbolic of the seven churches. In the tabernacle and the temple of Solomon, the seven-branched lampstand, the menorah, stood to the left opposite the table of showbread in the holy place (Exod 25:31–36; 40:22–25). The lamps were to be kept constantly lit because they symbolized God's abiding presence with Israel. In the New Testament, the church is described as the body of Christ, equipped to be his presence in the world (1 Cor 12:27–31; Eph 2:10; 4:11–16). This makes the lampstands an apt image for the churches, which are the body of Christ, his presence in the world.

In this first section of Revelation, we get a sense of the recipients and their role in the world. More importantly, we also get a sense of who is on their side and what the outcome of the future struggle is going to be. With this in mind, we can move on to the letters to the seven churches of Asia Minor. The literary order of the letters to the seven churches— Ephesus, Smyrna, Pergamum, Thyatira, Sardis, Philadelphia,

Laodicea—corresponds geographically to what might have been an itinerary of earlier pastoral travels of the author of the book.

In thinking about the relationship of the introduction to the rest of the book, it is helpful to keep in mind the two worlds that we find in apocalyptic and other literature in the Bible and to which we have drawn attention already. There is the earthly world that we inhabit and can know through the five senses, but there is also the heavenly or spiritual world, which is just as real, but is largely invisible to us. This connection between the earthly and the cosmic is indicated in part in that in the letters to the seven churches, Christ is introduced to each church using a portion of the description of the risen Christ given in chapter 1. The letters to the churches address those living in the earthly world, but importantly warn them of behaviors and events that have significance in the spiritual or heavenly realm. The cosmic significance of earthly behavior is what is spelled out when we come to the visions of the book that look directly into the goings-on in the heavenly realms. This connection between the letters and the visions is important to keep in mind as we venture further into the book.

*The Letters to the Seven Churches (Rev 2–3)*

Ephesus (Rev 2:1–7)

Ephesus was a major port city in the Roman province of Asia. From there goods from across western Anatolia could be sent by ship to Greece, Rome, and points beyond.[36] The apostle Paul clearly saw potential in this place, making it his base of operations for two to three years (Acts 19:1–20:1). Under Emperor Augustus, the city flourished and was awarded the title "First and greatest metropolis of Asia." The city was famous for its temple to Artemis (Diana), listed by Antipater of Sidon as one of the seven wonders of the world. It was several times larger than the Parthenon in Greece and featured a massive statue of the goddess (Antipater of Sidon, *Greek Anthology* 9.58).[37] While the port gave Ephesus its wealth, the temple of Artemis endowed it with prestige.

Temples in the ancient world were not just places of worship, but also functioned as financial institutions, and more than one ancient writer describes the temple of Artemis at Ephesus as functioning like a chartered bank (Aelius Aristides, *Orations* 23.24; Dio Chrysostom, *Discourse* 31.54–56). Income derived from outlying temple agricultural estates could be lent out at interest, and gold, silver, and other precious objects could be placed on deposit, safeguarded by temple administrators and the sanctity of the shrine itself. More obvious than its financial role was the function the temple served as a major pilgrimage destination, and like any such site, it supported a wide range of merchants and individuals who profited from the constant flow of worshipers. Evidence of this is found in Acts 19:23–41 where Paul's preaching is seen to threaten the financial well-being of the town's guild of silversmiths, whose livelihood came in part from making small silver copies of the great statue found in the shrine.

Following the death of Julius Caesar (r. 45–44 BC), a portion of a smaller temple to Artemis in the city was dedicated to the worship of the slain emperor. The forum of the city boasted a temple to Augustus and the goddess Roma.[38] The figure of emperor Domitian loomed large over the city, both during his lifetime and after his death. In AD 89/90, a temple to Domitian was consecrated, featuring a colossal statue of the emperor. In keeping with its devotion and status, the city was granted the title *neōkoros*, marking it as home to the imperial cult.[39]

| Church | Approval & Warning in Letters (2–3) | Cosmic Parallels | Final Reward/Penalty |
|---|---|---|---|
| Ephesus | tested *false* (*pseudeis*) apostles (2:2) | *false* prophet (*pseudo-prophētou*) appears (16:13) | the *false* (*pseudesin*) will be consigned to the lake of fire (21:8) |
| | steadfast *endurance* (*hypomonēn*; 2:2–3) | *endurance* (*hypomonē*) required (13:10; 14:12) | |
| | will eat of *tree of life* (*xylou tēs zōēs*) in paradise (2:7) | | *tree of life* (*xylon zōēs / xylon tēs zōēs / xylou tēs zōēs*) in a new Eden (22:2, 14, 19) |

*Table 8.1. The Letter to the Church at Ephesus*

To the church at Ephesus (table 8.1), Christ is described as the one who stands among the "lampstands" (*lychniōn*; Rev 2:1), an image that appears again in the body of the book in reference to the two martyred witnesses (11:4). The believers at Ephesus are praised for having tested and rejected the "false" (*pseudeis*) apostles who have tried to lead them astray (2:2). Later in the book, Satan will loose a "false prophet" (*pseudoprophētou*) on the world in an attempt to lure people away from God (16:13). In the conclusion of the book, the "liars" or the "false ones" (*pseudesin*) are among those thrown into the lake of fire (21:8). The Ephesians have endured steadfastly (*hypomonēn*) for Christ (2:2–3). Even so, they are not following Christ as they once did. This is important because perseverance or endurance (*hypomonē*) is exactly what is required of the faithful in the persecution that takes place in the central portion of the book (13:10; 14:12). Here and in each of the messages that follow, the emphasis is, "Get your act together in the present so you'll be ready for the challenges that I know lie in your future." The words to the Ephesians end with the promise that if they endure, Christ will give them the "right to eat from the tree of life [*xylou tēs zōēs*], which is in the paradise of God" (2:7). This reference to the tree of life and the garden connects this material with the conclusion of the book, where the "tree of life" (*xylou tēs zōēs*) appears again, and the new Jerusalem is described in terms reminiscent of the garden of Eden (22:2, 14, 19; see Gen 2:9). Here in the letter to the church of Ephesus, John introduces a danger that is cosmically depicted in the body of the book and a reward that is similarly depicted at the close of the book.

## Smyrna (Rev 2:8–11)

Smyrna lived in the shadow of the more successful port of nearby Ephesus. Even so, the Smyrnaeans could find solace in the thought that their city was the birthplace of the great poet Homer—a comfort they shared with at least half a dozen other Ionian towns and cities. More concretely, the people of Smyrna could take pride in the fact that of all of the cities of Asia, they were the first to establish the worship of the goddess Roma (ca. 195 BC)—and this long before they became part of the Roman Empire (Tacitus, *Annals* 4.56). Such a move was a solid vote in favor of the young Roman republic, since it came at a time when the Seleucid monarch Antiochus III (the Great) (r. 223–187 BC) was extending his empire into western Anatolia. In AD 26, in the reign of Tiberius (r. AD 14–37), and again during the reign of Hadrian (r. AD 117–38), the city's devotion was rewarded with the title *neōkoros*.[40]

| Church | Approval & Warning in Letters (2–3) | Cosmic Parallels | Final Reward/ Penalty |
|---|---|---|---|
| Smyrna | slandered (*tēn blasphēmian*) by the synagogue of Satan (2:9) | beast has heads with *blasphemous names* (*blasphēmias*; 13:1) & utters *blasphemies* (*blasphēmias*; 13:5–6)<br><br>Babylon rides beast with *blasphemous* names (*blasphēmias*; 17:3) | |
| | future *suffering* (*thlipsin*), imprisonment, persecution (2:9, 10) | martyrs emerge from the great *tribulation* (*thlipseōs*; 7:14) | |
| | be faithful to death, get crown of *life* (*zōēs*; 2:10) | martyred given *living* (*zōēs*) water (7:17) | faithful brought to *life* (*ezēsan*; verb *zaō*) in first resurrection (20:5–6) |
| | *victorious* (*nikōn*) avoid *second death* (*tou thanatou tou deuterou*; 2:11) | | *one who is victorious* (*nikōn*); (21:7) drinks from spring of *life* (*zōēs*; 21:6) & avoids *second death* (*ho thanatos ho deuteros*; 21:8; also 20:6, 14) |

*Table 8.2. The Letter to the Church at Smyrna*

To the Smyrnaeans, Christ is introduced as the "First and the Last" and the one who was dead but is now alive (2:8). The Christians at Smyrna had experienced oppression and poverty and had been slandered (*tēn blasphēmian*) by members of the Jewish community (2:9; see table 8.2). In the body of the book, the ultimate source of such slander is revealed as the beast who arises to utter "slander" (*blasphēmias*) against the name of God and is covered with blasphemous names (13:1, 5; 17:3). Unfortunately for the followers of Jesus at Smyrna, the future will be worse—they will suffer "tribulation" (*thlipsin*) to the point of death (2:10), and in the central section of the book "tribulation" (*thlipseōs*) and death are exactly what the faithful will experience (7:14). Those who are faithful to the point of death, however, will be rewarded with a crown of "life" (*zōēs*; 2:10) and will avoid the "second death" (*tou thanatou tou deuterou*; 2:11). In the body of Revelation we see the martyred restored to life, inhabiting the heavenly throne room and nourished with living (*zōēs*) water (7:17). Those at Smyrna who endure and are "victorious" (*nikōn*) will avoid the "second death" (2:11). At the end of the book, as John witnesses the creation of the new heaven and the new earth, the risen Christ declares that the one who is "victorious" (*nikōn*; 21:7) will receive water from the spring of life (*zōēs*; 21:6) and avoid the second death (*ho thanatos ho deuteros*; 21:8; also 20:6, 14), which awaits those who stand in unrelenting opposition to God.

## Pergamum (Rev 2:12–17)

Pergamum was the capital of a small independent kingdom whose final ruler was Attalus III (r. 138–33 BC). On his death, the childless Attalus willed his realm to the Roman republic, which used it as the basis of the Roman province of Asia (Strabo, *Geography* 13.4.1–2). Such a transfer is not all that surprising, since the dynasty of which Attalus was a part initially received its territory as part of the Treaty of Apamea (188 BC), in which the conquering Romans redistributed the Seleucid holdings in Asia Minor to trustworthy allies. The city had a library that rivaled that of Alexandria in Egypt and fittingly became a center for the production and export of parchment (Pliny the Elder, *Natural History* 13.21.70).[41] In 19 BC, the city became the first city in the province of Asia to be granted the status of *neōkoros*, an honor that accompanied the completion of its temple to the goddess Roma and Caesar Augustus.[42] The acropolis of the city towered an imposing one thousand feet above the surrounding river valley and was crowned by the temple of Zeus, a shrine that most interpreters identify as "the throne of Satan" referred to in Revelation 2:13.

Christ's words to the faithful of Pergamum note how they have endured persecution, with one of their number, a certain Antipas, having been executed for his faith (2:13). Despite their faithfulness, however, some were deceived by false teaching. Allusion to the Old Testament story of Balaam suggests that some have been led into idolatry and sexual immorality (2:14; see Num 22–24; 31:13–19). The appeal to the story of Balaam is apt, not only in the idolatry that threatened the faithful in both cases, but also in that, like the sacred precinct of Pergamum located atop the city's acropolis, Balaam's attempt to destroy Israel was launched from atop the cliffs of Moab, looking down on the Israelites spread out in the valley below (Num 23:6–30). Just as the Israelites were judged when lured into sexual immorality and idolatry with the Moabites, the church at Pergamum is at a similar risk if it is seduced by the teaching of the Nicolaitans (Rev 2:15–16).

Christ's letter identifies Pergamum as home to the "throne [*thronos*] of Satan" (2:13; see table 8.3). In the central portion of the book we read that the dragon (i.e., Satan) gives the beast a "throne" (*thronon*) and that the dragon is *worshiped* (13:2). At Pergamum, we see the faithful lauded for being true to the "name" (*onoma*) of Christ (2:13), but nonetheless facing the temptation of *idolatry* and sexual *immorality* (*porneusai*; 2:14). In the central part of the book, the faithful who have remained *sexually pure and virginal*[43] take the "name" (*onoma*) of the Lamb on their foreheads and *worship* before God's throne in heaven (14:1–4). In this same chapter is announced the fall of Babylon, who had made the nations participants in her

| Church | Approval & Warning in Letters (2–3) | Cosmic Parallels | Final Reward/ Penalty |
|---|---|---|---|
| Pergamum | strong for my *name* (*onoma*), did not renounce me (2:13) | faithful take *name* (*onoma*) of Lamb on their foreheads (7:4) | |
| | will receive a white stone with a new *name* (*onoma*; 2:17) | martyred with *name* (*onoma*), sing praise in heaven (14:1) | |
| | city is home to Satan & his *throne* (*thronos*; 2:13) | Dragon (Satan) gives the beast a *throne* (*thronon*; 13:2) | |
| | | Dragon (Satan) is worshiped (13:4) | |
| | some have fallen to idols & *sexual immorality* (*porneusai*; 2:14) | sexually pure & virginal take *name* (*onoma*) of Lamb & worship (14:1–4) Babylon, mother of *prostitutes* (*pornōn*) & abominations (17:5), causes nations & kings to commit *sexual immorality* (*porneias*; 14:8; 18:3, also 9) | |
| | Christ will fight unrepentant with the *sword of his mouth* (*en tē romphaia tou stomatos mou*; 2:16) | | Faithful & True strikes with the *sword of his mouth* (*ek tou stomatos autou ekporeuetai romphaia oxeia*; 19:15) |
| | hidden manna (2:17) | | wedding supper of the Lamb (19:9) |

*Table 8.3. The Letter to the Church at Pergamum*

immorality (*porneias*; 14:8; 18:3, 9). Those who do not separate from such sin may be caught up in God's judgment against it when he makes war "with the sword of [his] mouth" (*en tē romphaia tou stomatos mou*; 2:16), a weapon (*ek tou stomatos autou ekporeuetai romphaia oxeia*) wielded later in the book by the one called "Faithful and True" (19:15). Finally, the church at Pergamum is promised that, if they are victorious, they will eat of the hidden manna (2:17). Toward the end of the book, we learn that the faithful will be invited to the great wedding feast of the Lamb (19:7–9). Here and elsewhere in the book, we are reminded that correct doctrine is not just a matter of polite theological debate. Theology matters, because what we most sincerely believe determines what we do, and this can have serious ramifications for the course that the church sets for itself in the world.

## Thyatira (Rev 2:18–29)

The city of Thyatira was strategically located at a ford in the Lycus River, over which passed a Roman road connecting the ports of Smyrna and Ephesus to the south and the provincial capital of Pergamum to the north.[44] We know comparatively little about Thyatira, as it was not a prominent city in ancient times. Inscriptions related to the city mention trade guilds connected to work in wool, leather, bronze, armor, and, notably, purple cloth.[45] In Acts 16:14, we read of a convert of Paul's named Lydia, who was a resident of the city and a seller of purple cloth. Like many cities in the region, Thyatira was damaged in the earthquake of 27 BC and was rebuilt with assistance from Rome. First-century coins of the city featured busts of the emperors Claudius and Vespasian and the goddess Roma.[46]

The believers at Thyatira are lauded for their increasing faith, love, service, and perseverance (Rev 2:19). Nevertheless, they have also been seduced by and tolerate the teaching of a false prophetess, "Jezebel," who deceives some into sexual immorality (*porneusai*) and eating food offered to idols—the two things prohibited earlier by the council at Jerusalem (Acts 15:29; see table 8.4). Those who follow her will suffer her fate (Rev 2:23). Later, in the body of the book, the harlot Babylon is labeled (quite literally) the "MOTHER OF PROSTITUTES [*pornōn*] AND OF THE ABOMINATIONS [i.e., idols]," a reference to the same two sins (17:5). Toward the end of this letter, Christ states that the one who overcomes will be granted authority over "nations" (*ethnōn*) and "will rule them with an iron scepter" (*poimanei autous en rabdō sidēra*; 2:26–27), images that are repeated later when the victorious Christ arrives to strike the "nations" (*ethnē*) and "rule them with an iron scepter" (*autos poimanei autous en rabdō sidēra*; 19:15). Finally, at the end of the letter, Christ promises that he will give the "morning star" (*ton astera ton prōinon*) to the one who overcomes (2:28). In the conclusion to the book, we discover that it is Christ himself who arrives as "the bright Morning Star" (*ho astēr ho lampros, ho prōinos*; 22:16).

The warning about Jezebel (a woman tellingly named after the Israelite queen who sent an innocent Naboth to his death by means of lying witnesses) found in the letter to Thyatira, and the reflexes of this imagery that one sees in the cosmic center of the book in the person of Babylon, suggest that toleration of lies and sin in the present will make the faithful vulnerable to this threat when it strikes from outside in the future. Those who tolerate a false prophet locally in the present are more likely to succumb to such lies in the future when those lies are told from the perspective and power of the state (see 16:13; 19:20).

| Church | Approval & Warning in Letters (2–3) | Cosmic Parallels | Final Reward/ Penalty |
|--------|-------------------------------------|------------------|------------------------|
| Thyatira | you tolerate Jezebel, false prophetess who brings *sexual immorality* (*porneusai*) & idolatry (2:20) | great prostitute Babylon, mother of *prostitutes* (*pornōn*) & abominations (Ps 2; Rev 17:5) kings of the earth commit *adultery* (*porneusantes*) with Babylon (18:9, also 3) | |
| | authority over *nations* (*ethnōn*) given to those who overcome; Christ will *rule nations with an iron scepter* (*poimanei autous en rabdō sidēra*; 2:26–27) | Christ will strike the *nations* (*ethnē*) with an *iron scepter* (*autos poimanei autous en rabdō sidēra*) & rule them (19:15) | |
| | I will give you the *morning star* (*ton astera ton prōinon*; 2:28) | | Jesus is the *Morning Star* (*ho astēr ho lampros, ho prōinos*; 22:16) |

*Table 8.4. The Letter to the Church at Thyatira*

Sardis (Rev 3:1–6)

The city of Sardis was situated at a crossroad where several routes from the interior met those leading west to the ports of Ephesus and Smyrna.[47] The city had a storied history as the capital of Croesus (r. ca. 560–547 BC), the king of Lydia legendary for his wealth. After the fall of Sardis to the Persians in 547 BC, the city became the seat of the local Persian satrap. Later it became an administrative center during the Seleucid era. In AD 17, an earthquake devastated Sardis, but the city recovered due in no small part to financial assistance from the Roman emperors Tiberius and Claudius in the form of cash infusions and extended tax relief.[48] With support of this kind, one can imagine that the citizens of Sardis were grateful to Rome and forthcoming with their loyalty. Like the nearby city of Ephesus, Sardis featured a massive temple to Artemis, which, although smaller than the one boasted by its neighbor, still ranked as the eighth largest in the Greek world.[49] The Jewish community in Sardis was of such a size that Josephus could make note of the fact that Roman officials there issued decrees related to their freedom of worship and right to send money to Jerusalem (Josephus, *Jewish Antiquities* 14.235, 59–61; 16.171).

As concerns the church in Sardis, things are not good; the believers there are on spiritual life support (Rev 3:1–2). Nevertheless, a few have managed to remain pure and have not "defiled" (*emolynan*) their clothes but walk with Christ and will be dressed in "white" (*leukois*; 3:4; see table 8.5). Later, in the body of the book, those who are martyred are each given a "white" (*leukē*) robe (6:11; also 7:9, 13–14). Elsewhere, these 144,000 are identified as the ones who have not "defiled" (*emolynthēsan*) themselves (14:4). Those at Sardis who remain faithful will not have their name removed from "the book of life" (*tēs biblou tēs zōēs*; 3:5). In the body of the book, we find that those not in the "book of life" (*tō bibliō tēs zōēs*) are sent to destruction (13:8; also 17:8; 20:12, 15), and in the conclusion of the book it is announced that only those whose names are in the "book of life" (*tō bibliō tēs zōēs*) may enter the new Jerusalem (21:27).

| Church | Approval & Warning in Letters (2–3) | Cosmic Parallels | Final Reward/ Penalty |
|---|---|---|---|
| Sardis | you are almost dead, wake up! (3:2)<br><br>obey what you have heard (3:3)<br><br>have not *defiled* (*emolynan*) their clothes (3:4)<br><br>some will be dressed in *white* (*leukois*; 3:4)<br><br>name will stay in *book of life* (*tēs biblou tēs zōēs*; 3:5) | have not *defiled* (*emolynthēsan*) themselves (14:4)<br><br>faithful given *white* (*leukē, leukas*) robes (6:11; 7:9, 13)<br><br>those not in *book of life* (*tō bibliō tēs zōēs*) go to destruction (13:8; also 17:8; 20:12, 15) | only those who are in the *book of life* (*tō bibliō tēs zōēs*) enter the new Jerusalem (21:27) |

Table 8.5. The Letter to the Church at Sardis

## Philadelphia (Rev 3:7–13)

The city of Philadelphia was strategically situated at the southern end of the Cogamis River Valley at the point where the Roman road passed south across a saddle in the Messogis range to descend into the Meander Valley. Like its neighbor Sardis, Philadelphia was devastated by the earthquake of AD 17 and was similarly the beneficiary of assistance from the Roman state (Tacitus, *Annals* 2.47). As an acknowledgment of its gratitude for the generosity of Tiberius, the city was given the right to add the epithet "Neocaesarea" to its name. Later, the city added another name associated with the family of the emperor, "Flavius."[50]

| Church | Approval & Warning in Letters (2–3) | Cosmic Parallels | Final Reward/ Penalty |
|---|---|---|---|
| Philadelphia | you have endured already (3:10) | | |
| | hold on so no one takes your crown (3:11) | | |
| | you will be a pillar in the temple (3:12) | | faithful & Christ dwell together (21:3) |
| | I will write my *name* (*onoma*) on you (3:12) | faithful take *name* (*onoma*) of Lamb on their foreheads (7:4; 14:1) | |
| | dwell with God in *the new Jerusalem, descending out of heaven from God* (*tēs kainēs Ierousalēm hē katabainousa ek tou ouranou apo tou theou;* 3:12) | | *the Holy City, the new Jerusalem, coming down out of heaven from God* (*tēn hagian Ierousalēm kainēn eidon katabainousan ek tou ouranou apo tou theou;* 21:2, 10) |

Table 8.6. The Letter to the Church at Philadelphia

According to Revelation, the Christians at Philadelphia seem to have fallen out with the Jewish community there, who have rejected them as ones who have no relationship with the God of Israel (Rev 3:9; see table 8.6). Far from being rejected, however, the ones who endure will be made a pillar in the temple and have the "name" (*onoma*) of *God* and *Christ* written on them

(3:12). In the body of the book, the faithful take the "name" (*onoma*) of the *Lamb* and *God* on their foreheads (14:1; also 7:4), and in the conclusion of the book, the faithful and Christ dwell together (21:3). The faithful at Philadelphia have already endured persecution, and because of this they will be spared from the trials to come but will dwell with God in "the new Jerusalem, which is coming down out of heaven from my God" (*tēs kainēs Ierousalēm hē katabainousa ek tou ouranou apo tou theou*; 3:12), a reward that is realized almost verbatim in the conclusion of the book (21:2, 10).

## Laodicea (Rev 3:14–22)

Laodicea was located along the Roman road linking Sardis and Colossae and near the confluence of the Meander and Lycus rivers. To the west, a road running through the Meander Valley connected the city to the port of Ephesus. Strabo describes the water of the nearby rivers as being hard, but drinkable (*Geography* 12.8.20). The site itself lacked a spring, and remains of a siphon-style aqueduct suggest that the city sourced its water from the thermal springs at Denzili, eighteen kilometers to the south. The nature of this supply may lie behind the reference to water that is hot, cold, and lukewarm in Revelation 3:16.[51]

Like other cities in the earthquake-prone region, Laodicea was damaged in the quake of AD 17 and was restored with assistance granted by the emperor Tiberius (Strabo, *Geography* 12.8.18). The town was a wealthy one, for when a second earthquake struck in AD 60, it was able to rebuild without financial assistance from Rome (Tacitus, *Annals* 14.27). During this second rebuilding, a stadium was erected that was dedicated to the emperors Vespasian and Titus.[52] Just west of the city there existed a medical school at the sanctuary of Men Karou (Strabo, *Geography* 12.8.20). One of its graduates, Demosthenes

Philalethes, was the author of a famous ophthalmological text that saw use into the medieval period. Scattered ancient references suggest that the Lycus Valley was a center for the treatment of eye ailments and the production of medication, and this would seem to underlie the specific reference to the church's need for eye salve in Revelation 3:18.[53]

Strabo describes the territory around Laodicea as exceedingly fertile and notes the income it earned from sheep renowned for their soft black wool (*Geography* 12.8.16). Alongside wool production there existed a textile industry, in which local plants provided a red-purple dye that was a substitute for the more expensive purple derived from murex snails. The wealth that flowed from its businesses gave the city financial clout and enabled it to mint its own coins.[54] Coinage minted in Laodicea suggests that during the reign of Domitian, a temple to the cult of the emperor was erected there.[55] The city was home to a substantial Jewish community. The Roman statesman Cicero (106–43 BC) reports an incident in which the authorities seized twenty pounds of gold that the Jewish community had attempted to send to Jerusalem, presumably in support of the temple there (Cicero, *For Flaccus* 28).

This church seems to have bought into the Roman economic system and has consequently failed to recognize its own pathetic state. In a city famous for its black wool and medical expertise, the Christians of Thyatira need to buy white "robes" (*himatia*; see table 8.7) in order to cover their "shameful nakedness" (*hē aischynē tēs gymnotētos sou*) and eye salve so that they can "see" (*blepēs*; Rev 3:18). Later, in the body of the book, Christ announces blessing on those who remain "robed" (*himatia*) so that they do not go around "naked" (*gymnos*) and have their "shame" (*aschēmosynēn*) "seen" (*blepōsin*; 16:15). The faithful Christ disciplines the people because he loves them

| Church | Approval & Warning in Letters (2–3) | Cosmic Parallels | Final Reward/ Penalty |
|---|---|---|---|
| Laodicea | you are wretched, pitiful, poor, blind, & naked (3:17)<br><br>get white *robes* (*himatia*) to cover your *shameful nakedness* (*hē aischynē tēs gymnotētos sou*), eye salve to *see* (*blepēs*; 3:18)<br><br>the faithful & true *witness/martyr* (*ho martys*) promises they will *sit* (*kathisai*) with him on his *throne* (*thronō*; 3:21) | blessing on those who remain *robed* (*himatia*) so that they do not go around naked (*gymnos*) & have their shame (*aschē-mosynēn*) seen (*blepōsin*; 16:15) | *thrones* (*thronous*) are arranged for those who have borne *witness* (*martyr-ian*) for Christ, but who are now *seated* (*ekathisan*) to judge the wicked (20:4) |

Table 8.7. The Letter to the Church at Laodicea

and wants renewed relationship with them (3:19–20). In 3:21, Christ tells the Laodiceans that if they are victorious as he has been victorious—and he is the one introduced in 3:14 as the faithful and true "witness" or "martyr" (*ho martys*)—then they will "sit" (*kathisai*) with him on his "throne" (*thronō*; 3:21). Toward the end of the book, in 20:4, "thrones" (*thronous*) are arranged on which sit those who have borne "witness" (*martyrian*) for Christ, but who are now "seated" (*ekathisan*) to judge the wicked.

## WHAT TO EXPECT BASED ON CHAPTERS 1–3

One of the chief things that the letters to the seven churches do is prepare the reader for the body of the book and for its conclusion. The subtle connections between the here-and-now issues facing the churches and the visions of the body of the book demonstrate that the difficult and sacrificial choices we make in this world can have profound ramifications in the spiritual and cosmic realm. In the present, Christ promises the churches his support and assures them of victory. In the body of the book, we will see the Lamb meet every new satanic challenge with victory already in hand because of his work on the cross. The book of Revelation is given first to these seven first-century churches and relates to the peril they faced from an all-consuming empire that put itself in the place of God and dominated either by co-opting people into its economic system or by forcing subservience and even worship. The message of Revelation is that those who reject this power and follow Christ receive eternal life. While this message was given initially to the Christians of first-century Asia Minor, it remains valid for anyone who is faced with seduction or persecution by a system that would put itself in the place of God.

## THE BODY OF THE BOOK (4:1–20:15)

From here we move to the central section of the book (4:1–20:15). The core of the book differs from the introduction temporally as well as in genre and locale. Following the formulaic close of the letter to Laodicea (3:22), the words "after this I looked" (*meta tauta eidon*) in 4:1 indicate a passage in time and a shift from the epistolary genre to visionary material. In this new vision, there is a spatial move from the Isle of Patmos to heaven itself. This central, visionary section of the book is where most of the drama unfolds. One key to understanding the book as a whole is to understand how this material and the letters to the churches work together. In chapter 1 and the letters to the churches, the ascended Christ is presented as one who was dead but is now alive and enthroned. This picture demonstrates that he has already achieved victory over sin and death. At the outset of the book, therefore, the readers undergoing persecution are reminded that the one they follow has already achieved the victory. This shows that the risen Christ is keenly aware of the challenges besetting the faithful. In the visionary core of the book that follows, these followers are able to see that behind the struggles they face there is being waged a cosmic battle, in which the victory of Christ and the vindication of the faithful is foreordained.

As we have already noted, this portrayal of conflict on two levels of reality is similar to the technique used in the book of Job in which Job's righteousness attracts malevolent attention and his suffering is brought about by "the Satan" (Job 1:6–11). Throughout the book of Job, the real drama of consequence is the battle being waged in heaven between God and the Satan. Job's role on earth is to remain faithful so that in the end he will be vindicated. While Job remains oblivious to the cosmic battle, however, the book of Revelation allows its readers a glimpse behind the curtain by laying out the details of the cosmic battle in which they are earthly participants. The knowledge at the outset that what they do in the here and now is of cosmic importance, and that victory has been won by the risen Christ, encourages the faithful as they endure hardship in the present.

A great many proposals have been made regarding the structure of Revelation.[56] Our reading of Revelation has convinced us that the central section of the book (4:1–20:15) comprises a chiasm of the pattern A-B-C-D-C'-B'-A', in which each of the paired sections is introduced as a new vision by the phrase "and I saw" (*kai eidon*) and clearly connected by specific shared *vocabulary*, *imagery*, and *content*. Read with a sensitivity to these elements and their distribution, the book of Revelation is found to be organized as follows:

A Appearance of the Lamb and the initial judgment of the earth (4:1–6:17)

B 144,000 and six of seven trumpets (7:1–9:21)

C God's two witnesses (10:1–11:14)

D Victory! The incarnation and Satan's failure (11:15–12:17)

C' Satan's two witnesses (13:1–18)

B' 144,000 and seven bowls (14:1–19:10)

A' Appearance of "Faithful and True" and the final judgment of Satan (19:11–20:15)

So, what does this all mean? Chiasm is a literary technique in which sections of a piece of literature as small as a verse or as large as an entire book are paired. In a case in which there is an odd literary element that is left unpaired at the center, the aim is often to focus attention on what is *conveyed* in that section as being critical to the message of the book. In Revelation, this structural arrangement zooms in on the central section, "D" (11:15–12:17), which we have titled "Victory! The incarnation and Satan's failure." For the Christians of the province of Asia suffering at the hands of imperial Rome and its supporters, the central point of the book is perfectly suited to their need. At the sound of the seventh trumpet in 11:15, all heaven erupts with the declaration that "the kingdom of this world has become the kingdom of our Lord and of his Messiah, and he shall reign for ever and ever." So, in a sense, John spills the beans at the start of his book, and all the way through it, and if you somehow managed to miss the point, he also puts it at the center of the book—Jesus, the risen Christ, wins!

The first part of the chiastic pattern leads you into that central point—that is what the A-B-C sections do. Generally speaking, what occupies these sections is the *initiation* of the cosmic conflict, and what occurs in the C'-B'-A' is the *consummation* of that conflict, which takes the reader to the aftermath of the conflict in the conclusion of the book. So, let us move through the paired parts of the book to see how they are connected and how they help us zero in on the central section, D, in which the victory of Christ and the defeat of Satan are declared and celebrated. Once we have done this, we will finish by looking at the conclusion to the book (21:1–22:21).

*Sections A (4:1–6:17: The Appearance of the*
*Lamb and the Initial Judgment of the Earth) and*
*A' (19:11–20:15: The Appearance of "Faithful and*
*True" and the Final Judgment of Satan)*

The first element in the body of Revelation is A, 4:1–6:17, a section that depicts the appearance of the Lamb and the initial judgment of the earth. In the body of the book, it stands in parallel to A', the appearance of "Faithful and True" and the final judgment of Satan (19:11–20:15).

The big idea expressed here is as follows: as the battle is about to be joined in section A, God's throne room is full of worship and celebration. This makes it clear at the outset who the winner will be—the churches know the power of the one who is on their side. In chapter 5, the sealed scroll (God's battle plan) is opened by the Lamb, who, as the one slain but now alive, has already conquered death. As such, he has already redeemed humans from every nation, has been declared triumphant, and has been given power (5:5, 9, 12)—all before the battle is joined. The churches can stay faithful in the persecution to come because victory over death and hell has *already been won* at the cross. As the book has been structured, section A (4:1–6:17) introduces the judgment by the Lamb, while section A' (19:11–20:15) shows its completion (table 8.8).

These two blocks of material are connected in multiple ways. First, both commence with similar phrases. In 4:1, John begins the section noting, "*I looked* [*eidon*], and *there* before me *was* [*kai idou*] a door *standing open in heaven* [*ēneōgmenē en tō ouranō*]*." In 19:11, John encounters another vision introduced by a similar phrase. The object of the vision is different, but the framing is similar—"*I saw* [*eidon*] *heaven standing open* [*ton ouranon ēneōgmenon*] and *there* before me *was* [*kai idou*] a white horse." The shared elements continue. In both sections the flow of the narrative is characterized by the arrival of a figure who initiates judgment. In A, elders (who acted as judges in ancient Israel) are seated on thrones (*thronous*; 4:4). In A', thrones (*thronous*) are set out for the ones given authority to judge (20:4). In section A, the slain Lamb (i.e., Christ) initiates judgment on the earth by releasing four horsemen (5:1, 7). The first of these is a "white horse" (*hippos leukos*; 6:2). In A' we again encounter a "white horse" (*hippos leukos*; 19:11) and discover that the rider is none other than Christ himself. In section A, as the activity initiated by the horsemen progresses to the sixth seal, the stars of the "sky" (*ouranou*) fall to "earth" (*gēn*), and the "sky" (*ouranos*) itself is split apart (6:13–14). In

A', Christ arrives to judge, and at his presence the "earth" (*gē*) and "sky" (*ouranos*) flee (20:11).

| A and A' Compared: The Lamb against Satan | |
|---|---|
| **A**<br>**Appearance of the Lamb & the Initial Judgment of the Earth (4:1–6:17)** | **A'**<br>**Appearance of "Faithful & True" & the Final Judgment of Satan (19:11–20:15)** |
| *I looked (eidon) and there was (kai idou) ... a door opened in heaven (ēneōgmenē en tō ouranō; 4:1)* | *I saw (eidon) heaven open (ton ouranon ēneōgmenon), and there ... was (kai idou) a white horse (19:11)* |
| twenty-four elders seated on *thrones (thronous; 4:4)* | *thrones (thronous)* for those given authority to *judge (krima; 20:4)* |
| elders place *crowns (stephanous)* before the throne (4:10); Lamb (Christ) releases *white horse (hippos leukos)*, whose rider wears a *crown (stephanos; 6:2)* | Faithful & True (Christ) rides *white horse (hippos leukos)* & wears many *crowns (diadēmata; 19:11–13)* |
| stars of *sky (ouranou)* fall to *earth (gēn)*; *sky (ouranos)* is split apart (6:13–14) | *earth (gē)* & *sky (ouranos)* flee (20:11) |
| *kings (basileis), generals (chiliarchoi), mighty men (ischyroi),* every *slave (doulos),* & every *freemen (eleutheros)* hide (6:15) | *kings (basileōn), generàls (chiliarchōn), mighty men (ischyrōn), freemen (eleutherōn),* & *slaves (doulōn)* hide (19:18) |
| *Death (thanatos)* & *Hades (hadēs)* destroy (6:7–8) | *Death (thanatos)* & *Hades (hadēs)* surrender the dead (20:13) |
| How long until you *judge (krineis)?* (6:10) | Faithful & True *judges (krinei)* & "makes war" (19:11) |

*Table 8.8. Sections A (Rev 4:1–6:17) and A' (19:11–20:15) Compared*

For the original recipients of this book, the image of the four horsemen was not a source of *fear*, but *confidence*, because these figures represented God's *intervention* on their behalf. The character of the horsemen as agents of judgment is clear from the fact that they represent allusions to the covenant curses found in the Old Testament in Leviticus 26 and Deuteronomy 28 (you might remember this from our section on prophecy). In the Old Testament context, these curses of increasing severity were visited on Israel as warnings for them to abandon their wickedness and return to obedience. If rebellion persisted, then the final result was defeat and exile. In our section here, the first seal looses a rider on a white horse who charges forth to conquer (Rev 6:2; see Lev 26:24, 28, 31). The second seal releases a rider on a red horse who takes peace from the earth and who wields a sword (6:4; see Lev 26:16, 25a). The third seal yields a black horse that brings a famine represented by a scales and news of madly inflated prices for food (Rev 6:5–6; see Lev 26:6). The fourth seal reveals a pale horse that brings the covenant curse of death by sword, famine, plague, and wild animals (Rev 6:8; see Lev 26:22, 25–26). In Revelation 6:10, the martyred faithful cry out, "How long, Sovereign Lord ... until you judge [*krineis*] ... and avenge?"

Judgment consummated dominates the parallel section of A'. At the beginning of this section we immediately come upon the rider on the white horse loosed by the Lamb in chapter 4 and discover that the rider is none other than Christ himself (19:11–16). In this figure, the cry of the martyred in 6:10 is answered, for he arrives and "with justice he judges [*krinei*] and wages war" (19:11). In 19:20, Satan's acolytes, the beast and the false prophet, are captured and dispatched to the lake of burning sulfur. In 20:4, thrones are set up for those who had been given authority to "judge" (*krima*; 20:4). Satan and his allies are destroyed and sent to the lake of fire (20:10). Finally, a great white throne appears, and the dead are judged (*ekrithēsan*), with the guilty being sent to the second death (20:13–15). Other parallels of initiation and consummation connect the two sections. In section A, "kings," "generals," "mighty men," and "slave and free" (*basileis, chiliarchoi, ischyroi, doulos, eleutheros*) attempt to hide (6:15), while in section A' the same list is consigned to be devoured (19:18). In section A, "Death and Hades" ([*ho*] *thanatos, kai ho hadēs*) are allowed to destroy (6:8), while in A', "Death and Hades" (*ho thanatos kai hadēs*) are themselves subdued and forced to give up their dead (20:13).

So, what is the point of this pairing? Section A shows God to be attentive to the plight of his followers and establishes that he will *intervene* on their behalf. The throne room scene of praise exudes confidence and shows that *nothing* is in doubt or out of control. In fact, the arrival of the Lamb *alive* but clearly once having been *slain* reminds the readers that the victory over sin and death has already been achieved at the cross by the Lamb of God raised from the dead. The sealed scroll at first strikes modern readers as a literary Pandora's box, because once it is opened, nasty things begin to happen. In reality, however, the scroll is the Lamb's top-secret battle plan by which he will intervene on behalf of the faithful and bring judgment to their oppressors. In section A' we see the *result* of this secret battle plan—Christ is victorious, and justice is carried out. The one called the Lamb in section A appears here by the name "Faithful and True" because he has been just that—he kept his promise and has come to bring justice for the faithful and destroy the forces of evil who have murdered them.

*Sections B (7:1–9:21: The 144,000 and Six of Seven Trumpets) and B′ (14:1–19:10: The 144,000 and Seven Bowls)*

Section B begins at 7:1 with a temporal shift marked by the words "After this I saw" (*meta touto eidon*; see table 8.9). The vision John sees is of "144,000" (*hekaton tesserakonta tessares chiliades*) Israelites who are to receive the seal (*esphragismenōn*) of God on their foreheads (*metōpōn*; 7:3–4). This seal is given to protect them from the devastation that is to be wrought upon the earth. This group appears to be identical to the vast multitude described in 7:9, 14 as appearing before the throne having "washed their robes and made them white in the blood of the Lamb." Using the imagery of a shepherd and his sheep but flipping the roles, the angel states that the Lamb (*arnion*) will "shepherd" (*poimanei*) these saints and one day will lead them to "springs of living water" (*zōēs pēgas hydatōn*; 7:17).

Section B′ begins with the words "Then I looked" (*kai eidon*; 14:1) in a way that is a close parallel to the start of section B (7:1) and opens on a nearly identical scene. In this case, however, what is in *process* in chapter 7 is now seen to have been *accomplished*. Here, the 144,000 (*hekaton tesserakonta tessares chiliades*) have now been sealed with the name of God written on their foreheads (*metōpōn*), have been redeemed from the earth, and now appear before the throne (*thronou*) singing praises to God (14:3). This group is described as ones who have kept themselves pure. Picking up the inverted shepherd-sheep imagery from 7:17, the saints are described as ones who now "follow the Lamb [*arniō*] wherever he goes" (14:4). Immediately after this scene, in 14:7, an angel announces that all should praise God because he has made the "springs of water" (*pēgas hydatōn*; see 7:17).

| B and B' Compared: The Faithful Challenged & Vindicated | |
|---|---|
| **B**<br>**144,000 & Six of Seven Trumpets (7:1–9:21)** | **B'**<br>**144,000 & Seven Bowls (14:1–19:10)** |
| *After this I saw* (*meta touto eidon*; 7:1) | *and I looked* (*kai eidon*; 14:1) |
| *144,000* (*hekaton tesserakonta tessares chiliades*) with *seal* (*esphragismenōn*) of God on their *foreheads* (*metōpōn*) prepare for persecution (7:3–8) | *144,000* (*hekaton tesserakonta tessares chiliades*) with *name* of God on their *foreheads* (*metōpōn*) sing in heaven (14:1–5) |
| *Lamb* (*arnion*) as shepherd will lead them to springs of *living water* (*zōēs pēgas hydatōn*; 7:17) | Saints follow the *Lamb* (*arniō*) wherever he goes (14:4); God has made the *springs of water* (*pēgas hydatōn*; 14:7) |
| first trumpet—hail, fire, & blood *came upon* (*egeneto*) the *earth* (*eis tēn gēn*; 8:7) | first bowl—bowl poured *out on the earth* (*eis tēn gēn*) bringing *about* (*egeneto*) wounds & sores (16:2) |
| second trumpet—one-third of *sea* (*thalassēs*) turns to *blood* (*haima*), one-third of *creatures* (*echonta psychas*) in *sea* (*en tē thalassē*) *die* (*apethanen*), & one-third shipping is destroyed (8:8–9) | second bowl—*sea* (*thalassan*) turns to *blood* (*haima*), & every *living thing* (*psychē zōēs*) in sea (*en tē thalassē*) dies (*apethanen*; 16:3) |
| third trumpet—star falls & one-third of *rivers* (*potamōn*) & *springs of water* (*tas pēgas tōn hydatōn*) *become* (*egeneto*) bitter (8:10–11) | third bowl—all *rivers* (*potamous*) & *springs of water* (*tas pēgas tōn hydatōn*) become (*egeneto*) blood (16:4–7) |
| fourth trumpet—*sun* (*hēliou*), moon, & stars are struck; world in partial darkness (8:12–13) | fourth bowl—*sun* (*hēlion*) sends scorching fire against people of earth (16:8–9) |
| fifth trumpet—abyss ruled by *King* (*basilea*) Abaddon is opened; smoke *darkens* (*eskotōthē*) sun; humans in agony (9:1–12) | fifth bowl—*kingdom* (*basileia*) of beast plunged into *darkness* (*eskotōmenē*); humans in agony (16:10–11) |

*Continued*

| | |
|---|---|
| sixth trumpet—angels at *the Great River Euphrates* (*tō potamō tō megalō Euphratē*) released & lead army with horses that spew fire, smoke, & sulphur *out of their mouths* (*ek tōn stomatōn autōn*); survivors worship *demons* (*daimonia*) & idols, commit murder, & practice magic, sexual immorality, & *theft* (*klemmatōn*; 9:13–21) | sixth bowl—*the Great River Euphrates* (*ton potamon ton megan* [*ton*] *Euphratēn*) dries up; evil *spirits* (demons, *daimoniōn*) emerge *from mouth* (*ek tou stomatos*) of the dragon, beast, & false prophet; Christ will come like a *thief* (*kleptēs*; 16:12–16) |

*Table 8.9. Sections B (Rev 7:1–9:21) and B' (Rev 14:1–19:10) Compared*

Throughout the rest of sections B and B' there are significant parallels between the trumpets that are sounded in B and the bowls that are poured out in B'. While the character of each section is one of judgment, in general, the judgment begun in B is partial, while that brought to bear in B' is a judgment that is advanced further or is fully consummated. In B, the first trumpet is sounded and results in hail, fire, and blood brought to bear (*egeneto*) "on the earth" (*eis tēn gēn*), with the result that a third each of the earth, trees, and grass is consumed (8:7). In B', the first bowl is poured out "on the land" (*eis tēn gēn*), resulting in (*egeneto*) wounds or sores for those who had accepted the mark of the beast and worshiped him (16:2). The second trumpet is sounded in section B (8:8–9), with the result that a third of the "sea" (*thalassēs*) turns to "blood" (*haima*), one-third of all sea creatures "in the sea" (*en tē thalassē*) die (*apethanen*), and one-third of all maritime shipping is destroyed. In B', the second bowl is poured out to similar, but more devastating, effect—the "sea" (*thalassan*) turns to "blood" (*haima*), and every living thing "in the sea" (*en tē thalassē*) dies (*apethanen*) (16:3).

With the sounding of the third trumpet (B) (8:10–11), a star falls from heaven onto a third of the *rivers and springs of water* (*tōn potamōn kai epi tas pēgas tōn hydatōn*), turning (*egeneto*) them bitter and causing the death of many people. The pouring out of the third bowl (B′) (16:4–7) conveys a similar judgment, but one that goes further to affect all of the *rivers and springs of water* (*tous potamous kai tas pēgas tōn hydatōn*), turning (*egeneto*) them to blood (16:4). The substitution of blood for water is punishment for the way in which those affected had shed the blood of the saints and the prophets. The fourth trumpet blast (B) comes in 8:12–13, and the result is that a third each of the "sun" (*hēliou*), moon, and stars are struck, leaving the world in partial darkness. The pouring of the fourth bowl (B′) (16:8–9) also affects the "sun" (*hēlion*), but to fuller degree and opposite effect. Here the entire sun is conscripted to send scorching fire on the people of the earth. Rather than bringing repentance, this judgment causes humans to curse God all the more.

Section B continues with the fifth trumpet described in 9:1–12. In this judgment, the abyss is opened, and locusts given power to sting like scorpions pour out to torment for five months all who do not bear the protective seal of God on their foreheads (9:3–4). So great will be the agony of these wounds that humans will long for death. So great is the cloud of locusts that it "darkens" (*eskotōthē*) the sun (9:2). At the end of the description of the fifth trumpet, the abyss is ruled by a "king" (*basilea*), an angel named Abaddon or Apollyon (9:11). In B′, when the fifth bowl is poured out (16:10–11), a similar scene unfolds. This bowl is poured out on the "kingdom" (*basileia*) of the beast, which is plunged into "darkness" (*eskotōmenē*; 16:10). By means left unexplained, this darkness brings incredible torment, causing humans to gnaw at their own tongues in agony and to suffer from pains and wounds (16:10–11). While there is no direct verbal parallel here to the injuries that result from the fifth trumpet, the torment arising from the outpouring of the fifth bowl nonetheless parallels what is described in relation to the earlier locust stings (see 9:3, 5–6).

In section B, the sixth trumpet (9:13–21) releases four angels that have heretofore been bound at "the great river Euphrates" (*tō potamō tō megalō Euphratē*), but who are now loosed to kill one-third of humanity (9:14–15). Together, they lead a vast army made up of horses that spew fire, smoke, and sulfur "out of their mouths" (*ek tōn stomatōn autōn*; 9:17–18). Rather than repent, however, the survivors of this judgment continue to worship "demons" (*daimonia*) and idols, commit murder, and practice magic, sexual immorality, and *thefts* (*klemmatōn*; 9:20–21). When the sixth bowl is emptied in B' (16:12–16), another attack is initiated when "the great river Euphrates" (*ton potamon ton megan [ton] Euphratēn*) dries up, allowing the kings of the east to cross over. At this point, evil spirits emerge "out of the mouth" (*ek tou stomatos*) of the dragon, the beast, and the false prophet, respectively (16:13). These evil spirits are "demonic spirits" (*daimoniōn*) that perform signs to convince the kings of the world to gather for battle (16:14). In the midst of these events, Christ reminds the faithful that he will come like a "thief" (*kleptēs*) (16:15).

### Section C (10:1–11:14: God's Two Witnesses) and C' (13:1–18: Satan's Two Witnesses)—Who Will Be Worshiped?

Sections C and C' move us closer to the center of the book and its point of prime emphasis. Each of these parallel sections is marked by the presence of two witnesses who promote the interests of the ones they serve. The question developed here is one of worship and who is worthy to receive it. In 11:1 of section C, the *worshipers* in the temple are counted. Later, witnessing

| C and C' Compared: Who Will Be Worshiped? | |
|---|---|
| **C**<br>**Who Will Be Worshiped?**<br>**God's Two Witnesses**<br>**(10:1–11:14)** | **C'**<br>**Who Will Be Worshiped?**<br>**Satan's Two Witnesses (13:1–18)** |
| issue is worship: worshipers in temple counted & suffer, but even God's enemies will eventually give him glory (11:1, 13) | issue is worship: humans are deceived & compelled to worship the dragon & the beast (13:4, 8, 12, 15) |
| *Then I saw* (*kai eidon*; 10:1) | *Then I saw* (*kai eidon*; 13:1; see 13:11) |
| angel straddles *sea* (*thalassēs*) & *land* (*gēs*; 10:2) | beast emerges from *sea* (*thalassēs*) onto land (13:1) |
| *seven* (*hepta*) thunders speak (10:3–4) | beast has *seven* (*hepta*) heads, each inscribed with blasphemous name (13:1) |
| two prophets destroy opponents with *fire* (*pyr*) & have *power* (*exousian*) to strike the *earth* (*gēn*) with covenant curses (drought, plague, water to blood; 11:5–6) | dragon gives beast *power* (*exousian*) & makes *earth* (*gēn*) worship the first beast, & causes *fire* (*pyr*) to fall from heaven (13:2–13) |
| every *people, tribe, language, & nation* (*tōn laōn kai phylōn kai glōssōn kai ethnōn*) look at corpses of two prophets (11:9) | first beast given authority over every *tribe, people, language, & nation* (*phylēn kai laon kai glōssan kai ethnos*; 13:7) |
| God gives *breath* (*pneuma*) to resurrect two prophets (11:11) | first beast gives *breath* (*pneuma*) to second so that it comes to life to oppress & kill the faithful (13:15) |
| *inhabitants of earth* (*hoi katoikountes epi tēs gēs*) gloat over death of two prophets (11:10) | second beast causes *earth & its inhabitants* (*tous katoikountas epi tēs gēs*) to worship the first beast (13:12, 14) |
| resurrection of two prophets brings terror (11:11) | healing of beast's head brings false worship (13:3) |
| gentiles trample Holy City for 42 *months* (*mēgas tesserakonta* [*kai*] *duo*); prophets *prophesy* for 1,260 days (42 months; 11:2–3) | beast *blasphemes* & makes war on saints for 42 *months* (*mēgas tesserakonta* [*kai*] *duo*; 13:5) |

*Table 8.10. Sections C (10:1–11:14) and C' (13:1–18) Compared*

the resurrection of God's two witnesses and surviving the subsequent earthquake, the people give glory to God (11:13). In
chapter 13, in the parallel section, C', deceit and coercion are
the governing principles as men and women are deceived into
*worshiping* the dragon and the beast, and those who refuse to
do so are killed (13:14–15). As we go through the sections, we
will see that this is a battle of opposites.

As in previous sections, C and C' each begin with the words
"Then I saw" (*kai eidon*; 10:1; 13:1), an indication that this is a
new vision (table 8.10). As section C opens, an angel straddles
"sea" (*thalassēs*) and dry land (*gēs*) in an act showing possession, and when he speaks the sound is that of "seven" (*hepta*)
thunders (10:2–3). At the start of section C', a beast with "seven"
(*hepta*) heads emerges from the "sea" (*thalassēs*; the place of
chaos) onto dry "land." His seven heads are inscribed with
blasphemous names (13:1). In section C, the angel announces
the arrival of "two witnesses" (*dysin martysin*), "prophets"
(*prophētai*; 11:10) who are given "power" (*exousian*) over the
"earth" (*gēn*) to bring covenant curses of drought, plague, and
even turning water to blood (11:3, 6). When opponents try to
harm them, "fire" (*pyr*) comes out of their mouths (11:5). Only
when their work is completed are they allowed to be slain. Once
this happens, every "people, tribe, language and nation" (*tōn laōn
kai phylōn kai glōssōn kai ethnōn*) look at their corpses (11:9). The
prophets, however, are raised by the "breath of life from God"
(*pneuma zōēs ek tou theou*; 11:11). In C', the dragon (i.e., Satan)
employs *two* beasts—one coming out of the sea (*thalassēs*) and
the other out of the earth (13:1, 11)—to promote his interests in
the world. The first of these is given "power" (*exousia*) over every
"tribe, people, language and nation" (*phylēn kai laon kai glōssan kai
ethnos*), which leads to false worship on the earth (*gēn*; 13:7–8).
The second beast shares the "authority" (*exousian*; 13:12) of the

first beast and, in imitation of the miracles performed by God's two witnesses, is able to call "fire" (*pyr*) from heaven (13:13–14; see 11:6). Here, in imitation of the "breath of life from God" that raises God's two witnesses from the dead, the first beast gives his "breath" (*pneuma*) to enliven the image of the second beast to oppress and *kill* the faithful (13:15).

The death of the two prophets in section C leads the "inhabitants of the earth" (*hoi katoikountes epi tēs gēs*) to gloat (11:10). When the prophets *rise from the dead*, however, the people become terrified (11:11). In section C', the second beast causes the "inhabitants of the earth" (*tous katoikountas epi tēs gēs*) to worship the first beast (13:12–14). One of the things that prompts the worship of the first beast is that one of his seven heads is wounded, but then is *healed* (13:3, 12). While the people of the world are impressed, the effect of this is to show the beast to be a false Christ, a cheap imitation of what happened to the two prophets and to the once-slain Lamb, who now lives. Finally, in both C and C', we learn that this entire period of oppression is limited to forty-two months (*mēgas tesserakonta [kai] duo*; 11:2–3; 13:5). As in Daniel, God's sovereignty is demonstrated by the fact that he has power to declare a limit to this suffering and oppression (Dan 4:34; 9:24–26).

What the C and C' panels of the book clearly demonstrate is that the Lamb is worthy of worship and the beast is not. The two witnesses of God and the two beasts each ably represent their respective masters. The only way in which the beast is able to garner worship, however, is through oppression and deception. In the end, the number of the beast says it all—it is 666, the "number of a man" (Rev 13:18). You do not worship humans. As we have noted, this number corresponds to the numeric value of the title "Nero Caesar." In Hebrew, the symbols for numbers were letters of the alphabet, and if you take the Hebrew-Aramaic letters that spelled "Nero Caesar" and add them up, the total is 666—an interesting coincidence, since Nero was one of the first-century tormentors of the faithful and claimed to be a god. After his death it seems to apply to all who, like Nero, claim deity and sit on the throne of the Roman Empire. The whole of chapter 13 portrays the beast and his partner as spiritual counterfeits, something that is consistent with the number of the antichrist as 666, as each digit is one short of divine perfection.

## Section D (11:15–12:17): Victory!
### The Incarnation and Satan's Failure

With this we come to the center of the book, which we have labeled D, Victory! The incarnation and Satan's failure (fig. 8.9). The first verses of the central section of the book answer fully and finally the question raised in C–C'—"Who will be worshiped?" The answer is clear. It is here at the core of Revelation that the seventh and final trumpet (missing from section B, 7:1–9:21) is now finally sounded, completing a sequence that was initiated when the Lamb opened the first seal in 6:1. This last trumpet announces the victory of God and the establishment of his rule.

> The seventh angel sounded his trumpet, and there were
>     loud voices in heaven, which said:
> "The kingdom of the world has become
>     the *kingdom of our Lord and of his Messiah*,
>     and *he will reign for ever and ever*."
> And the twenty-four elders, who were seated on their
>     thrones before God, *fell on their faces and worshiped
>     God*, saying:
> "We give thanks to you, Lord God Almighty,
>     the One who is and who was,

because you have taken your great power
   and have begun to reign.
The nations were angry,
   and your wrath has come.
The time has come for judging the dead,
   and for rewarding your servants the prophets
and your people who revere your name,
   both small and great—
and for destroying those who destroy the earth."
   (Rev 11:15–18)

### Section D – God Alone Is Worshiped! Victory! The Incarnation and Satan's Failure (11:15–12:17)

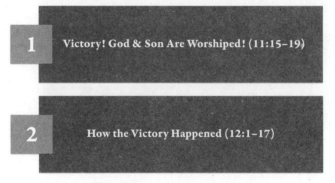

Fig. 8.9. Section D (Rev 11:15–12:17)

This central section of the book has two major components: in 11:15–19 we have *victory declared* and a wild celebration of victory over Satan. In 12:1–17 we see the *secret plan* that brought about that victory.

Zooming in on D.2 and the description of God's secret plan for victory, we see that it unfolds as a *cosmic depiction of the incarnation, into which is spliced an important word to the suffering faithful* (fig. 8.10). The surprise ending to the story is the discovery that despite Satan's continued violence, he had in fact been defeated years *earlier* in the incarnation. In 12:1–9 (D.2a), a woman gives birth to a son who is destined to rule the nations (Rev 12:5). When the child is threatened by a seven-headed red dragon (a presumed allusion to the power of Rome mediated through Herod),[57] he is taken up to heaven to God and his throne. This brief cosmic vignette portrays the incarnation and the ascension of Christ, not just to the safety of heaven, but to the *authority* that comes from occupying its throne room.

### Section D.2 – How the Victory Happened (12:1–17)

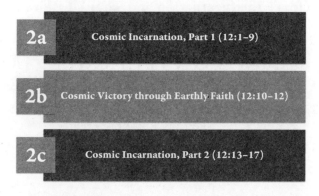

2a   Cosmic Incarnation, Part 1 (12:1–9)

2b   Cosmic Victory through Earthly Faith (12:10–12)

2c   Cosmic Incarnation, Part 2 (12:13–17)

*Fig. 8.10. Section D.2 (Rev 12:1–7)*

The *next* unit of this section (D.2b: Rev 12:10–12) is something of a retrospective in which the faithful followers of Christ are informed about how this earlier cosmic event has had direct consequences for them and how they have figured in its aftermath. These words represent the central theme of the book of Revelation and God's critical sustaining message to his persecuted church. They proclaim the reality of God's kingdom, the

cross, and the empty tomb, and show how the suffering followers of Christ used these truths to set their own lives in eternal
context and to overcome—even in death—as Christ overcame
in death. They are words describing a moment of divine victory that is worth pausing to meditate on and give thanks for.

Then I heard a loud voice in heaven say:
*"Now have come the salvation and the power*
*and the kingdom of our God,*
*and the authority of his Messiah.*
For the accuser of our brothers and sisters,
who accuses them before our God day and night,
has been hurled down.
*They triumphed over him*
*by the blood of the Lamb*
*and by the word of their testimony;*
*they did not love their lives so much*
*as to shrink from death.*
Therefore rejoice, you heavens
and you who dwell in them!
But woe to the earth and the sea,
because the devil has gone down to you!
He is filled with fury,
because he knows that his time is short."
(Rev 12:10–12)

Satan has lost, and the heavens rejoice. As we saw in Daniel,
the kingdom can be present and God can be in control, even if
it is not immediately evident to us. Satan is cast to earth, which
is where he has come to hunt the faithful. But the faithful have
defeated him through Christ. This is why the faithful are praised
with the words of Revelation 12:11, "They *triumphed over him*
*by the blood of the Lamb and by the word of their testimony;*

they did not love their lives so much as to shrink from death." Even though it is in the middle of the book and the literary conclusion is some way off, the past tense ("they *triumphed over* him") shows this interlude to be *retrospective*. The phrase also shows that, in part, it is the *faithful* who have defeated Satan through the *work of Christ* and their own *testimony*. The letters to the churches showed how the day-in-day-out faithfulness of Christ's followers leads to actions that have cosmic significance. Here we see that such faithfulness has helped win the victory.

The concluding part of the cosmic portrayal comes in 12:13–17 (D.2c), which continues the story suspended at verse 9 and looks at the effect the incarnation had on *Satan* and his reaction toward those who follow Christ. In short, Satan is hurled to earth, where he pursues the followers of Christ. If he cannot destroy the Christ child, then he can at least try to destroy his followers (12:17). The persecution of the faithful is real, but it is the vain lashing out of a Satan who has been defeated and whose doom is certain. The saints have been faithful in their witness in a world built on a lie, a world dominated by an empire and emperor that demanded worship and were willing to oppress and murder in order to ensure that it was given. In the midst of this, the faithful have achieved victory even in *death* because they have sided with the one who has power over *Death* and *Hades*.

This declaration of victory in chapter 12 takes us back to the beginning of the book and one of the most beautiful and profound passages in all of Scripture. We know of no other passage in Scripture that so beautifully and succinctly sums up the person and work of Christ and ties together Scripture from Genesis to Revelation. Through the disobedience of Adam and Eve in the garden, sin entered the world, bringing death in its train. But at the cross, sin and death were crushed. So, at the beginning of the book, when John falls to the ground undone, Christ himself approaches. "When I saw him, I fell at his feet as though dead. Then he placed his right hand on me and said: 'Do not be afraid. I am the First and the Last. I am the Living One; I was dead, and now look, I am alive for ever and ever! And I hold the keys of death and Hades'" (Rev 1:17–18). This is why the early church could triumph over oppression and could face martyrdom with faith and determination. Those who followed Jesus had a real sense that the one they served had defeated death already, and because he was the one who held the *keys* of death and Hades, they were victorious even in death.

## CONCLUSION (21:1–22:21)

The conclusion to the book, 21:1–22:21, comprises two sections (fig. 8.11). In 21:1–22:5, we witness the creation of a new heaven and a new earth. Already in 6:12–14, with the opening of the sixth seal, the current heaven and earth has begun to be dismantled. There, the sun, moon, and stars carefully positioned at creation fall away, and the sky stretched out by the divine word is rolled up like a scroll. With the end of chapter 20, all that has tainted creation and our relationship with God has been dealt with—the beast, the false prophet, and Satan himself have been fully and finally destroyed (19:20; 20:10). All those who committed themselves to rejecting God and who pledged themselves to his enemies have undergone the second death. Even Death and Hades themselves have been eliminated forever (20:14–15). With the complete removal of anyone and anything that might come between God and humanity, the way is clear for the creation of a new world where the Creator and creation can dwell together in perfect relationship. Since all that is evil has been eliminated, nothing remains in this new

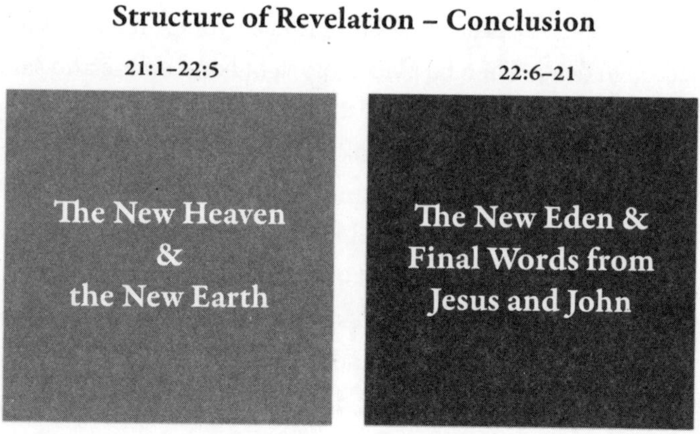

## Structure of Revelation – Conclusion

21:1–22:5                                    22:6–21

The New Heaven
&
the New Earth

The New Eden &
Final Words from
Jesus and John

*Fig. 8.11. The conclusion to Revelation (Rev 21–22)*

paradise to tempt humans into sin. The possibility of a second fall has been eliminated.

The whole new city expresses this restored relationship. The city itself descends from heaven—it is heaven come to earth. As we have already seen, its cubic dimensions recall the holy of holies and identify it as a place where God and his people finally come together in perfect communion. In chapter 22, the river, the tree of life, and the fact that there is "no curse" all recall the garden of Eden, where God and humans first dwelled together in perfect relationship. This is a place where God and his people can dwell together for eternity—as the Westminster Shorter Catechism puts it, "to glorify God and enjoy him forever." The scene of perfect peace and relationship with God is not yet realized, however, so this final section and the book as a whole concludes with the reminder and encouragement that Christ is coming soon. In the meantime, the faithful will need to endure so that when Christ's reign becomes visible, the faithful will enjoy the reward of new life with God in the holy city. The final word from Christ is, "Yes, I am coming soon." John's response comes back, "Amen. Come, Lord Jesus!" (22:20).

The book of Revelation reminds us of whom we serve. It reminds us that how we live—our determination to live for God in ordinary ways in the here and now—can have cosmic and eternal significance, and that even in the seemingly mundane events of our daily living we can be waging spiritual battles. It reminds us that even when things do not seem to be going our way, the victory has already been won because, at the cross, Christ conquered sin and death. Throughout the book, the Lamb that is alive but was obviously once slain is the risen Christ, who has conquered death. The enemy may not know it, but they are defeated already. For the early church, the message of Revelation was a profound call to endurance and resistance. Like the second half of Daniel, the book doesn't promise immediate victory or deliverance. In fact, the promise it makes *presumes* that some *will die*. In 12:11, at the heart of the book, the ones praised in heaven are *martyrs*, but they are martyrs who sing the praises of the victorious Christ: "They triumphed over him by the blood of the Lamb and by the word of their testimony; *they did not love their lives so much as to shrink from death.*"

The book of Revelation was first given to followers of Jesus struggling to live for Christ in the shadow of an oppressive Roman world. But today, the book of Revelation is for us. It reminds us that we belong to God and not the world. It reminds us that our citizenship and loyalty are not with the powers of this world. As Paul said to the Ephesians well before this book was written, "Our struggle is not against flesh and blood, but *against the rulers, against the authorities, against the powers of this dark world and against the spiritual forces of evil in the heavenly realms*" (Eph 6:12). As followers of Jesus, we face these challenges of loyalty every day. Today, however, the book of Revelation speaks most powerfully to the global persecuted church: the followers of Jesus beheaded on a Libyan beach by ISIS; the Pakistani Christians entrapped by antiblasphemy laws and sentenced to death for their faith; the Indian Christians driven from their villages; the Egyptian, Indonesian, and Chinese Christians who watch as their churches are burned to the ground. We could go on. All of these things are happening in the world today. So, while Revelation is for everyone, those in the developed and democratic world cannot fully appreciate the way in which the words, "Do not be afraid. I am the First and the Last. I am the Living One; I was dead, and now look, I am alive for ever and ever! And I hold the keys of death and Hades" continue to strengthen our persecuted brothers and sisters in Christ around the world today (Rev 1:17–18). That is why we say with them and with John, "Come, Lord Jesus."

# CONCLUSION

## THIRTEEN THESES FOR ENCOUNTERING
## THE END OF THE WORLD

If you are reading this, the end has not yet come, and the following thirteen theses remain relevant. We began this book with a look at end-times speculation and the nature and role of dispensationalism in popular end-times teaching today. Turning to prophecy and apocalyptic, we highlighted the importance of distinguishing literary genres and reading with an awareness of how and what each communicates. As a way of applying this, we took up Ezekiel, Daniel, and Revelation, delving into social and historical context and considering what we might learn by carefully considering the final form of each book. Throughout, we have tried to honor readers of Scripture who have preceded us, even when we have disagreed with their method or conclusions. Most importantly, we have approached the text of Scripture convinced of its authority and its power to transform lives. These thirteen theses and their explanation are our final thoughts on how we should read, think, and act on words that often mystify but were given to motivate us to greater love and labor for the Lamb, once slain but now alive and exalted.

1.  Using the Bible or biblical tropes to arrange and interpret human history is not new; dispensational arrangements are no older than the mid-nineteenth century and are peculiarly Anglo-American in their history.

2. Dispensationalism is one of many ways of engaging with Scripture that has had positive and negative impacts on the church.

3. It is wiser to use the Bible to interpret the news than the news to interpret the Bible; it is wiser to use the Bible to interpret our calendars than the calendar to interpret our Bibles.

4. Apocalyptic and prophetic texts are *different* genres that cannot be conflated and ought to be interpreted according to the guidelines unique to their literary types.

5. When reading apocalyptic and prophetic genres, a good reader will always read the text in its literal sense.

6. When reading Scripture, it is better to begin by asking how Old Testament prophecies and apocalyptic texts were understood by the original recipients than to speculate about how they might be fulfilled in our future.

7. The modern nation of Israel is not identical with biblical Israel.

8. We are on the surest interpretative footing when we consider the whole of a biblical book, not when we piece together tiny portions of different books.

9. Understanding some biblical passages symbolically is not to question the reliability, inspiration, or perfection of the Scriptures.

10. We should be on the lookout for the antichrist but should exercise wisdom in doing so. Identifying the antichrist with Nero or the Roman emperor does not prevent such identifications with present political systems or leaders but gives us the grammatical and theological rules to do so responsibly.

11. To live in expectation of Christ's return does not require knowing *when* Christ will return.

12. Questioning the idea of the rapture or other dispensational teachings is not to question the hope of Christ's promised return in glory to a creation made fit for eternal life.

13. Looking for Christ to come again should not distract us from his presence with and in the church by the Spirit in word and sacrament.

## THESES EXPLAINED

*1. Using the Bible or biblical tropes to arrange and interpret human history is not new; dispensational arrangements are no older than the mid-nineteenth century and are peculiarly Anglo-American in their history.*

Human beings are organizers. We order ourselves into societal groups, we create systems to simplify tasks, and we construct philosophical frameworks to help us understand our place and purpose in the world. In dispensationalism, J. N. Darby put forward a framework for understanding God's salvific work in history and the response of humans to it. In this he was not unique. Rabbinic Judaism believed in a six-thousand-year

schema that culminated in the coming of the Messiah and
a millennial Sabbath. Church father Irenaeus spoke of God
relating to humans across time through four principal cov-
enants (*Against Heresies* 3.11.8). Seventeenth-century French
mystic and philosopher Pierre Poiret compared the work of
God through history to the human stages of life from infancy
to old age and beyond. Puritan Congregationalists Jonathan
Edwards and Isaac Watts each offered up similar schema.
Darby was just one in a long line of Bible readers who saw
order in God's work in history and developed a schema that
made sense of Scripture's testimony to that work. Darby's
offering differed from those of his predecessors in spreading
around the globe, crossing denominational lines, and inspiring ongoing modification and speculation. Dispensationalism
should not be regarded as *the* way to understand Scripture,
but one of many attempts that Christians have made to unlock
God's word and understand his work in the world. Like all
human attempts at systematization, it deserves to be scruti-
nized and tested.

*2. Dispensationalism is one of many ways of
engaging with Scripture that has had positive
and negative impacts on the church.*

Within Judaism and throughout the history of the church, there
have been many attempts to make sense of God's work in history and varying approaches to reading Scripture. Like the day-
age view of history found in early Judaism and the allegorical
interpretative approach of Origen of Alexandria, the dispensational approach represents one more attempt to make sense
of God's word and its relevance to us—and like all systems of

our creation, it has had positive and negative consequences. Whatever its flaws, dispensationalism has encouraged the intense study of the Old and New Testaments. The emphasis on the any-moment return of Christ has spurred many to devote their money and energy to church planting and evangelistic and missionary outreach. While we may disagree with the way in which dispensationalism reads prophecy and the correlations it makes across the canon and its genres, we should not disparage the sincerity, passion, and faithfulness of those who have adopted it as their way into the Bible. To do so would be to ignore the advice of the apostle Paul, "The eye cannot say to the hand, 'I don't need you!' And the head cannot say to the feet, 'I don't need you!'" (1 Cor 12:21).

*3. It is wiser to use the Bible to interpret the news than the news to interpret the Bible; it is wiser to use the Bible to interpret our calendars than the calendar to interpret our Bibles.*

When Hal Lindsey, Jack Van Impe, and others scour the news for keys to unlock what Scripture teaches about end times, they get things backward—they are using the volatile to interpret what is unchanging. For years, end-times teachers saw Babylon the Great (Rev 18) as Rome; but when a coalition of thirty-five nations invaded Iraq in 1991, suddenly many came to see it as Baghdad. Scripture is steadfast and reliable, the news cycle ever-changing. Using the volatility of the news cycle to interpret Scripture is like setting out on a journey with a GPS that is constantly barking, "Recalibrating!" It is the reliability of Scripture and the principles we derive from it that ground us and help us interpret and navigate in a changing world.

*4. Apocalyptic and prophetic texts are different genres*
*that cannot be conflated and ought to be interpreted*
*according to the guidelines unique to their literary types.*

Reading the Bible "literally" includes being aware of the genre that is in front of us and reading and interpreting accordingly. When we encounter various genres within a newspaper or on social media, we instinctively adjust our reading and expectations as we flip from article to editorial or tweet to tweet. We easily distinguish the satirical from the serious, laughing at one and responding more soberly to another. Prophetic and apocalyptic writers each communicated an urgent word of God to his people by means of distinct genres. Prophets warned hearers to change present behavior to avoid disaster in the immediate future. For writers of apocalyptic, the context of defeat, exile, or oppression prompted a call to hope and perseverance. If we read prophecy and apocalyptic as if they are the same, we risk failing to grasp the life-changing message that God conveyed through each and stumbling in our efforts to apply it today.

*5. When reading apocalyptic and prophetic genres, a*
*good reader will always read the text in its literal sense.*

The literal sense is grounded in what we can know of the (human) author's mindset and circumstances and those of the author's intended audience. All these are provided by quality resources such as commentaries and Bible dictionaries. If we are serious about reading literally, the first questions are always, "What might this text have meant in its original setting? To its original hearers or readers?" When it comes to the literal sense, these are only the *first* questions. The next question to be asked is, "What does this text now mean as part of the canon of Scripture?" What happens when, for example, the apocalyptic passages of Daniel are read alongside the prophets of the Old Testament? Note that this dynamic is already at work *within* the canon because Revelation takes up and repurposes those very images, enriching their meaning. The final (related) question is then, "What does this text mean *about Jesus*?" If he is the one about whom the Scriptures testify, then if we are reading rightly, the texts should end up enriching our understanding of his person and work. None of this frees us from the literal sense; rather, it invites us to read with Christian readers throughout history, that is, within the rule of faith. Without this, our reading is at best truncated and at worst barren.

*6. When reading Scripture, it is better to begin by asking how Old Testament prophecies and apocalyptic texts were understood by the original recipients than to speculate about how they might be fulfilled in our future.*

In interpreting prophetic and apocalyptic passages, it makes sense to begin with the question, "How was this understood by those to whom it was first given?" Would a God who loves his people deliver to an endangered ancient audience a message that had no relevance for them and which only a distant future generation would have the ability to understand? To do so seems callous and nonsensical. We do well to acknowledge that Scripture is *for* us even if it was not written initially *to* us. This is most obvious with the New Testament Epistles—each first written to followers of Jesus in a specific Greco-Roman locale. The teaching, correction, and encouragement given to them, however, have relevance to us because of our shared faith in Christ. In Revelation, we find a book addressed to imperiled churches in Asia Minor. Reading how Christ steeled them for the challenges of their day, we learn how to remain faithful in a world that is at war with God and those who have pledged allegiance to him. To think that Daniel or Revelation is all about *us* and *our* future is to read with a hubris that ignores the experiences of our forebears in the faith.

### 7. The modern nation of Israel is not identical with biblical Israel.

God's word to Abram in Genesis 12:3—"I will bless those who bless you, and whoever curses you I will curse"—is not a call to uncritical support of a modern secular state but a warning about rejecting divine mercy. By the time God addresses Abram in Genesis 12, humans have made multiple unsuccessful attempts to reconnect with their creator and stand more alienated than ever. Now God steps in and chooses Abram as his intermediary so that the world might be blessed through him. What the NIV and other translations render "curse" is actually two separate Hebrew words, *qālal*, "to treat lightly or dismissively," followed by *'ārar*, "to curse." The first half of the verse lays out the prospects for those who welcome Abram in his mission and those who might reject him—"whoever treats you lightly (or dismissively) I will curse." This verse is not a call to unqualified support of the modern state of Israel, but to take heed to the ones (the first being Abram and his descendants) who bring the message of reconciliation with God. To receive such a messenger is to embrace blessing; to reject the messenger is to invite eventual curse.

### 8. We are on the surest interpretative footing when we consider the whole of a biblical book, not when we piece together tiny portions of different books.

Biblical authors wrote and shaped their works with the expectation that readers would encounter and consider the final form of a book. A careful reading of that form in relation to its original context, therefore, should be our first step in trying to make sense of Scripture. Biblical writers often alluded to images and passages found in earlier works, but to understand such references, the later book must first be considered in *its* final form. Sometimes such allusions point to an earlier work to establish a context for interpretation. At other times, an older image is repurposed to bring a new message to a new audience. If our primary way of reading Scripture is to relate a tiny portion of one book to an isolated snippet of another, we risk reading Scripture in a way that places our interests above the intentions of the biblical authors and what they intended to say to their first readers and to us.

*9. Understanding some biblical passages symbolically is not to question the reliability, inspiration, or perfection of the Scriptures.*

Those who seek to read the Bible "literally" do so because they value Scripture and want to take its message seriously. Such readers rightly chafe at an approach that avoids the plain teaching of Scripture by imposing a self-serving "symbolic" reading. Recognizing symbolism in Scripture, however, is not to devalue the Bible's authority. Biblical authors often employed symbolism to deliver a point with power and impact. Ezekiel's depiction of God's throne borne by a quartet of fantastic creatures (Ezek 1; 10) uses symbolism associated with Babylonian deities to emphasize God's ongoing sovereignty over Israel's then-captors. Recognizing that biblical writers sometimes used symbolism is not downgrading the truth of Scripture or a failure to take it seriously but recognizes a literary technique that the inspired writers used to bring God's message to his people.

*10. We should be on the lookout for the antichrist
but should exercise wisdom in doing so. Identifying
the antichrist with Nero or the Roman emperor does
not prevent such identifications with present political
systems or leaders but gives us the grammatical
and theological rules to do so responsibly.*

As we have argued, there is a good case to be made for emperor
Nero as the "beast" of Revelation 13, whose number was 666.
Identifying the antichrist, however, is not solely a game of
names and numbers, but of character. There was never just
one antichrist. In his epistles, John tells us what to look for.
Antichrist is a denier and a liar—anyone who insinuates himself
into the church to deny the Father and the Son or that Jesus is
Messiah come in the flesh (1 John 2:18, 22; 4:3; 2 John 7). Rather
than playing amateur cryptologist with the names of world leaders, we are wiser to be alert to what is said about Christ from
pulpits, in books, and over our airwaves. As John told his readers, we need to be careful to remain in the teaching of Christ
(2 John 9).

*11. To live in expectation of Christ's return does
not require knowing when Christ will return.*

An ongoing interest of many end-times teachers is speculation
about precisely when Christ will return. For William Miller and
his followers, it was 1843 or 1844. In *The Late Great Planet Earth*,
Hal Lindsey opined that Christ would return "within forty years
or so of 1948."[1] Such eschatological punditry can be exciting,
but it inevitably ends in disappointment and loss of credibility—and it's not what Christ called us to do. Given a deadline,
many of us leave things to the last minute. This tendency may
be why Jesus urged his disciples to "keep watch, because you
do not know the day or the hour" (Matt 25:13). Anticipation of

Christ's return primes us to order our lives and relationships so that we are living for God in the present. Date setting has always led to disappointment; anticipation leads to activity.

*12. Questioning the idea of the rapture or other dispensational teachings is not to question the hope of Christ's promised return in glory to a creation made fit for eternal life.*

The two-stage return of Christ championed by Darby proposed an initial rapturous appearance to retrieve the faithful from a doomed world, followed by a later return in triumph and judgment. While the dispensationalist view differs from the single-return view of the historic church and its creeds, both views share a common truth—Christ is risen, enthroned, and will one day return to judge the living and the dead. This is the blessed hope that all Christians share, which should inspire our worship and encourage us in faithfulness, evangelism, and holy living.

*13. Looking for Christ to come again should not distract us from his presence with and in the church by the Spirit in word and sacrament.*

There will be a time when evil and death will be destroyed, and God's rule will be fully and finally manifested over creation. That does not mean, however, that God's kingdom is not already present. In Daniel 2:44–45, the rock that destroys the statue, displacing the human kingdoms it represents, is a declaration of divine presence and authority. When the Pharisees asked Jesus when God's kingdom would arrive, he replied, "It is within you" or "in your midst" (Luke 17:20–21). The parallelism of the Lord's Prayer defines the coming of this kingdom as God's will being "done, on earth as it is in heaven" (Matt 6:10). Those who follow Jesus Christ in the here and now are the body of Christ, his presence in the world. While we wait in expectation of Christ's return—however that might happen—we should not overlook the reality of the kingdom that is present as those filled with his Spirit do his will.

A s followers of Christ, we are all members of the body of Christ. The different experiences that have shaped the different parts of the body have uniquely equipped each of us to serve God in ways that would be impossible were we all the same. We diminish the prospects of our congregations and the church as a whole, therefore, if we write off entire swaths of the body of Christ as somehow deficient or too misguided to be included. For dispensationalists, this means giving ear to the voices that, for almost two thousand years of church history, told a story about the return of Christ that was markedly different from the one proclaimed by Darby and those after him. For nondispensationalists, it may mean engaging the dispensationalists in their congregations and recognizing how their interest in Scripture and focus on Christ's return has given them a passion for reaching the lost that burns more intensely than in many other quarters of the church.

Finally, we hope that in coming to the end of this book and in thinking about Scripture and end times, you have a new appreciation for how important it is to read a biblical book first for its message as a whole before returning to consider its component parts and how they relate to other parts of the canon. Understanding and taking to heart the overarching message of the final form of a biblical book is essential and provides a corrective for how this or that portion of a book should be understood. In addition, as we read books such as Ezekiel, Daniel, and Revelation, we do well to temporarily step out of the twenty-first century and attempt to think like an ancient Israelite or a first-century Christian. In this way we can appreciate the experiences that the faithful of the past went through and how these words from God spoke first and foremost to them in their moment of need. Only when we do this can we appreciate the initial, essential message of these books and how that message translates to our world and the challenges faced by Christians today—not just in North America but around the world.

Amen. Come, Lord Jesus.

# Image Attributions

Figure 1.9, "The Salamander Safe," is held by the Library of Congress and is in the public domain; accessible at https://lccn.loc.gov/2008661406.

Figure 3.2 is from Larkin, Clarence, *Dispensational Truth, or God's Plan and Purpose in the Ages* (Glenside, PA: Rev. Clarence Larkin Est., 1920, n.p.), https://www.blueletterbible.org/images/larkin/.

Figure 3.3 is from Larkin, *Dispensational Truth*, p. 72.

Figure 3.4 is from adapted from Logos Bible Software.

Figure 7.1 is from Larkin, *Dispensational Truth*, p. 72.

Figure 7.2 is from Larkin, *Dispensational Truth*, p. 72.

Figure 8.2 is from Larkin, *Dispensational Truth*, n.p.

Figure 8.7 is from Siebold, Jim, "Orbis Terrarum," http://www.myoldmaps.com/maps-from-antiquity-6200-bc/118-agrippas-orbis-terrarum/118-agrippa.pdf. This version is itself derived from the black and white drawing in Raisz, Erwin, *General Cartography*, 2nd ed. (New York, NY: McGraw-Hill, 1948), fig. 10, p. 13.

Figure 8.8 shows the similarity between Brittania (on a British coin) and the goddess Roma (in a statue). The image showing the reverse side of the 1967 British penny is a scan by Retroplum, public domain, via Wikimedia Commons. https://commons.wikimedia.org/wiki/File:British_pre-decimal_penny_1967_reverse.png. The image of the statue, "Base della colonna antonina 04 personificazione di roma," was taken by I, Sailko, CC BY-SA 3.0, https://creativecommons.org/licenses/by-sa/3.0>, via Wikimedia Commons. https://commons.wikimedia.org/wiki/File:Base_della_colonna_antonina_04_personificazione_di_roma.JPG.

# NOTES

## INTRODUCTION

1. Hal Lindsey and C. C. Carlson, *The Late Great Planet Earth* (Grand Rapids: Zondervan, 1973).

2. Times Staff Writer, "John Walvoord, 92; His Bestseller Related Mideast Unrest to End-of-World Prophecies," *Los Angeles Times*, January 10, 2003, http://articles. latimes.com/2003/jan/10/local/me-walvoord10.

3. John F. Walvoord and John E. Walvoord, *Armageddon, Oil and the Middle East Crisis* (Grand Rapids: Zondervan, 1974).


## CHAPTER 1

1. Mayan civilization flourished during the eighth and ninth *bak'tuns* (ca. AD 250–900).

2. Robert K. Sitler, "The 2012 Phenomenon: New Age Appropriation of an Ancient Mayan Calendar," *Nova Religio* 9.3 (2006): 24–38.

3. Among the exhibits mounted during the height of this interest were "Maya 2012: Lords of Time" at Philadelphia's Penn Museum (May 12, 2012–January 13, 2013), "Maya 2012" at The National Museum of Korea (September 4–October 28, 2012), and "Maya: Secrets of their Ancient World" at the Royal Ontario Museum in Toronto (November 19, 2011–April 9, 2012) and the

Canadian Museum of Civilization in Ottawa, Ontario (May 18–October 28, 2012).

4. Mark A. Kellner, "New Dispensation? Camping: 'Leave Church': Family Radio Founder's Latest Teaching Prompts Church Defections," *Christianity Today* 46 (2002): 21.

5. Harold Camping, *1994?* (New York: Vantage, 1992).

6. C. Sarno et al., "Rationalizing Judgment Day: A Content Analysis of Harold Camping's Open Forum Program," *Sociology of Religion* 76 (2015): 199–221.

7. As expressed by third-century Babylonian rabbi Qattina, "The world will exist for six thousand years and be destroyed [i.e., lie fallow] for one thousand" (Babylonian Talmud Sanhedrin 97a).

8. The unsettledness preceding this event was regarded as the birth pangs of the Messiah (Babylonian Talmud Sanhedrin 98a; Babylonian Talmud Ketubot 111a; Genesis Rabbah 42:4; Matt 24:8).

9. Unless otherwise specified, all quotations of the Babylonian Talmud are taken from Jacob Neusner, trans. and ed., *The Babylonian Talmud: A Translation and Commentary* (Peabody, MA: Hendrickson, 2005). The Tannaite rabbis lived during the first two centuries AD, and their thought is contained in the Mishnah.

10. Sometime between AD 41 and 44, self-proclaimed prophet Theudas promised his followers that he would part the Jordan River and lead them across. Roman procurator Cuspius Fadus, however, captured and beheaded the would-be deliverer of Israel (Josephus, *Jewish Antiquities* 20.97–98). During the administration of procurator Marcus Antonius Felix (AD 52–60),

an Egyptian gathered an armed band atop the Mount of Olives hoping that God would bring the walls of Jerusalem down, allowing them entry. This effort, too, was thwarted by the Roman garrison (Josephus, *Jewish Antiquities* 20.167–72; Acts 21:38).

11. A tradition also known to church historian Eusebius, who states that Bar Kokhba claimed to have been a "luminary sent from heaven" (*Ecclesiastical History* 4.6.2).

12. The Lukan expression *stratias ouraniou* ("host/army of heaven") is the Greek equivalent of the Hebrew *ṣəbāʾ haššāmayim*, which, when it does not refer to constellations, identifies the heavenly army of God (e.g., 1 Kgs 22:19; 2 Chr 18:18). The choir of the "army of heaven" can be compared to the US Marine Corps Band or the Red Army Chorus. No wonder it instilled terror in shepherds used to working at night and fending off predators.

13. Kirsopp Lake, ed., *The Apostolic Fathers*, vol. 1, *I Clement, II Clement, Ignatius, Polycarp, Didache, Barnabas*, Loeb Classical Library (Cambridge: Harvard University Press, 1912).

14. The term *anno mundi* is abbreviated AM. Subsequent revisions of this system are designated by the addition of Roman numerals, e.g., AM I, AM II, AM III.

15. Richard Landes, "Lest the Millennium Be Fulfilled: Apocalyptic Expectations and the Pattern of Western Chronography, 100–800 CE," in *The Use and Abuse of Eschatology in the Middle Ages*, ed. Werner Verbeke, Daniel Verhelst, and Andries Welkenhuysen (Leuven: Leuven University Press, 1988), 145.

16. Landes, "Lest the Millennium Be Fulfilled," 148.

17. Landes, "Lest the Millennium Be Fulfilled," 159.

18. O. Irshai, "Dating the Eschaton: Jewish and Christian Apocalyptic Calculations in Late Antiquity," in *Apocalyptic Time*, ed. Albert I. Baumgarten and W. J. Hanegraaff (Leiden: Brill, 2000), 149.

19. Landes, "Lest the Millennium Be Fulfilled," 162; Irshai, "Dating the Eschaton," 151.

20. See Richard Kyle, *The Last Days Are Here Again: A History of the End Times* (Grand Rapids: Baker, 1998), 38.

21. Kyle, *Last Days Are Here Again*, 39.

22. Landes, "Lest the Millennium Be Fulfilled," 139, 168–70.

23. Landes, "Lest the Millennium Be Fulfilled," 191–92.

24. Landes, "Lest the Millennium Be Fulfilled," 193–94.

25. Richard Landes, *Relics, Apocalypse, and the Deceits of History: Ademar of Chabannes, 989–1034*, Harvard Historical Studies (Cambridge: Harvard University Press, 1995), 295.

26. See John M. Court, *Approaching the Apocalypse: A Short History of Christian Millenarianism* (London: Tauris, 2008), 84–91; Kyle, *Last Days Are Here Again*, 45–46.

27. Fifth Lateran Council, Session 11, "On How to Preach," December 19, 1516, www.papalencyclicals.net/Councils/ecum18.htm.

28. Kyle, *Last Days Are Here Again*, 60–62; Damian Thompson, *The End of Time: Faith and Fear in the Shadow of the Millennium* (Hanover, NH: University Press of New England, 1997), 83, 88.

29. Martin Luther, *Calculation of the Years of the World (Supputatio annorum mundi)*, trans. Kenneth K. Miller (1541, rev. 1545), 114, https://www.dropbox.com/s/y39wf8c pe8gn4o1/Luther-Chronikon%28KKM-English%29B.

pdf?dl=o; Luther, *Letter to John Ruhel* (1525); Luther, *Luther's Works*, vol. 49, *Letters II* (St. Louis: Concordia, 1972), 112. See also, Kyle, *Last Days Are Here Again*, 61–62, 192.

30. Martin Luther, *On War Against the Turks* (1529), in *Luther's Works*, vol. 46, *Christian in Society III* (St. Louis: Concordia, 1967), 181.

31. James Ussher, *The Annals of the World: Deduced from the Origin of Time, … Collected from All History, as Well Sacred, as Prophane, and Methodically Digested* (London: E. Tyler, for J. Crook, and for G. Bedell, 1658), 1, 792.

32. Sylvester Bliss, *Memoirs of William Miller, Generally Known as a Lecturer on the Prophecies and the Second Coming of Christ* (Boston: Himes, 1858), 66–67.

33. Bliss, *Memoirs of William Miller*, 76.

34. Bliss, *Memoirs of William Miller*, 97–98, 108–9.

35. Bliss, *Memoirs of William Miller*, 93–95, 206.

36. Bliss, *Memoirs of William Miller*, 139–45.

37. In early 1844, Miller himself estimated that since 1832 he had delivered over thirty-two hundred lectures on the return of Christ (Bliss, *Memoirs of William Miller*, 254).

38. Bliss, *Memoirs of William Miller*, 177–84.

39. Bliss, *Memoirs of William Miller*, 171.

40. Bliss, *Memoirs of William Miller*, 170–72.

41. Astronomers now refer to the comet as C/1843 D1.

42. Bliss, *Memoirs of William Miller*, 262–63.

43. Bliss, *Memoirs of William Miller*, 269–76.

44. A Genevese Traveller, "American Affairs," *Times* (London), October 31, 1844.

45. Bliss, *Memoirs of William Miller*, 288–91.

46. Bliss, *Memoirs of William Miller*, 329; Jack Van Impe, *A.D. 2000: The End?*, VHS (Troy, MI: Jack Van Impe Ministries, 1990).

## CHAPTER 2

1. For more on the portrayal of Christians in film, see Alicia Cohn, "The 'Scandalous,' Nonsensical Portrayal of Christian Faith on TV: Scripted Television Still Doesn't Get Evangelicals," *Christianity Today*, December 18, 2013, www.christianitytoday.com/women/2013/december/scandalous-nonsensical-portrayal-of-christian-faith-on-tv.html; and Yechiel Eckstein, "Hollywood's Anti-Christian Bias," *SBC Life*, April 1, 1997, www.sbclife.net/author/Rabbi%20Yechiel%20Eckstein/.

2. Catherine Wessinger, *How the Millennium Comes Violently: From Jonestown to Heaven's Gate* (New York: Seven Bridges, 2000), 35–37.

3. Jim Jones, "Q1053-4 Transcript of Jim Jones Sermon, Peoples Temple, San Francisco (1973)" (San Diego, CA: The Jonestown Institute, San Diego State University), www.jonestown.sdsu.edu/?page_id=27318.

4. On the story of the Jonestown and Waco tragedies and the apocalyptic aspects of each, see John R. Hall, Philip D. Schuyler, and Sylvaine Trinh, *Apocalypse Observed: Religious Movements and Violence in North America, Europe and Japan* (London: Routledge, 2000), 15–78.

5. For a fuller discussion of what best describes an evangelical today, see John G. Stackhouse, "Defining 'Evangelical,'" *Church and Faith Trends* 1 (2007): 1–5. A

similar definition can be found in George M. Marsden, *Understanding Fundamentalism and Evangelicalism* (Grand Rapids: Eerdmans, 1991), 4–5.

6.  Noted in David M. Haskell, *Through a Lens Darkly: How the News Media Perceive and Portray Evangelicals* (Toronto: Clements, 2009), 178–79.

7.  A. C. Dixon and R. A. Torrey, eds., *The Fundamentals: A Testimony to the Truth, Compliments of Two Christian Laymen*, 12 vols. (Chicago: Testimony, 1910–1915).

8.  For a full treatment of the origins of Christian fundamentalism, see George M. Marsden, *Fundamentalism and American Culture: The Shaping of Twentieth Century Evangelicalism, 1870–1925* (Oxford: Oxford University Press, 1982); Marsden, *Understanding Fundamentalism and Evangelicalism.*

9.  Sathianathan Clarke, *Competing Fundamentalisms: Violent Extremism in Christianity, Islam, and Hinduism* (Louisville: Westminster John Knox, 2017), 36–38.

10. Abraham Rabinovich, "The Strange Case of Denis Michael Rohan," *The Jerusalem Post*, November 14, 1969, A4.

11. E.g., Randall Price, *The Battle for the Last Days' Temple: Politics, Prophecy, and the Temple Mount* (Eugene, OR: Harvest House, 2004), 99; Ruth A. Tucker, *Another Gospel: Alternative Religions and the New Age Movement* (Grand Rapids: Zondervan, 1989), 191–216; Irvine Robertson, *What the Cults Believe* (Chicago: Moody, 1981), 87–96. Following Armstrong's death in 1986, his chosen successor, Joseph Tkach Sr., moved the church toward the teachings of evangelical Christianity. Today, the newly named Grace Communion International is a member of the National Association of Evangelicals.

Dissatisfied Worldwide Church of God members have dispersed across several small successor movements. See Walter Martin and Ravi Zacharias, *Kingdom of the Cults*, rev. and updated ed. (Bloomington, MN: Bethany House, 2003), 507–33.

12.　Herbert W. Armstrong, Letter to Supporters, September 26, 1969, www.wwcg-archives.com/wp-contentuploads/2018/08/Coworker/690926.htm.

13.　E.g., Yaakov S. Ariel, "Jews," in *Encyclopedia of Fundamentalism*, ed. Brenda E. Brasher (New York: Routledge, 2001), 251–53; Rivka Gonen, *Contested Holiness: Jewish, Muslim, and Christian Perspectives on the Temple Mount in Jerusalem* (Jersey City, NJ: KTAV, 2003), 157; Eric H. Cline, *Jerusalem Besieged: From Ancient Canaan to Modern Israel* (Ann Arbor: University of Michigan Press, 2004), 300; and Erik Freas, *Nationalism and the Haram Al-Sharif/Temple Mount: The Exclusivity of Holiness* (London: Palgrave Macmillan, 2017), 175.

14.　Similar to the story of Denis Rohan is the case of American Everett Adam Livvix, arrested in 2014 in connection with a plot to blow up several Muslim sites in Israel. Like Rohan, Livvix was psychologically evaluated, deemed mentally unfit for trial, and deported to the United States to face unrelated criminal charges. As he was neither Muslim nor Jewish, Israeli media reports of the day labeled Livvix as "Christian." Some more vividly identified him as an evangelical or fundamentalist Christian from Texas. Livvix, however, never identified his motives as being at all religious and while in Israel sometimes represented himself as Jewish.

15.　Donald Harman Akenson, *Discovering the End of Time: Irish Evangelicals in the Age of Daniel O'Connell* (Montreal: McGill-Queen's University Press, 2016), 3.

16.  Vaughn's social circle also included such American luminaries as Thomas Jefferson and George Washington (Akenson, *Discovering the End of Time*, 113).

17.  Akenson, *Discovering the End of Time*, 208–9.

18.  The best treatment of Darby's early life and career is now to be found in Akenson, *Discovering the End of Time*.

19.  William Kelly, ed., *The Collected Writings of J. N. Darby*, 35 vols. (Winschoten: Heijkoop, 1971).

20.  John Nelson Darby, "The Dispensations and the Remnants," in *Collectanea: Being Some of the Subjects Considered at Leamington, on 3d June and Four Following Days in the Year 1839* (Edinburgh: Robertson, 1882), 41.

21.  Darby, "Dispensations and the Remnants," 42.

22.  Darby, "Dispensations and the Remnants," 42–43.

23.  Darby never tidily lists the dispensations. Our sixfold arrangement is derived from several of his writings: John Nelson Darby, "Evidence from Scripture of the Passing Away of the Present Dispensation," in *The Collected Writings of J. N. Darby*, ed. William Kelly (Winschoten: Heijkoop, 1972), 89–121; "The Hopes of the Church of God, in Connection with the Destiny of the Jews and the Nations, as Revealed in Prophecy," in *The Collected Writings of J. N. Darby* (Winschoten: Heijkoop, 1972), 278–383; and "The Principles Displayed in the Ways of God, Compared with His Ultimate Dealings," in *The Collected Writings of J. N. Darby*, ed. William Kelly (Winschoten: Heijkoop, 1972), 383–91.

24.  Darby, "Hopes of the Church," 375; "Principles Displayed in the Ways," 384.

25.  Darby, "Hopes of the Church," 375; "Principles Displayed in the Ways," 385.

26. Darby, "Principles Displayed in the Ways," 384–85.

27. Darby, "Principles Displayed in the Ways," 385.

28. Darby, "Hopes of the Church," 375; "Principles Displayed in the Ways," 386.

29. Darby, "Hopes of the Church," 377.

30. Darby, "Hopes of the Church," 378.

31. Darby, "Principles Displayed in the Ways," 388–89.

32. Darby, "Evidence from Scripture," 90, 92, 117.

33. Darby, "Hopes of the Church," 378–79.

34. Darby, "Principles Displayed in the Ways," 389; Darby, "Hopes of the Church," 376.

35. Darby, "Evidence from Scripture," 99–100.

36. Darby, "Evidence from Scripture," 95.

37. John Nelson Darby, "The Public Ruin of the Church. Notes of a Public Meeting in London in September, 1847," in *The Collected Writings of J. N. Darby*, vol. 32, *Miscellaneous, No. 1*, ed. William Kelly (Winschoten: Heijkoop, 1972), 392–410.

38. See John Wade, ed., *The Black Book, or, Corruption Unmasked. Being an Account of Places, Pensions, and Sinecures ... and Corruption of the Borough Government* (London: Fairburn, 1828), 2:208–371.

39. Darby, "Evidence from Scripture," 97, 99.

40. Quoted in Harry A. Ironside, *A Historical Sketch of the Brethren Movement*, rev. ed. (Neptune, NJ: Loizeaux, 1985), 110.

41. Darby, "Hopes of the Church," 376; Darby, "Evidence from Scripture," 118.

42.   Darby, "Evidence from Scripture," 92, 98–99, 101–2.

43.   Charles C. Ryrie, *Dispensationalism Today* (Chicago: Moody, 1965), 65–85; Larry V. Crutchfield, "Rudiments of Dispensationalism in the Ante-Nicene Period, Part 1 (of 2 Parts): Israel and the Church in the Ante-Nicene Fathers," *BSac* 144.575 (1987): 254–76; Crutchfield, "Rudiments of Dispensationalism in the Ante-Nicene Period, Part 2 (of 2 Parts): Ages and Dispensations in the Ante-Nicene Fathers," *BSac* 144.576 (1987): 377–99; William C. Watson, *Dispensationalism before Darby: Seventeenth-Century and Eighteenth-Century English Apocalypticism* (Silverton, OR: Lampion, 2015).

44.   Reformed theology, for example, taught Israel's OT promises passed over to the church, which had in a sense corporately "superseded" Israel. See, for example, John Calvin, *Institutes of the Christian Religion* 3.21.6.

45.   John Nelson Darby, *The Hopes of the Church of God, in Connection with the Destiny of the Jews and the Nations, as Revealed in Prophecy. Eleven Lectures Delivered in Geneva, 1840*, new rev. ed. (London: Morrish, 1867), 112. "Sons of Israel," however, may be better rendered "sons of God" and refer to the divine council. See Michael S. Heiser, "Deuteronomy 32:8 and the Sons of God," *BSac* 158.629 (2001): 52–74.

46.   Darby, *Hopes of the Church*, 109.

47.   Darby, *Hopes of the Church*, 61–63, 88, 108–9.

48.   Darby, *Hopes of the Church*, 112–20; John Nelson Darby, *The Substance of a Lecture on Prophecy, Delivered at the Town Hall, at Sidmouth on Wednesday Evening, December 13th, 1843* (London: Whittaker, 1844), 23; Darby, *Hopes of the Church*, 75–76.

49.　Darby, *Hopes of the Church*, 76.

50.　Recently it has become a matter of some debate whether it was Darby or Scottish charismatic Edward Irving (1792–1834) who first developed the idea of the rapture. See Dave MacPherson, *The Incredible Cover-Up* (Meaford, OR: Omega, 1975). Regardless of who originated the idea, given Irving's limited travels, turbulent ministry, and early death, it was clearly Darby who was responsible for the global promulgation of the teaching.

51.　Darby, *Substance of a Lecture*, 16.

52.　Darby, *Substance of a Lecture*, 13; John Nelson Darby, "The Two Resurrections," in *The Collected Writings of J. N. Darby*, ed. William Kelly, vol. 10, *Doctrinal No. 3* (Winschoten: Heijkoop, 1972), 356.

53.　While the term "rapture" is now used almost exclusively to describe this event, Darby himself often referred to it by the phrases "first resurrection" or the "translation of the church."

54.　Darby, "Two Resurrections," 357; *Hopes of the Church*, 45.

55.　Darby, "Two Resurrections," 366.

56.　Darby, *Substance of a Lecture*, 14–15.

57.　Darby, *Substance of a Lecture*, 14.

58.　Darby, *Hopes of the Church*, 51–52; John Nelson Darby, "The Rapture of the Saints and the Character of the Jewish Remnant," in *The Collected Writings of J. N. Darby*, ed. William Kelly, vol. 11, *Prophetic, No. 4* (Winschoten: Heijkoop, 1972), 153.

59.　Darby, "Two Resurrections," 358–60. See Rev 20.

60.　Darby, *Substance of a Lecture*, 14–15; Darby, "Two Resurrections," 356, 360.

61. Darby, "Two Resurrections," 362.

62. See the chart of Darby's travels on page 66 of A. Christopher Smith, "J. N. Darby in Switzerland at the Crossroads of Brethren History and European Evangelism," *Christian Brethren Research Fellowship Journal* 34 (1983): 53–94.

63. R. Todd Mangum and Mark S. Sweetnam, *The Scofield Bible: Its History and Impact on the Evangelical Church* (Milton Keynes: Paternoster, 2009), 7–51. Another sympathetic assessment is Scofield's authorized biography, published shortly before his death: Charles G. Trumbull, *The Life Story of C. I. Scofield* (New York: Oxford University Press, 1920). Joseph M. Canfield, *The Incredible Scofield and His Book* (Vallecito, CA: Ross House, 1988), provides a thoroughly researched, acrimonious counterpoint. D. Jean Rushing's portrayal, "From Confederate Deserter to Decorated Veteran Bible Scholar: Exploring the Enigmatic Life of C. I. Scofield, 1861–1901" (MA thesis, East Tennessee State University, 2011), provides a balanced perspective.

64. Rushing, "From Confederate Deserter," 12–18.

65. Rushing, "From Confederate Deserter," 20.

66. Rushing, "From Confederate Deserter," 25–29.

67. Rushing, "From Confederate Deserter," 36.

68. Rushing, "From Confederate Deserter," 41–45.

69. Rushing, "From Confederate Deserter," 49–51, 56–58.

70. C. I. Scofield, *Rightly Dividing the Word of Truth (2 Tim. 2:15): Ten Outline Studies of the More Important Divisions of Scripture*, repr. ed. (New York: Loizeaux Brothers; Bible Truth Depot, n.d.).

71. Scofield, *Rightly Dividing the Word*, 18–23.

72.  Scofield, *Rightly Dividing the Word*, 7–17, 38–41.

73.  C. I. Scofield, ed., *The Scofield Reference Bible. The Holy Bible Containing the Old and New Testaments* (New York: Oxford University Press, 1909). The project's consulting editors were also active participants in the various summer Bible conferences that were held particularly throughout the northeastern United States in the latter quarter of the nineteenth century. This, along with their college and denominational affiliations, would have lent the work credibility with its intended audience.

74.  Rushing, "From Confederate Deserter," 92–97.

75.  Arno C. Gaebelein, *The History of the Scofield Reference Bible* (New York: Our Hope; Loizeaux Brothers, 1943), 62.

76.  This approach was one that Scofield borrowed from his mentor, James H. Brookes. See Rushing, "From Confederate Deserter," 77–80.

77.  Rushing, "From Confederate Deserter," 85.

78.  John D. Hannah, *An Uncommon Union: Dallas Theological Seminary and American Evangelicalism* (Grand Rapids: Zondervan, 2009), 67.

79.  Today Dallas Theological Seminary has a student population of over 2,300, which makes it one of the largest ATS-accredited theological seminaries in North America (Association of Theological Schools, "Association of Theological Schools: Dallas Theological Seminary," www.ats.edu/member-schools/dallas-theological-seminary.

80.  J. Dwight Pentecost, *Things to Come: A Study in Biblical Eschatology* (Grand Rapids: Zondervan, 1964).

81.  John F. Walvoord, *The Rapture Question* (Grand Rapids: Zondervan, 1979); Walvoord, *The Millennial Kingdom* (Grand Rapids: Zondervan, 1983); Walvoord, *Daniel:*

*The Key to Prophetic Revelation* (Chicago: Moody, 1971); Walvoord, *The Revelation of Jesus Christ: A Commentary* (Chicago: Moody, 1966).

82.    Walvoord and Walvoord, *Armageddon, Oil*.

83.    Peter Steinfels, "Gulf War Proving Bountiful for Some Prophets of Doom," *New York Times*, February 2, 1991, www.nytimes.com/1991/02/02/us/gulf-war-proving -bountiful-for-some-prophets-of-doom.html.

84.    Geraldine Baum, "Has Time Run Out? Religion: Some Worry Armageddon Is Near. But Most Evangelical Pastors Call the War a Prelude, Not the 'Main Event,'" *Los Angeles Times*, February 7, 1991, www.latimes.com/ archives/la-xpm-1991-02-07-vw-1003-story.html.

    Why would the elder Bush, a former US ambassador to the United Nations, onetime director of the CIA, and an Episcopalian, turn to a dispensationalist paperback at a moment of Middle East crisis? In the ten weeks prior to February 1991 Zondervan had sold six hundred thousand copies; Washington's request came from White House staff rather than the Defense or State Departments. Together, these suggest that presidential interest in Walvoord's book had more to do with understanding a significant slice of the electorate than with geopolitical concerns.

85.    E. Schuyler English, et al., eds., *The New Scofield Reference Bible: Holy Bible, Authorized King James Version, with Introductions, Annotations, Subject Chain References, and Such Word Changes in the Text as Will Help the Reader* (New York: Oxford University Press, 1967).

86.    Lindsey and Carlson, *Late Great Planet Earth*.

87.    Thor Heyerdahl, *The Ra Expeditions*, trans. Patricia Crampton (Garden City, NY: Doubleday, 1971); Eric von Däniken, *Chariots of the Gods? Unsolved Mysteries*

*of the Past*, trans. Michael Heron (New York: Berkley, 1969); Alvin Toffler, *Future Shock* (New York: Random House, 1970).

88.  Pentecost, *Things to Come*, 281.

89.  Lindsey, *Late Great Planet Earth*, 53–54.

90.  Van Impe, *A.D. 2000: The End?*; Jack Van Impe, *December 21st 2012: History's Final Day?*, DVD (Troy, MI: Jack Van Impe Ministries, 2008).

91.  "The Late Great Planet Earth (1978)," Internet Movie Database, www.imdb.com/title/tt0079445/business?ref_=tt_dt_bus.

92.  Pew Research Center, *Life in 2050: Amazing Science, Familiar Threats. Public Sees a Future Full of Promise and Peril* (Washington, DC: Pew Research Center, 2010), 15.

CHAPTER 3

1.  The sources featured offer a balance of characteristics. Dwight Pentecost's *Things to Come* is a classic of the dispensational world and encyclopedic in scope. Hal Lindsey's *Late Great Planet Earth* has shaped popular perceptions of eschatology since the 1970s. Ron Rhodes's book *The End Times in Chronological Order: A Complete Overview to Understanding Bible Prophecy* (Eugene, OR: Harvest House, 2012) is selected because of its clarity and availability.

2.  E.g., Lindsey, *Late Great Planet Earth*, 42–58; Rhodes, *End Times in Chronological Order*, 28–31.

3.  John Nelson Darby, "The Hopes of the Church of God, in Connection with the Destiny of the Jews and the Nations, as Revealed in Prophecy. Eleven Lectures Delivered in

Geneva, 1840," in *The Collected Writings of J. N. Darby*, vol. 2, *Prophetic, No. 1* (Winschoten: Heijkoop, 1972), 353–62; Darby, "Lectures on the Second Coming of Christ. Delivered at Toronto, Canada," in *Collected Writings of J. N. Darby*, vol. 11, *Prophetic, No. 4* (Winschoten: Heijkoop, 1972), 268–78.

4.    In 1922, the Jewish population of the British Mandate of Palestine stood at 83,790. A decade later, that figure had more than doubled, jumping to 174,606. See J. V. W. Shaw, ed., *A Survey of Palestine, Prepared in December 1945 and January 1946 for the Information of the Anglo-American Committee of Inquiry* (Jerusalem: Government Printer, Palestine, 1946), 1:141.

5.    E.g., Lindsey, *Late Great Planet Earth*, 43–54, 60–62; Grant R. Jeffrey, *Armageddon, Appointment with Destiny* (Toronto: Frontier Research, 1988), 34–43; Rhodes, *End Times in Chronological Order*, 28–30.

6.    Jeffrey, *Armageddon*, 108–27; Lindsey, *Late Great Planet Earth*, 55–57; Rhodes, *End Times in Chronological Order*, 96–97.

7.    International Department of the Temple Institute, "The Temple Institute," https://www.templeinstitute.org.

8.    The first temple was built by King Solomon, with the second temple erected following the return from exile and reconstructed by Herod the Great. The third temple will be built at some future date. Some writers count the postexilic temple and Herod's temple as the second and third temples respectively and so number the future temple as the fourth.

9.    International Department of the Temple Institute, "The Red Heifer: Fact & Fiction," https://www.templeinstitute.org/red-heifer-fact-and-fiction.htm.

10. Daniel C. Browning Jr., "The Strange Search for the Ashes of the Red Heifer," *The Biblical Archaeologist* 59.2 (1996): 74–89.

11. E.g., in the novels *Skinny Legs and All* and *Hunter*, Christians take destructive action to hasten the apocalypse. See Tom Robbins, *Skinny Legs and All* (New York: Bantam, 1990); Lackey Mercedes, *Hunter* (Los Angeles: Hyperion, 2015). In the 1991 film *The Rapture*, a mentally unbalanced character, Sharon (played by Mimi Rogers), takes her daughter out into the desert, where she kills her so that the girl can join her deceased father in heaven.

12. The term "rapture" is taken from the Vulgate *rapiemur* ("taken away") of 1 Thess 4:17. The Greek term is *harpazō*. Among critiques of the rapture doctrine it is common to point out that this term does not appear in the Greek NT. While this is true, this is not, in and of itself, an argument against the validity of this idea, since the church has a tradition of applying Latin terms to theological concepts. The term "sacrament," for example, is a term used by the Vulgate to translate the Greek *mystērion*, while the term "Trinity" is not a term that appears in Scripture at all. Any assessment of whether the rapture is scriptural must come from an examination of Scripture.

13. This question upended the long-running Niagara Bible Conference in 1900. See Larry Dean Pettegrew, "The Historical and Theological Contributions of the Niagara Bible Conference to American Fundamentalism" (ThD diss., Dallas Theological Seminary, 1976), 170–83.

14. Pentecost, *Things to Come*, 202–4; Rhodes, *End Times in Chronological Order*, 48.

15. For a comprehensive assessment of the various opinions that settles on the pretribulationist view, see Pentecost,

*Things to Come*, 156–218. See also Jeffrey, *Armageddon*, 131–39; Rhodes, *End Times in Chronological Order*, 41–53.

16. E.g., MacPherson, *Incredible Cover-Up*; Gary North, *Rapture Fever: Why Dispensationalism Is Paralyzed* (Tyler, TX: Institute for Christian Economics, 1993); Barbara R. Rossing, *The Rapture Exposed: The Message of Hope in the Book of Revelation* (New York: Basic, 2004). The three titles reflect the intense critique of dispensationalism and the rapture the books contain. While well researched, all are marred by vitriol. This is especially the case with Rossing, who is concerned with pointed social objections to the rapture doctrine. Actually refuting the doctrine is reserved for an epilogue, "Debunking the Rapture, Verse by Verse" (Rossing, *Rapture Exposed*, 173–86).

17. This is a dominant theme in Rossing's book.

18. Rossing, *Rapture Exposed*, 174–77. See Clinton E. Arnold, ed., *Zondervan Bible Background Commentary on the New Testament* (Grand Rapids: Zondervan, 2002), 3:422–23.

19. *NSRB*, 1235n2.

20. Pentecost, *Things to Come*, 219–26; Rhodes, *End Times in Chronological Order*, 67–71.

21. Pentecost, *Things to Come*, 26–28; Rhodes, *End Times in Chronological Order*, 71–72, 184–85.

22. Rhodes, *End Times in Chronological Order*, 71, 185.

23. Tim LaHaye and Jerry B. Jenkins, *Left Behind: A Novel of the Earth's Last Days* (Wheaton, IL: Tyndale House, 1989).

24. *NSRB*, 1294–95n1; Rhodes, *End Times in Chronological Order*, 55–66.

25. I.e., 445 BC; *NSRB*, 913n1 (5).

26.    This same understanding affects the interpretation of
       Ezekiel, in which chapter 33 is understood to refer to
       Ezekiel's own day and chapters 34–48 to the future resto-
       ration of Israel and beyond, with the intervening church
       age unrepresented.

27.    Clarence Larkin, *Dispensational Truth, or God's Plan
       and Purpose in the Ages*, rev. ed. (Glenside, PA: Rev.
       Clarence Larkin Est., 1920), 140; *NSRB*, 898–99n1;
       Pentecost, *Things to Come*, 239–50; Rhodes, *End Times
       in Chronological Order*, 87–88.

28.    We continue to present the pretribulation rapture theory,
       with Christians removed prior to the seventieth week of
       Daniel and the tribulation. While this is most popular
       view within dispensationalism, some believe that the
       church will go through at least part of the tribulation.

29.    Lindsey, *Late Great Planet Earth*, 151–53; Rhodes, *End
       Times in Chronological Order*, 88.

30.    Rhodes, *End Times in Chronological Order*, 76. Many dis-
       pensationalists explain the absence of the United States
       from end-times prophecy by suggesting that the loss of
       its substantial Christian population will send the country
       into decline, taking it off the world stage.

31.    *NSRB*, 908n4, 1364n2; Jeffrey, *Armageddon*, 140–41, 143;
       Lindsey, *Late Great Planet Earth*, 88–97; Pentecost, *Things
       to Come*, 318–23; Rhodes, *End Times in Chronological
       Order*, 93–94.

32.    E.g., Albert Close, *"Babylon": The Scarlet Woman: Or, the
       Divine Foreview of the Rise, Reign and Destiny of the Church
       of Rome. A Study Historic and Prophetic of Revelation XVII*,
       2nd ed. (London: Marshall Brothers, 1910).

33. The history of this rapprochement can be traced from the 1970s, in the common cause that evangelicals such as Francis Schaeffer found with Roman Catholics in opposing abortion, through to the 1994 ecumenical document *Evangelicals and Catholics Together*, the leading signatories of which were Charles Colson and Richard John Neuhaus. See "Evangelicals and Catholics Together: The Christian Mission in the Third Millennium," *First Things* (May 1994), https://www.firstthings.com/article/1994/05/evangelicals-catholics-together-the-christian-mission-in-the-third-millennium.

34. Lindsey, *Late Great Planet Earth*, 114–34; Pentecost, *Things to Come*, 368; Rhodes, *End Times in Chronological Order*, 124–25. Dispensationalist Bible teacher Walter Scott modified this view slightly by maintaining that Babylon "is not the papal system alone, but the fusion of parties bearing the christian name into one vast system of evil. The characteristics of the papacy in the Middle Ages are evidently witnessed in the whore of the Apocalypse." See Scott, *Exposition of the Revelation of Jesus Christ*, 4th ed. (Grand Rapids: Kregel, n.d.), 342. In its note on this passage, *The New Scofield Reference Bible* identifies Babylon as "all apostate Christendom, in which the Papacy will undoubtedly be prominent; it may well be that this union will anticipate all the religions of the world" (*NSRB*, 1369–70n2).

35. The term "Chrislam" first appears in the 1914 novel *The Flying Inn*, by G. K. Chesterton, which pictures a future England dominated by a progressive form of Islam. As an actual religious movement, it is represented by several syncretistic religious groups in Nigeria. In North America, the late end-times teacher Jack Van Impe

warned of the interfaith movement as a dangerous move toward melding Christianity and Islam into a single religion. Van Impe and others have pointed to interfaith overtures by American megachurch pastor and author Rick Warren as evidence of a move toward Chrislam.

36. Rhodes, *End Times in Chronological Order*, 107.

37. Rhodes, *End Times in Chronological Order*, 113–14.

38. Rhodes, *End Times in Chronological Order*, 116, 136–37.

39. "The Annals of Thutmose III," in *The Context of Scripture*, ed. William W. Hallo and K. Lawson Younger Jr. (Leiden: Brill, 1997–2002), 2.2A, lines 90–94a.

40. On the history of conflict related to Megiddo, see Eric H. Cline, *The Battles of Armageddon: Megiddo and the Jezreel Valley From the Bronze Age to the Nuclear Age* (Ann Arbor, MI: University of Michigan, 2000).

41. Pentecost lists eight theories regarding the character of the battle of Armageddon (*Things to Come*, 343–44).

42. Rhodes, *End Times in Chronological Order*, 76–79. Others are unclear about the timing, e.g., Jeffrey, *Armageddon*, 106. For the range of possible views and an assessment of each see Pentecost, *Things to Come*, 342–55.

43. Pentecost, *Things to Come*, 340, 50–55; also Lindsey, *Late Great Planet Earth*, 153–61.

44. Pentecost, *Things to Come*, 354–58.

45. Pentecost, *Things to Come*, 350.

46. Lindsey, *Late Great Planet Earth*, 154–57, 61.

47. Some end-times teachers argue that since the aftermath of the battle described in Ezek 38–39 involves seven months of burying the dead and seven years of

burning the leftover military hardware (Ezek 39:9–13), this engagement is an earlier one that is unrelated to the battle of Armageddon, and that the attack that occurs at this point is the one described in Jer 50:9, 41–42 (Rhodes, *End Times in Chronological Order*, 73–85, 167–68).

48. Pentecost, *Things to Come*, 354.

49. *NSRB*, 973–74n5.

50. Lindsey, *Late Great Planet Earth*, 161.

51. Pentecost, *Things to Come*, 357.

52. Jeffrey, *Armageddon*, 104.

53. *NSRB*, 1361n1; Lindsey, *Late Great Planet Earth*, 162–66; Pentecost, *Things to Come*, 356–57; Rhodes, *End Times in Chronological Order*, 165.

54. Pentecost, *Things to Come*, 341.

55. Pentecost, *Things to Come*, 240–42.

56. E.g., Lindsey, *Late Great Planet Earth*, 64–66; Pentecost, *Things to Come*, 326–28; Rhodes, *End Times in Chronological Order*, 77. An exception to this tendency is Charles H. Dyer, *World News and Bible Prophecy* (Wheaton, IL: Tyndale House, 1993), 109–13. For some writers, this connection is so assured that no effort is made to explain the reason for such connections, e.g., Walvoord and Walvoord, *Armageddon, Oil*, 121–29; Jeffrey, *Armageddon*, 97–107.

57. Wilhelm Gesenius, *Lexicon Manuale Hebraicum Et Chaldaicum in Veteris Testamenti Libros* (Lipsiae: Sumtibus typisque F.C.G. Vogelii, 1833), 916–17.

58. E.g., Francis Brown, S. R. Driver, and Charles A. Briggs, *A Hebrew and English Lexicon of the Old Testament … Based*

*on the Lexicon of William Gesenius as Translated by Edward Robinson* (Oxford: Oxford University Press, 1952).

59. Most significant among the relatively few translations that render "Rosh" as a place name are ERV (1885), ASV (1901), Darby (1890), NASB (1971), and Young's Literal Translation (1862).

60. For a refutation of the Rosh = Russia equation from the pen of a dispensational OT scholar, see Ralph H. Alexander, "A Fresh Look at Ezekiel 38 and 39," *Journal of the Evangelical Theological Society* 17 (1974): 161–62.

61. *NSRB*, 137n1; Pentecost, *Things to Come*, 395–97.

62. Pentecost, *Things to Come*, 396–97.

63. *NSRB*, 1373–74 nn. 2–3.

64. Rhodes, *End Times in Chronological Order*, 187–204.

65. Pentecost covers this era in immense detail (*Things to Come*, 427–546).

66. Pentecost, *Things to Come*, 549; Rhodes, *End Times in Chronological Order*, 206.

67. Pentecost, *Things to Come*, 549.

68. Pentecost, *Things to Come*, 397–407; Rhodes, *End Times in Chronological Order*, 210–11.

69. Rhodes, *End Times in Chronological Order*, 212–13.

70. Pentecost, *Things to Come*, 563–83; Rhodes, *End Times in Chronological Order*, 218–27.

71. Based on the ratio given in Marvin A. Powell, "Weights and Measures," in *The Anchor Bible Dictionary*, ed. David Noel Freedman (New York: Doubleday, 1992), 6:901.

72. Rhodes, *End Times in Chronological Order*, 223. See also Walvoord, *Revelation*, 323–24. Not all dispensational interpreters are so literalistic, however. For his part,

Scott understands the new Jerusalem to be the glorified church and so considers it to be a "mystical" city (Scott, *Revelation*, 421).

73. This parallel is noted by Rhodes as an outside possibility, but even so, he seems not to recognize the relational ramifications of such a correspondence (*End Times in Chronological Order*, 223).

74. Rhodes, *End Times in Chronological Order*, 218–20.

## CHAPTER 4

1. Pentecost, *Things to Come*, 476–511.

2. George Eldon Ladd, *Crucial Questions on the Kingdom of God* (Grand Rapids: Eerdmans, 1961), 49.

3. The disturbing story of how mainline American Protestants became entangled with the eugenics movement is detailed in Christine Rosen, *Preaching Eugenics: Religious Leaders and the American Eugenics Movement* (Oxford: Oxford University Press, 2004).

## CHAPTER 5

1. Richard A. Taylor, *Interpreting Apocalyptic Literature: An Exegetical Handbook* (Grand Rapids: Kregel Academic, 2016).

2. Gordon D. Fee and Douglas Stuart, *How to Read the Bible for All Its Worth* (Grand Rapids: Zondervan, 2014), 197.

3. Jeffrey, *Armageddon*, 10. See, similarly, Tim LaHaye and Thomas Ice, *Charting the End Times: A Visual Guide to Understanding Bible Prophecy* (Eugene, OR: Harvest House, 2001), 12–14; Lindsey, *Late Great Planet Earth*, 19–26, 32–41.

4. Pentecost, *Things to Come*, 49.

5. *NSRB*, 876n1; Pentecost, *Things to Come*, 142, 442, 476, 495–511.

6. John J. Collins, "Towards the Morphology of a Genre: Introduction," *Semeia* 14 (1979): 9.

7. In Babylonian iconography, the chief deity Marduk was sometimes represented as an ox; the underworld deity, Nergal, as a lion; Ninib, god of war, as an eagle; and Nabu, the revealer, as a human. See further Brian Neil Peterson, *Ezekiel in Context: Ezekiel's Message Understood in Its Historical Setting of Covenant Curses and Ancient Near Eastern Mythological Motifs*, Princeton Theological Monograph Series 182 (Eugene, OR: Pickwick, 2012), 116–24. That the living creatures act at the prompting of the spirit further indicates their subservient status (Ezek 1:12).

8. Pentecost, *Things to Come*, 441–42.

9. Charles H. Dyer, *The Rise of Babylon: Sign of the End Times* (Wheaton, IL: Tyndale House, 1991).

CHAPTER 6

1. Walvoord and Walvoord, *Armageddon, Oil*, 121–29, 63.

2. Walvoord, *Daniel*, 11–27, 174–76.

3. For a survey of these campaigns see Rainey and Notley, *Sacred Bridge*, 261–63.

4. It is significant to note that among the final kings of Judah, Jehoiachin was the only one who acted in keeping with the prophetic word that identified Babylon as God's instrument of judgment and surrendered in keeping with the divine command (2 Kgs 24:10–12; Jer

1:14–19; 25:1–14; cf. 38:17–18). It is likely for this reason that Ezekiel gives most of his dates from the year of the exile of King Jehoiachin. This dating format suggests that Ezekiel considers Jehoiachin, rather than his successor, Zedekiah, to be the last legitimate ruler of Judah.

5. In Ezek 4–5, the prophet acts out two pantomimes for the exiles showing how Jerusalem will be besieged and its inhabitants starved and struck down. In Ezek 11:16, Ezekiel tells the exiles how God himself has made their exile a sanctuary for them.

6. *CTA* 19 i–ii (*KTU* 1.19 i–ii). For English translations of this story see Dennis Pardee, "The ʾAqatu Legend (1.103)," in Hallo and Younger, *Context of Scripture*, 1:343–56; Nicolas Wyatt, *Religious Texts from Ugarit: The Words of Ilimilku and His Colleagues*, The Biblical Seminar 53 (Sheffield: Sheffield Academic, 1998), 246–312.

7. E.g., Lindsey, *Late Great Planet Earth*, 48–52. This view is not universally held, however. Pentecost—typically resistant to connecting Scripture to current events—sees Ezek 37 as referring to an event of the tribulation period (Pentecost, *Things to Come*, 231, 280).

8. Lindsey, *Late Great Planet Earth*, 43.

9. If Sheshbazzar is to be equated with Shenazzar (Ezra 5:14; cf. 1 Chr 3:18), then the first governor was a son of Jehoiachin. Zerubbabel (Hag 1:14; 2:2) was a grandson. Names of the later governors Elnathan and Yehezekiah (known from seals) correspond to Judean royal family names. See generally Rainey and Notley, *Sacred Bridge*, 285–86, 295–96.

10. Pentecost, *Things to Come*, 326–31; Lindsey, *Late Great Planet Earth*, 59–71.

11. Such is the argument of Walvoord and Walvoord, *Armageddon, Oil.*

12. Margaret S. Odell, *Ezekiel,* Smyth & Helwys Bible Commentary (Macon, GA: Smyth & Helwys, 2005), 468–69.

13. Pentecost, *Things to Come,* 512–17. Some rabbis also saw these differences in measurement as a problem and questioned the inspiration of the book on the basis of this. According to tradition, the question was settled when Rabbi Hanina ben Hezekiah locked himself in an upper room and burned three hundred barrels of lamp oil as he worked to reconcile the differences between Ezekiel and the Torah (Babylonian Talmud Shabbat 13b).

14. Pentecost, *Things to Come,* 487–511.

## CHAPTER 7

1. An early twentieth-century defense of the conservative position aimed at a popular audience is found in Robert Anderson, *Daniel in the Critics' Den: A Defense of the Historicity of the Book of Daniel* (Grand Rapids: Kregel, 1990). A presentation of the critical view at the same period is found in S. R. Driver, *The Book of Daniel: With Introduction and Notes* (Cambridge: Cambridge University Press, 1900).

2. See John H. Hayes and Frederick Prussner, *Old Testament Theology: Its History and Development* (Atlanta: John Knox, 1985), 139–40.

3. Porphyry's *Adversus Christianos (Against Christians)* is preserved in fragments in Jerome's commentary on Daniel. Porphyry presumed that predictive prophecy was impossible and concluded that Daniel was written during the time of Antiochus IV Epiphanes.

4.   For an overview of critical issues and the second-century dating of Daniel see John J. Collins, *Daniel: A Commentary on the Book of Daniel* (Minneapolis: Fortress, 1993), 24–39.

5.   Among other concerns were (1) the use of the term "Chaldean" as an ethnic designation as opposed to a technical term meaning "astrologer," (2) the lack of historical evidence for Nebuchadnezzar's madness, (3) evidence from Qumran suggesting that Nabonidus was actually the monarch who became ill, (4) the erroneous designation of Belshazzar as king at the fall of Babylon to Cyrus, and (5) the existence of a ruler named Darius the Mede. For a list of these criticisms and a conservative response, see Roland K. Harrison, *Introduction to the Old Testament* (Grand Rapids: Eerdmans, 1969), 1112–23.

6.   E.g., Robert Dick Wilson, "The Aramaic of Daniel," in *Biblical and Theological Studies, by Members of the Faculty of Princeton Theological Seminary* (New York: Scribner's Sons, 1912), 261–306; Kenneth A. Kitchen, "The Aramaic of Daniel," in *Notes on Some Problems in the Book of Daniel*, ed. D. J. Wiseman (London: Tyndale, 1965), 31–79.

7.   Josh McDowell, *Prophecy, Fact or Fiction? Historical Evidence for the Authenticity of the Book of Daniel* (San Bernardino: Campus Crusade for Christ, 1979).

8.   See, for example, the commentary by John Goldingay, *Daniel*, WBC 30 (Dallas: Word, 1989).

9.   Jeffrey, *Armageddon*, 26–33. For a comparison of several proposals, see Thomas Ice, "The 70 Weeks of Daniel," in *The End Times Controversy: The Second Coming under Attack*, ed. Tim LaHaye and Thomas Ice (Eugene, OR: Harvest House, 2003), 321–30.

10.  This takes a lunar month of 29.53 days and rounds it up to thirty days. (Most lunar calendars used a thirty-day

month and added an intercalary month every several years to bring the lunar year into line with the solar year.) According to Larkin, "the 5 months from the 17th day of the 2d month, until the 17th day of the 7th month, are reckoned as 150 days, or 30 days to a month" (Larkin, *Dispensational Truth*, 71). Grant Jeffrey notes that in Esth 1:4, the six-month-long feast given by King Xerxes lasted 180 days (*Armageddon*, 224).

11.      Nehemiah is reckoned to have received his command on March 14, 445 BC. The additional twenty-nine days is the number of days between March 14 and April 2, AD 30.

12.      While impressive, Anderson's calculations represent just one possible take. His resort to a lunar/prophetic year of 360 days ignores the fact that the Jewish lunar calendar periodically added an additional month to the year to bring it into sync with the solar year. In addition, the end point changes depending on the starting date chosen. Should the starting point be 587 BC and the prophecy of Jeremiah that Jerusalem would eventually be rebuilt (Jer 30:18-22; 31:38-40) or the 538 BC decree of Cyrus which granted the Judeans permission to return to Jerusalem to rebuild the temple and city (Ezra 1:1-4; 2 Chron 36:23; Isa 44:28; 45:13)? Several other starting dates have also been suggested. So wearying is the problem that one scholar has described the 70 weeks of Daniel as the "dismal swamp of Old Testament criticism." For a discussion of the chronological alternatives see Ernest C. Lucas, *Daniel* (Downers Grove, IL: InterVarsity, 2002), 245–48.

13.      Pentecost, *Things to Come*, 200–201, 246–49; Ice, "70 Weeks of Daniel," 332–34.

14.  Stanley D. Walters, "The End (of What?) Is at Hand," *Toronto Journal of Theology* 2 (1986): 23–46. The presentation of the basic structure and theme of Daniel offered here owes much to Walters's analysis. See also Brian P. Irwin, "The Book of Daniel and the Roots of New Testament Mission," in *Christian Mission: Old Testament Foundations and New Testament Developments*, ed. Stanley E. Porter and Cynthia Long Westfall (Eugene, OR: Pickwick, 2010), 42–63.

15.  That this is the case is clear not only from the content but also from the summary of Daniel's career conveyed by the notation that Daniel entered foreign service in the reign of Nebuchadnezzar (Dan 1:5–6) and that he continued to serve until the reign of Cyrus the Persian (Dan 1:21).

16.  Daniel 1:9: *wayyittēn hā'ĕlōhîm 'et-dānîyyē'l ləḥesed ûləraḥămîm lipnê śar hassārîsîm* ("God granted Daniel favor and compassion before the chief of the officials"). Unless otherwise specified, all Hebrew quotations are from Karl Elliger and W. Rudolph, eds., *Biblia Hebraica Stuttgartensia*, Minor ed. (Stuttgart: Deutsche Bibelgesellschaft, 1984). Septuagint quotes are based on Alfred Rahlfs, ed., *Septuaginta* (Stuttgart: Deutsche Bibelgesellschaft, 1979). Greek NT quotations are taken from Kurt Aland et al., eds., *The Greek New Testament*, 27th ed., 2nd printing; 4th rev. ed. (Stuttgart: Deutsche Bibelgesellschaft, 1994).

17.  It is also possible that this action is intended by the king to humiliate the astrologers who were so quick to shrink from the royal challenge.

18.  The designation of the rock as "not carved by human hands" (*hitgəzeret 'eben dî-lā' bîdayin*, 2:34) establishes that these kingdoms are not destroyed by accident or human power but by divine intent.

19.     That the stone grows into a mountain likely reflects a
        dependence on the same Sinai imagery found in the NT
        in contexts such as the transfiguration (Matt 17:1–13;
        Mark 9:2–13; Luke 9:28–36). For a summary of the
        connections between Matthew 17:1–13 and Sinai see
        W. D. Davies and Dale C. Allison Jr., *The Gospel according
        to Saint Matthew*, vol. 2, *Commentary on Matthew VIII–
        XVIII*, ICC (Edinburgh: T&T Clark, 1991), 684–709;
        and Terence L. Donaldson, *Jesus on the Mountain: A Study
        in Matthean Theology*, Journal for the Study of the New
        Testament Supplement Series 8 (Sheffield: JSOT Press,
        1985), 142–43.

20.     As noted above, the extent to which the kingdom of God
        has begun to intrude into the earthly realm is indicated
        by the fact that the king himself receives a partial inter-
        pretation of the dream. In 4:15b–17 (Heb. 4:12b–14), the
        angel announcing the destruction of the tree abandons
        the image of the tree and declares that an unnamed
        person will be temporarily deposed and given over to
        madness. This will be accomplished, the angel continues,
        to establish "that the Most High is sovereign over human
        kingdoms" (4:17; Heb. 4:14).

21.     This is indicated in 4:34 (Heb. 4:31) by the phrase
        *wəliqṣāt yômayyâ* ("At the end of that time …").

22.     This framing is emphasized by the use of *inclusio* in which
        the expression *malkûtēh malkût ʿālam wəšolṭānēh ʿim-dār
        wədār* ("his kingdom is eternal and his dominion exists
        generation to generation," 4:3; Heb. 3:33) is inversely
        repeated in 4:34 (Heb. 4:31) as *šolṭānēh šolṭān ʿālam
        ûmalkûtēh ʿim-dār wədār* ("his dominion is eternal and
        his kingdom exists generation to generation").

23.     See the repetition in 2:21 and 7:25 of the terms *šnh*
        ("to change"), *zəmon* ("fixed time/season"), and *ʿiddān*

("time"). Present also in both passages are near-identical phrases emphasizing the eternal nature of God's kingdom. Compare *malkû dî lǝ ʿolmîn lā ʾ titḥabbal* ("an eternal kingdom, not to be destroyed," 2:44) and *ûmalkûtēh dî-lā ʾ titḥabbal* ("his kingdom [is one] which will not be destroyed," 7:14).

24.  On the characteristics of apocalyptic see John J. Collins, *The Apocalyptic Imagination: An Introduction to the Jewish Matrix of Christianity* (New York: Crossroad, 1984), 1–8; and Paul D. Hanson, *Old Testament Apocalyptic* (Nashville: Abingdon, 1987), 25–34.

25.  The attempt on the part of the fourth beast to "alter the seasons" (*wǝyisbar lǝhašnāyâ zimnîn*) represents a direct challenge to the sovereignty of God, whose right to exercise this kind of authority has already been recognized in Nebuchadnezzar's declaration that only God "changes the times and the seasons" (*wǝhû ʾ mǝhašnē ʾ ʿiddānayyā ʾ wǝzimnayyā ʾ*, 2:21). The connection between these two sections is further confirmed by the presence in 7:25 of various forms of ʿiddān ("time"), which appears also in 2:21.

26.  This is the obvious implication of the statement that this kingdom will be destroyed, "but not by human power" (8:25). See also 2:34, 45.

27.  In 8:13, one angel asks of another, *ʿad-mātay heḥāzôn hattāmîd wǝhappeša ʿ šōmēm tēt wǝqōdeš wǝṣābā ʾ mirmās* ("How long will the vision of the regular sacrifice and the rebellion that causes desolation, and the trampling of the holy place and the host endure?"). In response to this, Daniel uses the same key vocabulary to ask God to rectify this situation (*wǝhā ʾēr pānêkā ʿal-miqdoškā haššāmēm*; "Shine your face upon your desolate holy place," 9:17).

28.     If the first month mentioned in 10:4 is Tishri, then the three weeks of mourning undertaken by Daniel coincide with both the Day of Atonement and the Feast of Tabernacles, the former being an appropriate backdrop for Daniel's time of penitence.

29.     The vision that begins in chapter 11 comes from the "Book of Truth" (11:21) and is a chronicle of the history of the ancient Near East from the end of the Persian Empire to the Hasmonean era. Figures and events that seem to be indicated here are Alexander the Great (336–323 BC; Dan 11:3), the Diadochi (11:4), the Ptolemies and the Syrian Wars (ca. 274–198 BC; Dan 11:5–13), Antiochus III (223–187 BC), the Battle of Ipsus (301 BC), and the Peace of Apamaea (188 BC; Dan 11:14–19), Seleucus IV Philapator (187–175 BC; Dan 11:20), and Antiochus IV Epiphanes (175–163 BC; Dan 11:21–45). See, in general, Goldingay, *Daniel*, 292–305. For the history of this period in general, see F. F. Bruce, *Israel and the Nations: The History of Israel from the Exodus to the Fall of the Second Temple*, rev. ed. (Carlisle, UK: Paternoster, 1997), 116–43.

30.     This policy of forcibly removing aboriginal Canadian children from their families and sending them to be educated in English in residential schools lasted from the late nineteenth to the mid to late twentieth century and was the subject of a royal commission, which produced a six-volume report in 2015. The ongoing work arising from this commission is now administered through the National Centre for Truth and Reconciliation at the University of Manitoba (https://nctr.ca/map.php). The report of the commission is available at http://nctr.ca/reports.php.

31.     See https://www.opendoorsca.org/world-watch-list/country-profiles/.

CHAPTER 8

1.    A comparison of these four perspectives can be found
      in Steve Gregg, *Revelation, Four Views: A Parallel
      Commentary* (Nashville: Thomas Nelson, 2013);
      Marvin C. Pate, *Four Views on the Book of Revelation*
      (Grand Rapids: Zondervan, 1998).

2.    E.g., Larkin, *Dispensational Truth*.

3.    In the introductory comments to Revelation in his 1522
      translation of the NT, Luther voiced doubts as to the
      book's value as prophecy and to its apostolic character.
      By 1530, however, with the Ottoman emperor Suleiman
      threatening Vienna, Luther was able to see the rise of
      the Turks as clearly foretold in the text. See Irena Backus,
      *Reformation Readings of the Apocalypse: Geneva, Zurich,
      and Wittenberg* (New York: Oxford University Press,
      2000), xv–xvii, 6–11; Winfried Vogel, "The Eschatological
      Theology of Martin Luther, Part II: Luther's Exposition
      of Daniel and Revelation," *Andrews University Seminary
      Studies* 25 (1987): 183–99. In this he was anticipated by
      earlier Catholic writers Nicholas of Lyra (1270–1349),
      Alexander Minorita (d. 1271), and Pierre Auriol (1280–
      1322), all of whom saw Rev 13:1 and its depiction of the
      beast arising from the sea as predicting the rise of Islam
      in the seventh century. See Philip D. Krey, "Nicholas of
      Lyra: Apocalypse Commentator, Historian, and Critic,"
      *Franciscan Studies* 52 (1992): 53–84.

4.    Sir Isaac Newton, *Observations Upon the Prophecies
      of Daniel, and the Apocalypse of St. John: In Two Parts*
      (Dublin: Printed by S. Powell for George Risk, George
      Ewing, and William Smith, 1733).

5.    William Miller, *Evidence From Scripture and History of
      the Second Coming of Christ, about the Year 1843: Exhibited*

*in a Course of Lectures* (Troy, NY: Elias Gates, 1838). One of the few recent commentaries from this perspective is Oral E. Collins, *The Final Prophecy of Jesus: An Introduction, Analysis, and Commentary on the Book of Revelation* (Eugene, OR: Wipf & Stock, 2007).

6.   Francisco Ribera, *In Sacrum Beati Ioannis Apostoli, & Evangelistiae Apocalypsin Commentarij* (Salamanica: Petrus Lassus, 1591).

7.   Notable futurist commentaries include Scott, *Exposition of the Revelation*; Harry A. Ironside, *Lectures on the Revelation* (New York: Loizeaux Brothers, 1930); Walvoord, *Revelation of Jesus Christ*; John F. MacArthur, Jr., *Revelation*, 2 vols. (Chicago: Moody, 1999–2000).

8.   Luis Alcazar, *Vestigatio Arcani Sensus in Apocalypsi* (Antwerp: Ioannem Keerbergium, 1614).

9.   This view was widely disseminated through the work of Scottish Congregationalist clergyman J. Stuart Russell in *The Parousia: A Critical Inquiry into the New Testament Doctrine of Our Lord's Second Coming*, new ed. (London: Unwin, 1887).

10.  E.g., David Chilton, *The Days of Vengeance: An Exposition of the Book of Revelation* (Fort Worth, TX: Dominion, 1987); Kenneth L. Gentry, Jr., *The Book of Revelation Made Easy: You Can Understand Bible Prophecy* (Powder Springs, GA: American Vision, 2008). On individual issues of eschatology addressed from a preterist perspective, see Gary DeMar, *Last Days Madness: The Folly of Trying to Predict When Christ Will Return* (Centerville, TN: American Vision, 1999).

11.  E.g., Raymond Calkins, *The Social Message of the Book of Revelation* (New York: Womans Press, 1920); Elisabeth Schüssler Fiorenza, *Revelation: Vision of a Just World*

(Minneapolis: Fortress, 1991); William Hendriksen, *More Than Conquerors: An Interpretation of the Book of Revelation* (Grand Rapids: Baker, 1967); Bruce M. Metzger, *Breaking the Code: Understanding the Book of Revelation* (Nashville: Abingdon, 1993); N. T. Wright, *Revelation for Everyone* (Louisville: Westminster John Knox, 2011); G. K. Beale, *The Book of Revelation: A Commentary on the Greek Text*, New International Greek Testament Commentary (Grand Rapids: Eerdmans, 1999).

12. Examples of recent eclectic commentaries on Revelation include Leon Morris, *Revelation*, Tyndale New Testament Commentaries 20 (Grand Rapids: Eerdmans, 1987); Robert H. Mounce, *The Book of Revelation* (Grand Rapids: Eerdmans, 1998); Grant R. Osborne, *Revelation* (Grand Rapids: Baker Academic, 2002). Beale may also be construed as falling into this category (*Book of Revelation*).

13. Leszek Jańczuk, "Dating the Book of Revelation in Light of Tradition," *Ruch Biblijny i Liturgiczny* 71 (2018): 44.

14. This attestation is found in the editions produced by Philoxenus of Mabbug and Thomas of Heraclea but is lacking in earlier texts. Regardless, the book of Revelation was among the last books to appear as part of the Syriac NT. See Jańczuk, "Dating the Book," 47–49.

15. Jańczuk, "Dating the Book," 48.

16. Brian W. Jones, *The Emperor Domitian* (New York: Routledge, 1992), 114–17. While Eusebius may have been prone to exaggeration on this point, Jones's conclusion would also seem to imply that he fabricated the testimony of the three sources that he cites. In addition, the idea that there was no persecution of Christians during this

era must contend with the tradition of the church, which places the martyrdom of figures such as Justin Martyr in the reign of Domitian.

17. Paul Keresztes, "Marcus Aurelius a Persecutor?," *Harvard Theological Review* 61 (1968): 321–41.

18. For an authoritative annual report on the global persecution of Christians consult the Open Doors World Watch list (https://www.opendoorsusa.org/christian-persecution/world-watch-list/).

19. If this is the case, then the murdered emperors would include (1) Julius Caesar, (2) Caligula, (3) Nero (possible suicide during the revolt of Galba), (4) Galba, and (5) Vitellius.

20. According to this view, if one takes the Greek form of Nero's title, "Neron Caesar," transliterates it into Aramaic (*nrwn qsr*), and reckons each letter as its corresponding number (from right to left, 50 + 6 + 200 + 50 and 200 + 60 + 100), then the phrase totals 666. See Charles, *Critical and Exegetical Commentary*, 364–68, and Delbert R. Hillers, "Revelation 13:18 and a Scroll from Murabbaʿat," *Bulletin of the American Schools of Oriental Research* 170 (1963): 65.

21. Adela Yarbro Collins, "Dating the Apocalypse of John," *Biblical Research* 26 (1981): 33–45; Morris, *Revelation*, 35–41; Metzger, *Breaking the Code*, 15–17; Simon J. Kistemaker, *Exposition of the Book of Revelation* (Grand Rapids: Baker Academic, 2001), 26–38; Mark Hitchcock, "A Defense of the Domitianic Date of the Book of Revelation" (PhD diss., Dallas Theological Seminary, 2005); Albert A. Bell, "Date of John's Apocalypse: The Evidence of Some Roman Historians Reconsidered," *New Testament Studies* 25 (1978): 93–102; Paul Trudinger, "The

'Nero Redivivus' Rumour and the Date of the Apocalypse of John," *St Mark's Review* 131 (1987): 43–44; J. Christian Wilson, "The Problem of the Domitianic Date of Revelation," *New Testament Studies* 39 (1993): 587–605; Mark W. Wilson, "The Early Christians in Ephesus and the Date of Revelation, Again," *Neotestamentica* 39 (2005): 163–93.

22.    David E. Aune, *Revelation 1–5*, WBC 52A (Dallas: Word, 1997), cxvii–cxxxiv.

23.    LaHaye and Ice, *Charting the End Times*, 56–62.

24.    Pentecost, *Things to Come*, 149–53.

25.    E.g., Larkin, *Dispensational Truth*, 128–32; Scott, *Exposition of the Revelation*, 83–84; Pentecost, *Things to Come*, 151–53; Walvoord, *Revelation*, 50–100; LaHaye and Ice, *Charting the End Times*, 43–45.

26.    LaHaye and Ice, *Charting the End Times*, 57–62.

27.    Pentecost, *Things to Come*, 215, 359–69.

28.    Pentecost, *Things to Come*, 226–28; Rhodes, *End Times in Chronological Order*, 184–85.

29.    Pentecost, *Things to Come*, 467–77; LaHaye and Ice, *Charting the End Times*, 124–25; Rhodes, *End Times in Chronological Order*, 187–204.

30.    Pentecost, *Things to Come*, 547–63; LaHaye and Ice, *Charting the End Times*, 126–28; Rhodes, *End Times in Chronological Order*, 205–27.

31.    For how the status of *neōkoros* affected municipal life and societal expectations, see Steven J. Friesen, *Twice Neokoros: Ephesus, Asia, and the Cult of the Flavian Imperial Family*, Religions in the Graeco-Roman World 116 (Leiden: Brill, 1993), 52–58.

32. For more detail on, and reconstructions of, Marcus Agrippa's Orbis Terrarum, see the monograph by Jim Siebold, "Orbis Terrarum," http://www.myoldmaps. com/maps-from-antiquity-6200-bc/118-agrippas-orbis -terrarum/118-agrippa.pdf. See also David A. deSilva, *Unholy Allegiances: Heeding Revelation's Warning* (Peabody, MA: Hendrickson, 2013), 21–25.

33. DeSilva, *Unholy Allegiances*, 30–34; J. Nelson Kraybill, *Apocalypse and Allegiance: Worship, Politics, and Devotion in the Book of Revelation* (Grand Rapids: Brazos, 2010), 56–59.

34. In 30/29 BC the people of Asia requested permission to worship the emperor Augustus Octavian (63 BC– AD 14) as their deliverer. See further deSilva, *Unholy Allegiances*, 21–32; Wes Howard-Brook and Anthony Gwyther, *Unveiling Empire: Reading Revelation Then and Now* (Maryknoll, NY: Orbis, 1999), 102–19; Kraybill, *Apocalypse and Allegiance*, 54–69.

35. Benjamin Mazar, "The Archaeological Excavations near the Temple Mount," in *Jerusalem Revealed: Archaeology in the Holy City 1968–1974*, ed. Yigael Yadin (Jerusalem: Israel Exploration Society, 1976), 26–27, 34–35.

36. For a historical-geographical overview of the city, see David A. deSilva, "The Social and Geographical World of Ephesus," in *Lexham Geographic Commentary on Acts through Revelation*, ed. Barry J. Beitzel (Bellingham, WA: Lexham, 2019), 537–53. See more fully Jerome Murphy-O'Connor, *St. Paul's Ephesus: Texts and Archaeology* (Collegeville, MN: Liturgical Press, 2008).

37. The temple and its dimensions are described by Pliny the Elder, *Natural History* 36.21.95–97. See also Strabo, *Geography* 14.1.22–23.

38. deSilva, "Social and Geographical World of Ephesus," 541.

39. deSilva, "Social and Geographical World of Ephesus," 549–51.

40. David A. deSilva, "The Social and Geographical World of Smyrna," in Beitzel, *Lexham Geographic Commentary*, 630–32, 34–35.

41. Gaëlle Coqueugniot, "Where Was the Royal Library of Pergamum? An Institution Found and Lost Again," in *Ancient Libraries*, ed. Jason König, Katerina Oikonomopoulou, and Greg Woolf (Cambridge: Cambridge University Press, 2013), 109–23.

42. David A. deSilva, "The Social and Geographical World of Pergamum," in Beitzel, *Lexham Geographic Commentary*, 642–45.

43. These are those "who did not defile themselves with women, for they remained virgins" (*hoi meta gynaikōn ouk emolynthēsan, parthenoi gar eistin*, 14:4).

44. David H. French, "Roman Roads and Milestones of Asia Minor, Vol. 4: The Roads, Fasc. 4.1 Notes on the Itineraria," *British Institute of Archaeology at Ankara Electronic Monograph* 10 (2016), 24, map 4a, https://biaa.ac.uk/ckeditor/filemanager/userfiles/electronic_publications/Vol.%204%20The%20Roads-Fasc.%204.1.pdf.

45. Mark Wilson, "The Social and Geographical World of Thyatira," in Beitzel, *Lexham Geographic Commentary*, 659–60.

46. Wilson, "Social and Geographical World of Thyatira," 658, 61.

47. French, "Roman Roads and Milestones," 24, map 4a.

48. David A. deSilva, "The Social and Geographical World of Sardis," in Beitzel, *Lexham Geographic Commentary*, 668.

49. DeSilva, "Social and Geographical World of Sardis," 667–68.

50. Mark Wilson, "The Social and Geographical World of Philadelphia," in Beitzel, *Lexham Geographic Commentary*, 678–79.

51. Rudwick and Green have suggested that the water imagery derives from the distinction that "hot water heals, cold water refreshes, but lukewarm water is useless for either purpose, and can serve only as an emetic," and that in contrast to the hot and cold waters of nearby Hierapolis and Colossae, respectively, the water of Laodicea was useless. See M. J. S. Rudwick and E. M. B. Green, "The Laodicean Lukewarmness," *Expository Times* 69.6 (1958): 176–78. The meaning of the temperature imagery used by John has become the subject of much recent debate. For a discussion see Cyndi Parker, "The Social and Geographical World of Laodicea," in Beitzel, *Lexham Geographic Commentary*, 684–96.

52. Parker, "Social and Geographical World of Laodicea," 689.

53. Ulrich Huttner, *Early Christianity in the Lycus Valley*, trans. David Green (Leiden: Brill, 2013), 170–73.

54. Huttner, *Early Christianity in the Lycus Valley*, 164–70.

55. Huttner, *Early Christianity in the Lycus Valley*, 160, 80–81.

56. A sampling of various structural approaches is conveniently provided in Mark W. Wilson, *Charts on the Book of Revelation: Literary, Historical, and Theological Perspectives* (Grand Rapids: Kregel, 2007), 31, 120.

57.    In the case of Herod's attempt to destroy the newborn Christ-child, the issue revolved around who was the true "king of the Jews" and who would be honored (Matt 2:1–12).

## CONCLUSION

1.    Lindsey, *Late Great Planet Earth*, 54.

# Bibliography

*2017 Missionary Prayer Handbook*. Wall, NJ: Christian
    Missions in Many Lands, 2017.
"IX: Assemblies of Brethren." *The Ecumenical Review* 24.2
    (1972): 130–44.
Adams, John Quincy. *His Apocalypse—Where in Is Set Forth
    a Detailed Panorama of the Prophetic Wonders of Daniel
    and Revelation*. Dallas: Prophetical Society, 1925.
Akenson, Donald Harman. *Discovering the End of Time: Irish
    Evangelicals in the Age of Daniel O'Connell*. Montreal:
    McGill-Queen's University Press, 2016.
———. *Exporting the Rapture: John Nelson Darby and the
    Victorian Conquest of North American Evangelicalism*.
    Montreal: McGill-Queen's University Press, 2018.
Aland, Kurt, et al., eds. *The Greek New Testament*. 27th
    ed., 2nd printing; 4th rev. ed. Stuttgart: Deutsche
    Bibelgesellschaft, 1994.
Alcazar, Luis de. *Vestigatio Arcani Sensus in Apocalypsi*.
    Antwerp: Ioannem Keerbergium, 1614.
Alexander, Philip S. "The King Messiah in Rabbinic Judaism."
    In *King and Messiah in Israel and the Ancient Near East:
    Proceedings of the Oxford Old Testament Seminar*, edited
    by John Day, David J. A. Clines, and Philip R. Davies,
    456–73. Sheffield: Sheffield University Press, 1998.
Alexander, Ralph H. "A Fresh Look at Ezekiel 38 and 39."
    *Journal of the Evangelical Theological Society* 17 (1974):
    161–62.

Anderson, Robert. *Daniel in the Critics' Den: A Defense of the Historicity of the Book of Daniel*. Grand Rapids: Kregel, 1990.

Ariel, Yaakov S. "Jews." In *Encyclopedia of Fundamentalism*, edited by Brenda E. Brasher, 251–53. New York: Routledge, 2001.

Arnold, Clinton E., ed. *Zondervan Bible Background Commentary on the New Testament*. Vol. 3. Grand Rapids: Zondervan, 2002.

"Association of Theological Schools. Dallas Theological Seminary." http://www.ats.edu/member-schools/dallas-theological-seminary.

Aune, David E. "The Apocalypse of John and the Problem of Genre." *Semeia* 36 (1986): 65–96.

———. *Revelation 1–5*. WBC 52A. Dallas: Word, 1997.

Backus, Irena. *Reformation Readings of the Apocalypse: Geneva, Zurich, and Wittenberg*. New York: Oxford University Press, 2000.

Baum, Geraldine. "Has Time Run Out? Religion: Some Worry Armageddon Is Near. But Most Evangelical Pastors Call the War a Prelude, Not the 'Main Event.'" *Los Angeles Times*, www.latimes.com/archives/la-xpm-1991-02-07-vw-1003-story.html.

Bayer, Oswald. "Rupture of Times: Luther's Relevance for Today." *Lutheran Quarterly* 13 (1999): 35–50.

Beale, G. K. *The Book of Revelation: A Commentary on the Greek Text*. New International Greek Testament Commentary. Grand Rapids: Eerdmans, 1999.

Beitzel, Barry J., ed. *Lexham Geographic Commentary on Acts through Revelation*. Bellingham, WA: Lexham, 2019.

Bell, Albert A. "Date of John's Apocalypse: The Evidence of Some Roman Historians Reconsidered." *New Testament Studies* 25 (1978): 93–102.

BeVier, William A. "C. I. Scofield: Dedicated and Determined." *Fundamentalist Journal* 2.9 (1983): 37–39.

Blaising, Craig A., and Darrell L. Bock. *Progressive Dispensationalism*. Wheaton, IL: Bridgepoint, 1993.

Bliss, Sylvester. *Memoirs of William Miller, Generally Known as a Lecturer on the Prophecies and the Second Coming of Christ*. Boston: Himes, 1858.

Bostick, Curtis V. *The Antichrist and the Lollards: Apocalypticism in Late Medieval and Reformation England*. Leiden: Brill, 1998.

Bowman, John Wick. "Bible and Modern Religions, Pt 2: Dispensationalism." *Interpretation* 10.2 (1956): 170–87.

Boyer, Paul. *When Time Shall Be No More: Prophecy Belief in Modern American Culture*. Cambridge, MA: Belknap, 1992.

Brown, Francis, S. R. Driver, and Charles A. Briggs. *A Hebrew and English Lexicon of the Old Testament ... Based on the Lexicon of William Gesenius as Translated by Edward Robinson*. Oxford: Oxford University Press, 1952.

Browning, Daniel C., Jr. "The Strange Search for the Ashes of the Red Heifer." *The Biblical Archaeologist* 59.2 (1996): 74–89.

Bruce, F. F. *Israel and the Nations: The History of Israel from the Exodus to the Fall of the Second Temple*. Rev. ed. Carlisle, UK: Paternoster, 1997.

Calkins, Raymond. *The Social Message of the Book of Revelation*. New York: Womans Press, 1920.

Callaway, Carl D. "Cosmogony and Prophecy: Maya Era Day Cosmology in the Context of the 2012 Prophecy." *PIAU* 7.S278 (2011): 192–202.

Camping, Harold. *1994?* New York: Vantage, 1992.

Campion, Nicholas. "The 2012 Mayan Calendar Prophecies in the Context of the Western Millenarian Tradition." *PIAU* 7.S278 (2011): 249–54.

Canfield, Joseph M. *The Incredible Scofield and His Book.* Vallecito, CA: Ross House, 1988.

Carlson, John B., and Mark Van Stone. "The 2012 Phenomenon: Maya Calendar, Astronomy, and Apocalypticism in the Worlds of Scholarship and Global Popular Culture." *PIAU* 7.S278 (2011): 178–85.

Chalmers, Aaron. *Interpreting the Prophets: Reading, Understanding and Preaching from the Worlds of the Prophets.* Downers Grove, IL: InterVarsity, 2015.

Charles, R. H. *A Critical and Exegetical Commentary on the Revelation of St. John, with Introduction, Notes, and Indices, Also the Greek Text and English Translation.* 2 vols. ICC. T&T Clark: Edinburgh, 1920.

Chilton, David. *The Days of Vengeance: An Exposition of the Book of Revelation.* Fort Worth, TX: Dominion, 1987.

Clarke, Sathianathan. *Competing Fundamentalisms: Violent Extremism in Christianity, Islam, and Hinduism.* Louisville: Westminster John Knox, 2017.

Cline, Eric H. *The Battles of Armageddon: Megiddo and the Jezreel Valley from the Bronze Age to the Nuclear Age.* Ann Arbor: University of Michigan Press, 2000.

———. *Jerusalem Besieged: From Ancient Canaan to Modern Israel.* Ann Arbor: University of Michigan Press, 2004.

Close, Albert. *"Babylon": The Scarlet Woman: Or, the Divine Foreview of the Rise, Reign and Destiny of the Church of Rome. A Study Historic and Prophetic of Revelation XVII.* 2nd ed. London: Marshall Brothers, 1910.

Clouse, Robert G., Robert N. Hosack, and Richard V. Pierard. *The New Millennium Manual: A Once and Future Guide.* Grand Rapids: Baker, 1999.

Cohen, Gili, and Harel, Amos. "Israel Indicts U.S. Citizen
        Suspected of Planning Attacks on Muslim Holy Sites."
        Haaretz, December 9, 2014. http://www.haaretz.com/
        israel-news/1.630795.

Cohn, Alicia. "The 'Scandalous,' Nonsensical Portrayal
        of Christian Faith on TV: Scripted Television
        Still Doesn't Get Evangelicals." Christianity Today,
        December 18, 2013. http://www.christianitytoday.
        com/women/2013/december/scandalous-nonsensical
        -portrayal-of-christian-faith-on-tv.html.

Collins, John J. "Apocalypse: The Morphology of a Genre."
        Semeia 14 (1979): 1–217.

———. "Apocalyptic Genre and Mythic Allusions in Daniel." Journal
        for the Study of the Old Testament 6.21 (1981): 83–100.

———. The Apocalyptic Imagination: An Introduction to Jewish
        Apocalyptic Literature. Grand Rapids: Eerdmans, 1998.

———. The Apocalyptic Imagination: An Introduction to the Jewish
        Matrix of Christianity. New York: Crossroad, 1984.

———. Daniel: A Commentary on the Book of Daniel.
        Minneapolis: Fortress, 1993.

———. "The Genre Apocalypse Reconsidered." Zeitschrift für
        antikes Christentum 20 (2016): 21–40.

———. "The Place of Apocalypticism in the Religion of
        Israel." In Ancient Israelite Religion: Essays in Honor
        of Frank Moore Cross, edited by Paul D. Hanson,
        S. Dean McBride Jr., and Patrick D. Miller, Jr., 539–58.
        Philadelphia: Fortress, 1987.

———. "Towards the Morphology of a Genre: Introduction."
        Semeia 14 (1979): 1–20.

Collins, Oral E. The Final Prophecy of Jesus: An Introduction,
        Analysis, and Commentary on the Book of Revelation.
        Eugene, OR: Wipf & Stock, 2007.

Cook, Stephen L. *The Apocalyptic Literature.* Nashville: Abingdon, 2003.

———. *Prophecy and Apocalypticism: The Postexilic Social Setting.* Minneapolis: Fortress, 1995.

Copeland, Corey. "So You Don't Like the Way Christians Are Portrayed on TV? Why We Must Be the Change We Wish to See on the Screen." *Relevant*, January 10, 2014. https://www.relevantmagazine.com/culture/so-you -dont-way-christians-are-portrayed-tv/.

Coqueugniot, Gaëlle. "Where Was the Royal Library of Pergamum? An Institution Found and Lost Again." In *Ancient Libraries*, edited by Jason König, Katerina Oikonomopoulou, and Greg Woolf, 109–23. Cambridge: Cambridge University Press, 2013.

Court, John M. *Approaching the Apocalypse: A Short History of Christian Millenarianism.* London: Tauris, 2008.

Crutchfield, Larry V. "C. I. Scofield." In *Twentieth-Century Shapers of American Popular Religion*, edited by Charles H. Lippy, 371–81. New York: Greenwood, 1989.

———. *The Origins of Dispensationalism: The Darby Factor.* Lanham, MD: University Press of America, 1992.

———. "Rudiments of Dispensationalism in the Ante-Nicene Period, Part 1 (of 2 Parts): Israel and the Church in the Ante-Nicene Fathers." *BSac* 144.575 (1987): 254–76.

———. "Rudiments of Dispensationalism in the Ante-Nicene Period, Part 2 (of 2 Parts): Ages and Dispensations in the Ante-Nicene Fathers." *BSac* 144.576 (1987): 377–99.

Däniken, Eric von. *Chariots of the Gods? Unsolved Mysteries of the Past.* Translated by Michael Heron. New York: Berkley, 1969.

Darby, John Nelson. "The Antichrist, Properly So Called."
In *Critical, 1*. Vol. 13 of *The Collected Writings of J. N.
Darby*, edited by William Kelly, 254–57. Winschoten:
Heijkoop, 1972.

———. "The Dispensations and the Remnants." In *Collectanea:
Being Some of the Subjects Considered at Leamington, on
3d June and Four Following Days in the Year 1839*, 41–49.
Edinburgh: Robertson, 1882.

———. "Evidence from Scripture of the Passing Away of the
Present Dispensation." In *Prophetic, No. 1.*, vol. 2 of
*The Collected Writings of J. N. Darby*, edited by William
Kelly, 89–121. Winschoten: Heijkoop, 1972.

———. "Hints on the Tabernacle. Exodus 25–34." In *Expository,
No. 1*. Vol. 19 of *The Collected Writings of J. N. Darby*,
edited by William Kelly, 184–96. Winschoten:
Heijkoop, 1972.

———. *The Hopes of the Church of God, in Connection with the
Destiny of the Jews and the Nations, as Revealed in
Prophecy. Eleven Lectures Delivered in Geneva, 1840*.
New rev. ed. London: Morrish, 1867.

———. "The Hopes of the Church of God, in Connection with
the Destiny of the Jews and the Nations, as Revealed
in Prophecy. Eleven Lectures Delivered in Geneva,
1840." In *Prophetic, No. 1*, vol. 2 of *The Collected
Writings of J. N. Darby*, edited by William Kelly,
278–383. Winschoten: Heijkoop, 1972.

———. *Lectures on the Second Coming, Delivered in Canada*.
London: W. H. Broom, 1868.

———. "Lectures on the Second Coming of Christ. Delivered
at Toronto, Canada." In *Prophetic, No. 4*, vol. 11 of *The
Collected Writings of J. N. Darby*, edited by William
Kelly, 206–332. Winschoten: Heijkoop, 1972.

———. "The Principles Displayed in the Ways of God, Compared with His Ultimate Dealings." In *Prophetic, No. 2*, vol. 5 of *The Collected Writings of J. N. Darby*, edited by William Kelly, 383–91. Winschoten: Heijkoop, 1972.

———. "The Public Ruin of the Church. Notes of a Public Meeting in London in September, 1847." In *Miscellaneous, No. 1*, vol. 32 of *The Collected Writings of J. N. Darby*, edited by William Kelly, 392–410. Winschoten: Heijkoop, 1972.

———. "The Rapture of the Saints and the Character of the Jewish Remnant." In *Prophetic, No. 4*, vol. 11 of *The Collected Writings of J. N. Darby*, edited by William Kelly, 118–67. Winschoten: Heijkoop, 1972.

———. *Seven Lectures on the Second Coming of the Lord: Delivered in Toronto, in 1863*. Toronto: Gospel Tract Depository, 1863.

———. *The Substance of a Lecture on Prophecy, Delivered at the Town Hall, at Sidmouth on Wednesday Evening, December 13th, 1843*. London: Whittaker, 1844.

———. "The Two Resurrections." In *Doctrinal No. 3*, vol. 10 of *The Collected Writings of J. N. Darby*, edited by William Kelly, 355–69. Winschoten: Heijkoop, 1972.

Davies, Philip R. "Judaisms in the Dead Sea Scrolls: The Case of the Messiah." In *The Dead Sea Scrolls in Their Historical Context*, edited by Timothy H. Lim et al., 219–32. Edinburgh: T&T Clark, 2000.

Davies, W. D., and Dale C. Allison, Jr. *Commentary on Matthew VIII–XVIII*. Vol. 2 of *The Gospel according to Saint Matthew*. ICC. Edinburgh: T&T Clark, 1991.

Dawson, Lorne. "Prophetic Failure in Millennial Movements." In *The Oxford Handbook of Millennialism*, edited by

Catherine Wessinger, 150–70. New York: Oxford University Press, 2011.

DeClaissé-Walford, Nancy L. "Addendum: The Scofield Reference Bible." *Review & Expositor* 106 (2009): 47–50.

DeMar, Gary. *Last Days Madness: The Folly of Trying to Predict When Christ Will Return*. Centerville, TN: American Vision, 1999.

deSilva, David A. "The Social and Geographical World of Ephesus." In *Lexham Geographic Commentary on Acts through Revelation*, edited by Barry J. Beitzel, 537–53. Bellingham, WA: Lexham, 2019.

———. "The Social and Geographical World of Pergamum." In *Lexham Geographic Commentary on Acts through Revelation*, edited by Barry J. Beitzel, 638–54. Bellingham, WA: Lexham, 2019.

———. "The Social and Geographical World of Sardis." In *Lexham Geographic Commentary on Acts through Revelation*, edited by Barry J. Beitzel, 665–73. Bellingham, WA: Lexham, 2019.

———. "The Social and Geographical World of Smyrna." In *Lexham Geographic Commentary on Acts through Revelation*, edited by Barry J. Beitzel, 629–37. Bellingham, WA: Lexham, 2019.

———. *Unholy Allegiances: Heeding Revelation's Warning*. Peabody, MA: Hendrickson, 2013.

Dixon, A. C., and R. A. Torrey, eds. *The Fundamentals: A Testimony to the Truth, Compliments of Two Christian Laymen*. 12 vols. Chicago: Testimony, 1910.

Donaldson, Terence L. *Jesus on the Mountain: A Study in Matthean Theology*. Journal for the Study of the Old Testament Supplement Series 8. Sheffield: JSOT Press, 1985.

Driver, S. R. *The Book of Daniel: With Introduction and Notes.* Cambridge: Cambridge University Press, 1900.

Dyer, Charles H. *The Rise of Babylon: Sign of the End Times.* Wheaton, IL: Tyndale House, 1991.

———. *World News and Bible Prophecy.* Wheaton, IL: Tyndale House, 1993.

Eckstein, Yechiel. "Hollywood's Anti-Christian Bias." *SBC Life,* April 1, 1997. http://www.sbclife.net/Articles/1997/04/sla4.

Efird, James M. *Left Behind? What the Bible Really Says about the End Times.* Macon, GA: Smyth & Helwys, 2006.

Elliger, Karl, and W. Rudolph, eds. *Biblia Hebraica Stuttgartensia.* Minor ed. Stuttgart: Deutsche Bibelgesellschaft, 1984.

Emmerson, Richard Kenneth. *Antichrist in the Middle Ages: A Study of Medieval Apocalypticism, Art, and Literature.* Manchester: Manchester University Press, 1981.

English, E. Schuyler, et al., eds. *The New Scofield Reference Bible: Holy Bible, Authorized King James Version, with Introductions, Annotations, Subject Chain References, and Such Word Changes in the Text as Will Help the Reader.* New York: Oxford University Press, 1967.

Evans, Craig A. *Jesus and His Contemporaries: Comparative Studies.* Leiden: Brill, 1995.

———. "Was Simon Bar Kosiba Recognized as Messiah." In *Jesus and His Contemporaries: Comparative Studies,* edited by Martin Hengel et al., 183–211. Leiden: Brill, 1995.

Fahey, Michael A. "What Makes a Fundamentalist." *Ecumenism* 91 (1988): 7–8.

Fee, Gordon D., and Douglas Stuart. *How to Read Bible for All Its Worth.* Grand Rapids: Zondervan, 2014.

Festinger, Leon, Henry Reicken, and Stanley Schacter. *When Prophecy Fails: A Social and Psychological Study of a Modern Group That Predicted the Destruction of the World*. New York: Harper & Row, 1956.

Flesher, LeAnn Snow. "The Historical Development of Premillennial Dispensationalism." *Review & Expositor* 106 (2009): 35–45.

Forbes, Bruce David, and Jeanne Halgren Kilde. *Rapture, Revelation, and the End Times: Exploring the Left Behind Series*. New York: Palgrave Macmillan, 2004.

Freas, Erik. *Nationalism and the Haram Al-Sharif/Temple Mount: The Exclusivity of Holiness*. London: Palgrave Macmillan, 2017.

French, David H. "Roman Roads and Milestones of Asia Minor, Vol. 4: The Roads, Fasc. 4.1 Notes on the Itineraria." *British Institute of Archaeology at Ankara Electronic Mongraph* 10 (2016). https://biaa.ac.uk/ckeditor/filemanager/userfiles/electronic_publications/Vol.%204%20The%20Roads-Fasc.%204.1.pdf.

Friesen, Steven J. *Twice Neokoros: Ephesus, Asia, and the Cult of the Flavian Imperial Family*. Religions in the Graeco-Roman World 116. Leiden: Brill, 1993.

Fuller, Robert C. *Naming the Antichrist: The History of an American Obsession*. New York: Oxford University Press, 1996.

Gaebelein, Arno C. "Fulfilled Prophecy a Potent Argument for the Bible." In vol. 11 of *The Fundamentals: A Testimony to the Truth, Compliments of two Christian Laymen*, edited by A. C. Dixon and R. A. Torrey, 55–86. Chicago: Testimony, 1910.

——. *The History of the Scofield Reference Bible*. New York: Our Hope; Loizeaux Brothers, 1943.

A Genevese Traveller. "American Affairs, New York, Oct. 15,"
       *Times* (London), October 31, 1844.

Gentry, Kenneth L., Jr. *The Book of Revelation Made Easy: You
       Can Understand Bible Prophecy*. Powder Springs, GA:
       American Vision, 2008.

Gesenius, Wilhelm. *Lexicon Manuale Hebraicum Et
       Chaldaicum in Veteris Testamenti Libros*. Lipsiae:
       Sumtibus typisque F.C.G. Vogelii, 1833.

Goldingay, John. *Daniel*. WBC 30. Dallas: Word, 1989.

Gonen, Rivka. *Contested Holiness: Jewish, Muslim, and
       Christian Perspectives on the Temple Mount in Jerusalem*.
       Jersey City, NJ: KTAV, 2003.

Gregg, Steve. *Revelation, Four Views: A Parallel Commentary*.
       Nashville: Thomas Nelson, 2013.

Gribben, Crawford, and Mark S. Sweetnam. *Left Behind
       and the Evangelical Imagination*. Sheffield: Sheffield
       Phoenix, 2011.

Griffin, William. *End-Time: The Doomsday Catalogue*. New
       York: Collier, 1979.

Guggenheimer, Heinrich W. *Seder Olam: The Rabbinic View
       of Biblical Chronology; Translated and with Commentary*.
       Northvale, NJ: Aronson, 1998.

Gumerlock, Francis X. "Millennialism and the Early
       Church Councils: Was Chiliasm Condemned at
       Constantinople." *Fides et Historia* 36.2 (2004): 83–95.

Hall, John R., Philip D. Schuyler, and Sylvaine Trinh.
       *Apocalypse Observed: Religious Movements and
       Violence in North America, Europe and Japan*. London:
       Routledge, 2000.

Hallo, William W., and K. Lawson Younger Jr. *The Context of
       Scripture*. 3 vols. Leiden: Brill, 1997–2002.

Hannah, John D. "A Review of the Incredible Scofield and
       His Book." *BSac* 147.587 (1990): 351–64.

——. "The Social and Intellectual History of the Origins of the Evangelical Theological College." PhD diss., University of Texas at Dallas, 1988.

——. *An Uncommon Union: Dallas Theological Seminary and American Evangelicalism*. Grand Rapids: Zondervan, 2009.

Hanson, Paul D. "Messiahs and Messianic Figures in Proto-Apocalypticism." In *The Messiah: Developments in Earliest Judaism and Christianity*, edited by James H. Charlesworth, 67–75. Minneapolis: Fortress, 1992.

——. *Old Testament Apocalyptic*. Nashville: Abingdon, 1987.

Harrison, Roland K. *Introduction to the Old Testament*. Grand Rapids: Eerdmans, 1969.

Hartman, Lars. "Survey of the Problem of Apocalyptic Genre." In *Apocalypticism in the Mediterranean World and the Near East*, edited by David Hellholm, 329–43. Tübingen: Mohr Siebeck, 1983.

Harvey, Richard. *Mapping Messianic Jewish Theology: A Constructive Approach*. Milton Keynes: Paternoster, 2009.

Haskell, David M. *Through a Lens Darkly: How the News Media Perceive and Portray Evangelicals*. Toronto: Clements, 2009.

Hayes, John H., and Frederick Prussner. *Old Testament Theology: Its History and Development*. Atlanta: John Knox, 1985.

Hays, Richard B., and Stefan Alkier. *Revelation and the Politics of Apocalyptic Interpretation*. Waco, TX: Baylor University Press, 2012.

Heick, Otto William. "The Antichrist in the Book of Revelation." *Consensus* 11 (1985): 27–30.

Heiser, Michael S. "Deuteronomy 32:8 and the Sons of God." *BSac* 158.629 (2001): 52–74.

Hellholm, David. "The Problem of Apocalyptic Genre and the Apocalypse of John." *Semeia* 36 (1986): 13–64.

Hendriksen, William. *More Than Conquerors: An Interpretation of the Book of Revelation*. Grand Rapids: Baker, 1967.

Heyerdahl, Thor. *The Ra Expeditions*. Garden City, NY: Doubleday, 1971.

Hillers, Delbert R. "Revelation 13:18 and a Scroll from Murabba'at." *Bulletin of the American Schools of Oriental Research* 170 (1963): 65.

Hippolyte. *Commentaire Sur Daniel*. Paris: Cerf, 1947.

Hitchcock, Mark. "A Defense of the Domitianic Date of the Book of Revelation." PhD diss., Dallas Theological Seminary, 2005.

Holst, Robert. "The 'Cry of Dereliction': Another Point of View." *The Springfielder* 35.4 (1972): 286–89.

Hoopes, John W. "A Critical History of 2012 Mythology." *PIAU* 7.S278 (2011): 240–48.

Horsley, Richard A. "'Messianic' Figures and Movements in First-Century Palestine." In *The Messiah: Developments in Earliest Judaism and Christianity*, edited by James H., 276–95. Charlesworth. Minneapolis: Fortress, 1992.

Horsley, Richard A., and John S. Hanson. *Bandits, Prophets, and Messiahs: Popular Movements in the Time of Jesus*. Minneapolis: Winston, 1985.

House, H. Wayne. *Charts of Bible Prophecy*. Grand Rapids: Zondervan, 2003.

———. *Charts of Christian Theology and Doctrine*. Grand Rapids: Zondervan, 1992.

Howard-Brook, Wes, and Anthony Gwyther. *Unveiling Empire: Reading Revelation Then and Now*. Maryknoll, NY: Orbis, 1999.

Huttner, Ulrich. *Early Christianity in the Lycus Valley*.
        Translated by David Green. Leiden: Brill, 2013.
Ice, Thomas. "The 70 Weeks of Daniel." In *The End Times
        Controversy: The Second Coming under Attack*, edited
        by Tim LaHaye and Thomas Ice, 307–53. Eugene, OR:
        Harvest House, 2003.
Inboden, Will. "It's Impossible to Count the Things Wrong
        with the Negligent, Spurious, Distorted New
        Biography of George W. Bush." *Foreign Policy*, 2016.
        http://foreignpolicy.com/2016/08/15/its-impossible-
        to-count-the-things-wrong-with-the-negligent
        -spurious-distorted-new-biography-of-george-w-bush
        /?utm_content=buffere1499&utm_medium=
        social&utm_source=facebook.com&utm_
        campaign=buffer.
Ironside, Harry A. *A Historical Sketch of the Brethren
        Movement*. Rev. ed. Neptune, NJ: Loizeaux, 1985.
———. *Lectures on the Revelation*. New York: Loizeaux Brothers,
        1930.
Irshai, O. "Dating the Eschaton: Jewish and Christian
        Apocalyptic Calculations in Late Antiquity." In
        *Apocalyptic Time*, edited by Albert I. Baumgarten and
        W. J. Hanegraaff, 113–54. Leiden: Brill, 2000.
Irwin, Brian P. "The Book of Daniel and the Roots of
        New Testament Mission." In *Christian Mission:
        Old Testament Foundations and New Testament
        Developments*, edited by Stanley E. Porter and Cynthia
        Long Westfall, 42–63. Eugene, OR: Pickwick, 2010.
Isaac, E. "1 (Ethiopic Apocalypse of) Enoch." In *Apocalyptic
        Literature and Testaments*, vol. 1 of *The Old Testament
        Pseudepigrapha*, edited by James H. Charlesworth,
        5–100. Garden City, NY: Doubleday, 1983.

Jackson, Alicia R. "Wesleyan Holiness and Finished Work
        Pentecostal Interpretations of Gog and Magog Biblical
        Texts." *Journal of Pentecostal Theology (Online)* 25.2
        (2016): 168–83.

Jańczuk, Leszek. "Dating the Book of Revelation in Light of
        Tradition." *Ruch Biblijny i Liturgiczny* 71 (2018): 37–52.

Jeffrey, Grant R. *Armageddon, Appointment with Destiny.*
        Toronto: Frontier Research, 1988.

———. *Russia's Secret Agenda.* VHS. Toronto: Frontier
        Research.

Johnson, Elliott E. "Apocalyptic Genre in Literal
        Interpretation." In *Essays in Honor of J. Dwight
        Pentecost,* edited by Stanley D. Toussaint and
        Charles H. Dyer, 197–210. Chicago: Moody, 1986.

Jones, Brian W. *The Emperor Domitian.* London:
        Routledge, 1992.

Jones, Jim. "Q1053–4 Transcript of Jim Jones Sermon,
        Peoples Temple, San Francisco (1973)." San Diego,
        CA: The Jonestown Institute, San Diego State
        University. www.jonestown.sdsu.edu/?page_id=27318.

Jones, Timothy Paul, David Gundersen, and Benjamin Galan.
        *The Rose Guide to End-Times Prophecy.* Torrance, CA:
        Rose, 2011.

Kelhoffer, James A. "The Relevance of Revelation's Date and
        the Imperial Cult for John's Appraisal of the Value
        of Christians' Suffering in Revelation 1–3." In *Die
        Johannesapokalypse: Kontexte – Konzepte – Rezeption,*
        edited by Franz Tóth, Jörg Frey, and James A.
        Kelhoffer, 553–85. Wissenschaftliche Untersuchungen
        zum Neuen Testament 287. Tübingen: Mohr Siebeck,
        2012.

Kellner, Mark A. "New Dispensation? Camping: 'Leave Church': Family Radio Founder's Latest Teaching Prompts Church Defections." *Christianity Today* 46 (2002): 21.

Kelly, William, ed. *The Collected Writings of J. N. Darby.* 35 vols. Winschoten: Heijkoop, 1971.

Keresztes, Paul. "Marcus Aurelius a Persecutor?" *Harvard Theological Review* 61 (1968): 321–41.

Kistemaker, Simon J. *Exposition of the Book of Revelation.* Grand Rapids: Baker Academic, 2001.

Kitchen, Kenneth A. "The Aramaic of Daniel." In *Notes on Some Problems in the Book of Daniel,* edited by D. J. Wiseman, 31–79. London: Tyndale, 1965.

Klausner, Joseph. *The Messianic Idea in Israel, from Its Beginning to the Completion of the Mishnah.* New York: Macmillan, 1955.

Kraybill, J. Nelson. *Apocalypse and Allegiance: Worship, Politics, and Devotion in the Book of Revelation.* Grand Rapids: Brazos, 2010.

Kreider, Dallas. "Darby, John Nelson (1800–1882)." In vol. 2 of *Encyclopedia of Protestantism,* edited by Hans J. Hillerbrand, 3–5. London: Routledge, 2004.

Krey, Philip D. "Nicholas of Lyra: Apocalypse Commentator, Historian, and Critic." *Franciscan Studies* 52 (1992): 53–84.

Kulik, Alexander. "Genre without a Name? Was There a Hebrew Term for 'Apocalypse.'" *Journal for the Study of Judaism in the Persian, Hellenistic and Roman Period* 40 (2009): 540–50.

Kyle, Richard. *The Last Days Are Here Again: A History of the End Times.* Grand Rapids: Baker, 1998.

Ladd, George Eldon. *Crucial Questions on the Kingdom of God*. Grand Rapids: Eerdmans, 1961.

LaHaye, Tim. *The Beginning of the End*. Wheaton, IL: Tyndale House, 1972.

LaHaye, Tim, and Thomas Ice. *Charting the End Times: A Visual Guide to Understanding Bible Prophecy*. Eugene, OR: Harvest House, 2001.

——. "Charting the End Times CD: A Visual Guide to Understanding Bible Prophecy." *Tim LaHaye Prophecy Library*. CD-ROM. Eugene, OR: Harvest House, 2006.

——. *Charting the End Times Prophecy Study Guide*. Eugene, OR: Harvest House, 2002.

——. *The End Times Controversy: The Second Coming under Attack*. Eugene, OR: Harvest House, 2003.

LaHaye, Tim, and Jerry B. Jenkins. *Left Behind: A Novel of the Earth's Last Days*. Wheaton, IL: Tyndale House, 1989.

Lake, Kirsopp, ed. *The Apostolic Fathers*. Vol. 1, *I Clement, II Clement, Ignatius, Polycarp, Didache, Barnabas*. Loeb Classical Library. Cambridge: Harvard University Press, 1912.

Landes, Richard. "Lest the Millennium be Fulfilled: Apocalyptic Expectations and the Pattern of Western Chronography, 100–800 CE." In *The Use and Abuse of Eschatology in the Middle Ages*, edited by Werner Verbeke, Daniel Verhelst, and Andries Welkenhuysen, 136–211. Leuven: Leuven University Press, 1988.

——. *Relics, Apocalypse, and the Deceits of History: Ademar of Chabannes, 989–1034*. Harvard Historical Studies. Cambridge: Harvard University Press, 1995.

Landry, Lauren. "Boston University Professor Reminds Us: The Mayan Calendar Doesn't Say the World Will

End." December 11, 2012. http://bostinno.streetwise.
co/2012/12/11/mayan-calendar-end-of-the-world-
december-21-2012/?utm_source=twitterfeed&utm_
medium=twitter.

Larkin, Clarence. *Dispensational Truth, or God's Plan and
Purpose in the Ages*. Rev. ed. Glenside, PA: Rev.
Clarence Larkin Est., 1920.

Leighton, Cadoc. "Finding Antichrist: Apocalypticism
in Nineteenth-Century Catholic England and the
Writings of Frederick Faber." *Journal of Religious
History* 37 (2013): 80–97.

Lewis, Scott M. *What Are They Saying about New Testament
Apocalyptic?* New York: Paulist, 2004.

Lindberg, Carter. "Eschatology and Fanaticism in the
Reformation Era: Luther and the Anabaptists."
*Concordia Theological Quarterly* 64.4 (2000): 259–78.

Lindsey, Hal, and C. C. Carlson. *The Late Great Planet Earth*.
Grand Rapids: Zondervan, 1973.

Lucas, Ernest C. *Daniel*. Apollos Old Testament Commentary.
Downers Grove, IL: InterVarsity, 2002.

Lucass, Shirley. *The Concept of the Messiah in the Scriptures of
Judaism and Christianity*. London: T&T Clark, 2011.

Luther, Martin. *Calculation of the Years of the World
(Supputatio Annorum Mundi)*. Translated by
Kenneth K. Miller. 1541. https://www.dropbox.com/s/
y39wf8cpe8gn401/Luther-Chronikon%28KKM
-English%29B.pdf?dl=0.

———. *Letter to John Ruhel* (1525). In *Luther's Works*, vol. 49,
*Letters II*, 112. St. Louis: Concordia, 1972.

———. *On War Against the Turks* (1529). In *Luther's Works*, vol.
46, *Christian in Society III*, 181. St. Louis: Concordia,
1967.

Lutzweiler, David. *The Praise of Folly: The Enigmatic Life and Theology of C. I. Scofield*. Draper, VA: Apologetics Group Media, 2009.

MacArthur, John F., Jr. *Revelation*. 2 vols. Chicago: Moody, 1999–2000.

MacLeod, David J. "Walter Scott, a Link in Dispensationalism between Darby and Scofield." *BSac* 153.610 (1996): 155–78.

MacPherson, Dave. *The Incredible Cover-Up*. Meaford, OR: Omega, 1975.

Maddaus, Gene. "Everett Adam Livvix, Figure in Israeli Mosque Plot, Is Released from Mental Facility and Returned to U.S." *LA Weekly*, July 10, 2015. http://www.laweekly.com/news/everett-adam-livvix-figure-in-israeli-mosque-plot-is-released-from-mental-facility-and-returned-to-us-5788862.

———. "A Westside High School Grad Went Searching for Meaning and Ended Up in an Israeli Military Prison." *LA Weekly*, July 8, 2015. http://www.laweekly.com/news/a-westside-high-school-grad-went-searching-for-meaning-and-ended-up-in-an-israeli-military-prison-5775576.

Mangum, R. Todd, and Mark S. Sweetnam. *The Scofield Bible: Its History and Impact on the Evangelical Church*. Milton Keynes: Paternoster, 2009.

Marrow, Stanley B. "Apocalyptic Genre and Eschatology." In *The Word in the World: Essays in Honor of Frederick L. Moriarty, S.J*, edited by Frederick L. Moriarty, Richard J. Clifford, and George W. MacRae, 71–81. Cambridge, MA: Weston College Press, 1973.

Marsden, George M. *Fundamentalism and American Culture: The Shaping of Twentieth Century Evangelicalism, 1870–1925*. Oxford: Oxford University Press, 1982.

————. *Understanding Fundamentalism and Evangelicalism.*
    Grand Rapids: Eerdmans, 1991.

Martin, Walter, and Ravi Zacharias. *Kingdom of the Cults.* Rev.
    and updated ed. Bloomington, MN: Bethany House,
    2003.

Mazar, Benjamin. "The Archaeological Excavations near the
    Temple Mount." In *Jerusalem Revealed: Archaeology in
    the Holy City 1968–1974*, edited by Yigael Yadin, 25–40.
    Jerusalem: Israel Exploration Society, 1976.

McDowell, Josh. *Prophecy, Fact or Fiction? Historical Evidence
    for the Authenticity of the Book of Daniel.* San Bernardino:
    Campus Crusade for Christ, 1979.

McGinn, Bernard, John J. Collins, and Stephen J. Stein,
    eds. *The Encyclopedia of Apocalypticism.* New York:
    Continuum, 2000.

McIver, Tom. *The End of the World: An Annotated Bibliography.*
    Jefferson, NC: McFarland, 1999.

Mercedes, Lackey. *Hunter.* Los Angeles: Hyperion, 2015.

Metzger, Bruce M. *Breaking the Code: Understanding the Book
    of Revelation.* Nashville: Abingdon, 1993.

————. "The Fourth Book of Ezra." In *Apocalyptic Literature
    and Testaments*, vol. 1 of *The Old Testament
    Pseudepigrapha*, edited by James H. Charlesworth,
    517–59. Garden City, NY: Doubleday, 1983.

Miller, William. *Evidence from Scripture and History of the
    Second Coming of Christ, about the Year 1843: Exhibited
    in a Course of Lectures.* Troy, NY: Elias Gates, 1838.

Morris, Leon. *Revelation.* Tyndale New Testament
    Commentaries 20. Grand Rapids: Eerdmans, 1987.

Mounce, Robert H. *The Book of Revelation.* Grand Rapids:
    Eerdmans, 1998.

Murphy-O'Connor, Jerome. *St. Paul's Ephesus: Texts and
    Archaeology.* Collegeville, MN: Liturgical Press, 2008.

Neusner, Jacob, trans. and ed. *The Babylonian Talmud: A Translation and Commentary*. Peabody, MA: Hendrickson, 2005.

Neusner, Jacob, William Scott Green, and Ernest S. Frerichs. *Judaisms and Their Messiahs at the Turn of the Christian Era*. Cambridge: Cambridge University Press, 1987.

Newton, Sir Isaac. *Observations Upon the Prophecies of Daniel, and the Apocalypse of St. John: In Two Parts*. Dublin: Printed by S. Powell for George Risk, George Ewing, and William Smith, 1733.

North, Gary. *Rapture Fever: Why Dispensationalism Is Paralyzed*. Tyler, TX: Institute for Christian Economics, 1993.

Novenson, Matthew V. "Why Does R Akiba Acclaim Bar Kokhba as Messiah." *Journal for the Study of Judaism in the Persian, Hellenistic and Roman Periods* 40 (2009): 551–72.

Odell, Margaret S. *Ezekiel*. Smyth & Helwys Bible Commentary. Macon, GA: Smyth & Helwys, 2005.

O'Leary, Stephen D. *Arguing the Apocalypse: A Theory of Millennial Rhetoric*. New York: Oxford University Press, 1998.

Oropeza, B. J. *99 Reasons Why No One Knows When Christ Will Return*. Downers Grove, IL: InterVarsity, 1996.

Osborne, Grant R. *Revelation*. Grand Rapids: Baker Academic, 2002.

Parker, Cyndi. "The Social and Geographical World of Laodicea." In *Lexham Geographic Commentary on Acts through Revelation*, edited by Barry J. Beitzel, 684–96. Bellingham, WA: Lexham, 2019.

Pate, C. Marvin. *Interpreting Revelation and Other Apocalyptic Literature: An Exegetical Handbook*. Grand Rapids: Kregel Academic, 2016.

Pentecost, J. Dwight. Review of *The New Scofield Reference Bible*, by C. I. Scofield, ed. *BSac* 124.494 (1967): 169–70.

———. *Things to Come: A Study in Biblical Eschatology*. Grand Rapids: Zondervan, 1964.

Peters, Ted. "Why Didn't Jesus Come." *Theology and Science* 10 (2012): 1–2.

Peterson, Brian Neil. *Ezekiel in Context: Ezekiel's Message Understood in Its Historical Setting of Covenant Curses and Ancient Near Eastern Mythological Motifs*. Princeton Theological Monographs Series 182. Eugene, OR: Pickwick, 2012.

Pettegrew, Larry Dean. "The Historical and Theological Contributions of the Niagara Bible Conference to American Fundamentalism." ThD diss., Dallas Theological Seminary, 1976.

———. "The Rapture Debate at the Niagara Bible Conference." *BSac* 157.627 (2000): 331–47.

Pew Research Center. *Life in 2050: Amazing Science, Familiar Threats. Public Sees a Future Full of Promise and Peril*. Washington, DC: Pew Research Center, 2010.

Phil, Torres. "Apocalypse Soon." *Skeptic* 21.2 (2016): 56.

Powell, Marvin A. "Weights and Measures." In vol. 6 of *Anchor Bible Dictionary*, edited by David Noel Freedman, 897–908. New York: Doubleday, 1992.

Price, Randall. *The Battle for the Last Days' Temple: Politics, Prophecy, and the Temple Mount*. Eugene, OR: Harvest House, 2004.

Pugh, Jeffrey C. *Homebrewed Christianity Guide to the End Times: Theology after You've Been Left Behind*. Minneapolis: Fortress, 2016.

Rabinovich, Abraham. "The Man Who Torched the Al-Aksa Mosque." *Jerusalem Post*, September 5, 2014. https://

www.jpost.com/Magazine/The-man-who-torched-al
-Aksa-Mosque-374403.

———. "The Strange Ease of Denis Michael Rohan." *Jerusalem Post*, November 14, 1969, A4.

Rahlfs, Alfred, ed. *Septuaginta*. Stuttgart: Deutsche Bibelgesellschaft, 1979.

Rainey, Anson F., and R. Steven Notley. *The Sacred Bridge: Carta's Atlas of the Biblical World*. Jerusalem: Carta, 2006.

Raisz, Erwin. *General Cartography*. New York: McGraw-Hill, 1948.

Reddish, Mitchell G. *Apocalyptic Literature: A Reader*. Peabody, MA: Hendrickson, 1995.

Rhodes, Ron. *The Eight Great Debates of Bible Prophecy: Understanding the Ongoing Controversies*. Eugene, OR: Harvest House, 2014.

———. *The End Times in Chronological Order: A Complete Overview to Understanding Bible Prophecy*. Eugene, OR: Harvest House, 2012.

Ribera, Francisco. *In Sacrum Beati Ioannis Apostoli, & Evangelistiae Apocalypsin Commentarij*. Salamanica: Petrus Lassus, 1591.

Robbins, Tom. *Skinny Legs and All*. New York: Bantam, 1990.

Roberts, J. W. "Revision of Scofield Bible." *Restoration Quarterly* 10.3 (1967): 161–66.

Robertson, Irvine. *What the Cults Believe*. Chicago: Moody, 1981.

Robinson, George L. "One Isaiah." In vol. 7 of *The Fundamentals: A Testimony to the Truth, Compliments of Two Christian Laymen*, edited by A. C. Dixon and R. A. Torrey, 70–87. Chicago: Testimony, 1910.

Rochat, Jocelyn. "George W. Bush et le Code Ezéchiel." *Allez Savoir* 39 (2007): 34–41.

Rosen, Christine. *Preaching Eugenics: Religious Leaders and the American Eugenics Movement*. Oxford: Oxford University Press, 2004.

Rossing, Barbara R. *The Rapture Exposed: The Message of Hope in the Book of Revelation*. New York: Basic, 2004.

Rudwick, M. J. S., and E. M. B. Green. "The Laodicean Lukewarmness." *Expository Times* 69.6 (1958): 176–78.

Rushing, D. Jean. "From Confederate Deserter to Decorated Veteran Bible Scholar: Exploring the Enigmatic Life of C. I. Scofield, 1861–1901." MA thesis, East Tennessee State University, 2011.

Russell, J. Stuart. *The Parousia: A Critical Inquiry into the New Testament Doctrine of Our Lord's Second Coming*. London: Unwin, 1887.

Ryrie, Charles C. *Dispensationalism Today*. Chicago: Moody, 1965.

Sandy, D. Brent. *Plowshares and Pruning Hooks: Rethinking the Language of Biblical Prophecy and Apocalyptic*. Downers Grove, IL: InterVarsity, 2002.

Sarno, C., B. Shestakofsky, H. Shoemaker, and R. Aponte. "Rationalizing Judgment Day: A Content Analysis of Harold Camping's Open Forum Program." *Sociology of Religion* 76 (2015): 199–221.

Sarno, Charles, and Helen Shoemaker. "Church, Sect, or Cult? The Curious Case of Harold Camping's Family Radio and the May 21 Movement." *Nova Religio: The Journal of Alternative and Emergent Religions* 19.3 (2016): 6.

Saturno, William A., David Stuart, Anthony F. Aveni, and Franco Rossi. "Ancient Maya Astronomical Tables from Xultun, Guatemala." *Science* 336.6082 (2012): 714–17.

Saucy, Robert L. *The Case for Progressive Dispensationalism: The Interface between Dispensational and Non-dispensational Theology*. Grand Rapids: Zondervan, 1993.

Schüssler Fiorenza, Elisabeth. *Revelation: Vision of a Just World*. Minneapolis: Fortress, 1991.

Scofield, C. I. "The Last World Empire and Armageddon." *BSac* 108.431 (1951): 355–62.

———. "The Return of Christ in Relation to the Church." *BSac* 109.433 (1952): 77–89.

———. "The Return of Christ in Relation to the Jew and the Earth." *BSac* 108.432 (1951): 477–87.

———. *Rightly Dividing the Word of Truth (2 Tim. 2:15): Ten Outline Studies of the More Important Divisions of Scripture*. Repr. ed. New York: Loizeaux Brothers; Bible Truth Depot, n.d.

———. *The Scofield Reference Bible. The Holy Bible Containing the Old and New Testaments*. New York: Oxford University Press, 1909.

———. *The Scofield Reference Bible. The Holy Bible Containing the Old and New Testaments*. New and improved ed. New York: Oxford University Press, 1917.

———. "The Times of the Gentiles." *BSac* 107.427 (1950): 343–55.

Scott, Walter. *Exposition of the Revelation of Jesus Christ*. 4th ed. Grand Rapids: Kregel, n.d.

Shaw, J. V. W., ed. *A Survey of Palestine, Prepared in December 1945 and January 1946 for the Information of the Anglo-American Committee of Inquiry*. Vol. 1. Jerusalem: Government Printer, Palestine, 1946.

Siebold, Jim. "Orbis Terrarum." http://www.myoldmaps.com/maps-from-antiquity-6200-bc/118-agrippas

-orbis-terrarum/118-agrippa.pdf.

Silver, Abba Hillel. *A History of Messianic Speculation in Israel: From the First through the Seventeenth Centuries.* Boston: Beacon, 1959.

Sitler, Robert K. "The 2012 Phenomenon: New Age Appropriation of an Ancient Mayan Calendar." *Nova Religio* 9.3 (2006): 24–38.

Smith, A. Christopher. "J. N. Darby in Switzerland at the Crossroads of Brethren History and European Evangelism." *Christian Brethren Research Fellowship Journal* 34 (1983): 53–94.

Smith, Erin A. "The Late Great Planet Earth Made the Apocalypse a Popular Concern." *Humanities* 38.1 (2017).

Socrates of Constantinople. *Ecclesiastical History, Comprising a History of the Church, in Seven Books, from the Accession of Constantine, A.D. 305, to the 38th Year of Theodosius II, Including a Period of 140 Years.* London: Bohn, 1853.

Spencer, Stephen R. "Scofield, C(yrus) I. (1845–1921)." In *Historical Handbook of Major Biblical Interpreters,* edited by Donald K. McKim, 610–15. Downers Grove, IL: InterVarsity, 1998.

Stackhouse, John G. "Defining 'Evangelical.'" *Church and Faith Trends* 1 (2007): 1–5. https://www.evangelicalfellowship.ca/getattachment/About-us/About-Evangelicalism/About-Evangelicals/Defining_Evangelical.pdf.aspx?lang=en-US.

Steinfels, Peter. "Gulf War Proving Bountiful for Some Prophets of Doom." *New York Times,* February 2, 1991. https://www.nytimes.com/1991/02/02/us/gulf-war-proving-bountiful-for-some-prophets-of-doom.html.

Stone, Michael E. "Apocalyptic Literature." In *Jewish Writings of the Second Temple Period: Apocrypha, Pseudepigrapha, Qumran Sectarian Writings, Philo, Josephus,* edited by Michael E. Stone, 383–441. Assen, Netherlands: Van Gorcum, 1984.

Stunt, Timothy C. F. "Irvingite Pentecostalism and the Early Brethren." *Christian Brethren Research Fellowship Journal* 10 (1965): 40–48.

Sutherland, Winston Terrance. "John Nelson Darby: Scholarship That Influenced the Bible College Movement." *Christian Higher Education* 9 (2010): 271–85.

Sutton, Matthew Avery. *American Apocalypse: A History of Modern Evangelicalism.* Cambridge, MA: Belknap, 2014.

Sweetnam, Mark S. "Defining Dispensationalism: A Cultural Studies Perspective." *The Journal of Religious History* 34 (2010): 191–212.

———. "Hal Lindsay and the Great Dispensational Mutation." *Journal of Religion and Popular Culture* 23 (2011): 217–35.

Sweetnam, Mark S., and Crawford Gribben. "J. N. Darby and the Irish Origins of Dispensationalism." *Journal of the Evangelical Theological Society* 52 (2009): 569–77.

Talmon, Shemaryahu. "The Concept of Māšîah and Messianism in Early Judaism." In *The Messiah: Developments in Earliest Judaism and Christianity,* edited by James H. Charlesworth, 79–115. Minneapolis: Fortress, 1992.

Taylor, Richard A. *Interpreting Apocalyptic Literature: An Exegetical Handbook.* Grand Rapids: Kregel Academic, 2016.

Thompson, Damian. *The End of Time: Faith and Fear in the*

*Shadow of the Millennium*. Hanover, NH: University Press of New England, 1997.

Times Staff Writer. "John Walvoord, 92; His Bestseller Related Mideast Unrest to End-of-World Prophecies." *Los Angeles Times*, January 10, 2003. https://www.latimes.com/archives/la-xpm-2003-jan-10-me-walvoord10-story.html.

Toffler, Alvin. *Future Shock*. New York: Random House, 1970.

Tregelles, Samuel Prideaux. *Heads of Hebrew Grammar: Containing All the Principles Needed by a Learner*. London: Bagster & Sons, 1852.

Trudinger, Paul. "The 'Nero Redivivus' Rumour and the Date of the Apocalypse of John." *St Mark's Review* 131 (1987): 43–44.

Trumbull, Charles G. *The Life Story of C. I. Scofield*. New York: Oxford University Press, 1920.

Tucker, Ruth A. *Another Gospel: Alternative Religions and the New Age Movement*. Grand Rapids: Zondervan, 1989.

Ulmer, Rivka. "The Culture of Apocalypticism: Is the Rabbinic Work *Pesiqta Rabbati* Intertextually Related to the New Testament Book the Revelation to John." *The Review of Rabbinic Judaism* 14 (2011): 37–70.

Unger, Walter. "'Earnestly Contending for the Faith': The Role of the Niagara Bible Conference in the Emergence of American Fundamentalism, 1875–1900." PhD diss., Simon Fraser University (Canada), 1981.

Ussher, James. *The Annals of the World: Deduced From the Origin of Time, and Continued to the Beginning of the Emperour Vespasians Reign, and the Totall Destruction and Abolition of the Temple and Common-Wealth of the Jews: Containing the Historie of the Old and New Testament, With That of the Macchabees, Also the Most*

*Memorable Affairs of Asia and Egypt, and the Rise of the Empire of the Roman Caesars Under C. Julius, and Octavianus: Collected From All History, as Well Sacred, as Prophane, and Methodically Digested*. London: E. Tyler, for J. Crook, and for G. Bedell, 1658.

Van Impe, Jack. *A.D. 2000: The End?*, VHS. Troy, MI: Jack Van Impe Ministries, 1990.

———. *December 21st 2012: History's Final Day?* DVD. Troy, MI: Jack Van Impe Ministries, 2008.

———. "Jack Van Impe Presents." December 14, 2012. YouTube video, 28:28. https://www.youtube.com/watch?v=TQM4O8-ZiIk.

Van Stone, Mark. "It's Not the End of the World: Emic Evidence for Local Diversity in the Maya Long Count." *PIAU* 7.S278 (2011): 186–91.

Various Authors. "Evangelicals and Catholics Together: The Christian Mission in the Third Millennium." *First Things*, May 1994, https://www.firstthings.com/article/1994/05/evangelicals-catholics-together-the-christian-mission-in-the-third-millennium.

Verbeke, Werner, D. Verhelst, and Andries Welkenhuysen. *The Use and Abuse of Eschatology in the Middle Ages*. Leuven: Leuven University Press, 1988.

Vine, W. E. *Expository Dictionary of New Testament Words: A Comprehensive Dictionary of the Original Greek Words with Their Precise Meanings for English Readers*. London: Oliphants, 1939.

———. *New Testament Greek Grammar: A Course of Self-Help*. London: Pickering & Inglis, 1930.

Vogel, Winfried. "The Eschatological Theology of Martin Luther, Part II: Luther's Exposition of Daniel and Revelation." *Andrews University Seminary Studies* 25 (1987): 183–99.

Volker, Kurt. "Bush, Chirac, and the War in Iraq." *Foreign Policy*, http://foreignpolicy.com/2016/11/15/bush-chirac-and-the-war-in-iraq.

Wade, John. *The Black Book, or, Corruption Unmasked. Being an Account of Places, Pensions, and Sinecures … and Corruption of the Borough Government*. 2 vols. London: Fairburn, 1828.

Wainwright, Arthur W. *Mysterious Apocalypse: Interpreting the Book of Revelation*. Nashville: Abingdon, 1993.

Waldrep, B. Dwain. "Lewis Sperry Chafer and the Roots of Nondenominational Fundamentalism in the South." *Journal of Southern History* 73 (2007): 807–36.

Wallis, Wilber B. "The Coming of the Kingdom: A Survey of the Book of Revelation." *Presbyterion* 8 (1982): 13–70.

Walls, Jerry L. *The Oxford Handbook of Eschatology*. New York: Oxford, 2008.

Walters, Stanley D. "The End (of What?) Is at Hand." *Toronto Journal of Theology* 2 (1986): 23–46.

Walvoord, John F. *Daniel: The Key to Prophetic Revelation*. Chicago: Moody, 1971.

——. *The Millennial Kingdom*. Grand Rapids: Zondervan, 1983.

——. *The Rapture Question*. Grand Rapids: Zondervan, 1979.

——. *The Revelation of Jesus Christ: A Commentary*. Chicago: Moody, 1966.

Walvoord, John F., and John E. Walvoord. *Armageddon, Oil and the Middle East Crisis*. Grand Rapids: Zondervan, 1974.

Watson, William C. *Dispensationalism before Darby: Seventeenth-Century and Eighteenth-Century English Apocalypticism*. Silverton, OR: Lampion, 2015.

Weitzman, Steven. "Religious Studies and the FBI: Adventures in Academic Interventionalism." *Journal of the American Academy of Religion* 81 (2013): 959–95.

Wessinger, Catherine. *How the Millennium Comes Violently: From Jonestown to Heaven's Gate*. New York: Seven Bridges, 2000.

Westbrook, Raymond, and Bruce Wells. *Everyday Law in Biblical Israel: An Overview*. Louisville: Westminster John Knox, 2009.

Wilkinson, Paul Richard. "Dispensationalism and Love for Israel." *BSac* 169.676 (2012): 412–26.

———. *For Zion's Sake: Christian Zionism and the Role of John Nelson Darby*. Milton Keynes: Paternoster, 2007.

Williams, Michael D. "C. I. Scofield and Lewis Sperry Chafer: Dispensationalism as Social and Cultural Critique." PhD diss., University of St. Michael's College, 1986.

Wilson, J. Christian. "The Problem of the Domitianic Date of Revelation." *New Testament Studies* 39 (1993): 587–605.

Wilson, Joseph D. "The Book of Daniel." In vol. 7 of *The Fundamentals: A Testimony to the Truth, Compliments of Two Christian Laymen*, edited by A. C. Dixon and R. A. Torrey, 88–100. Chicago: Testimony, 1910.

Wilson, Mark W. *Charts on the Book of Revelation: Literary, Historical, and Theological Perspectives*. Grand Rapids: Kregel, 2007.

———. "The Early Christians in Ephesus and the Date of Revelation, Again." *Neotestamentica* 39 (2005): 163–93.

———. "The Social and Geographical World of Philadelphia." Pages 674–83 in *Lexham Geographic Commentary on Acts through Revelation*. Edited by Barry J. Beitzel. Bellingham, WA: Lexham, 2019.

———. "The Social and Geographical World of Thyatira." In *Lexham Geographic Commentary on Acts through Revelation*, edited by Barry J. Beitzel, 655–64.

Bellingham, WA: Lexham, 2019.

Wilson, Robert Dick. "The Aramaic of Daniel." In *Biblical and Theological Studies, by Members of the Faculty of Princeton Theological Seminary*, 261–306. New York: Scribner's Sons, 1912.

Wintermute, O. S. "Jubilees." In *Expansions of the "Old Testament" and Legends, Wisdom and Philosophical Literature, Prayers, Psalms, and Odes, Fragments of Lost Judeo-Hellenistic Works*, vol. 2 of The Old Testament Pseudepigrapha, edited by James H. Charlesworth, 35–142. Garden City, NY: Doubleday, 1985.

Witherington, Ben, III. *Revelation and the End Times: Unraveling God's Message of Hope*. Nashville: Abingdon, 2010.

Wojcik, Daniel. *The End of the World as We Know it*. New York: New York University Press, 1997.

Wright, George Frederick. "The Mosaic Authorship of the Pentateuch." In vol. 9 of *The Fundamentals: A Testimony to the Truth, Compliments of Two Christian Laymen*, edited by A. C. Dixon and R. A. Torrey, 10–21. Chicago: Testimony, 1910.

Wright, N. T. *The Millennium Myth*. Louisville: Westminster John Knox, 1999.

———. *Revelation for Everyone*. Louisville: Westminster John Knox, 2011.

Wyatt, Nicolas. *Religious Texts from Ugarit: The Words of Ilimilku and His Colleagues*. The Biblical Seminar 53. Sheffield: Sheffield Academic, 1998.

Yarbro Collins, Adela. "Apocalypse Now: The State of Apocalyptic Studies near the End of the First Decade of the Twenty-First Century." *Harvard Theological Review* 104 (2011): 447–57.

———. "Dating the Apocalypse of John." *Biblical Research* 26 (1981): 33–45.

Zimbaro, Valerie P. *Encyclopedia of Apocalyptic Literature.* Santa Barbara: ABC-CLIO, 1996.

# SUBJECT INDEX

# Scripture Index

## Old Testament

### Genesis

### Exodus

### Leviticus

# Ancient Sources Index

## Old and New Testament Pseudepigrapha

## Early and Medieval Christian Writings

## Greco-Roman Literature

## Ancient Jewish Writers

## Rabbinic Literature

## Ugaritic Literature

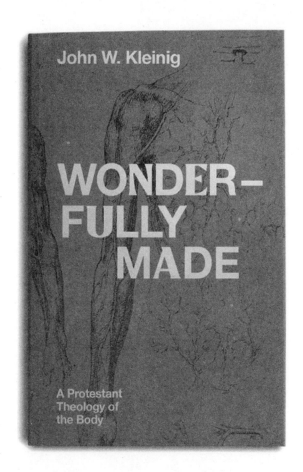

John W. Kleinig

# WONDER–FULLY MADE

A Protestant Theology of the Body

## ALSO AVAILABLE FROM LEXHAM PRESS

*Think deeply about God's word and the body*

—

**Visit lexhampress.com to learn more**